D1320588

禪

ZEN of WONDER

Hatter M • Volume 4

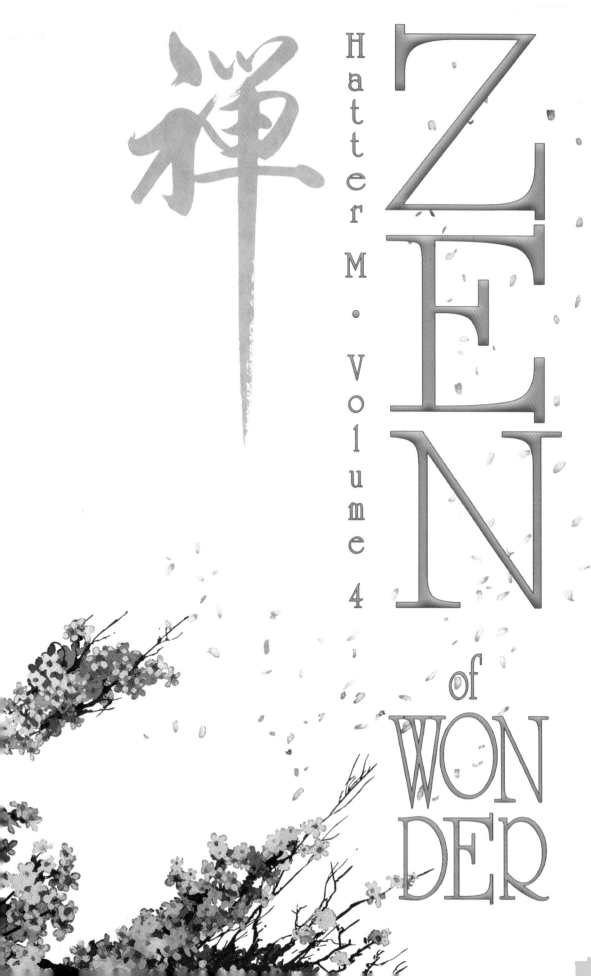

To Japan and the survivors of Fukushima.

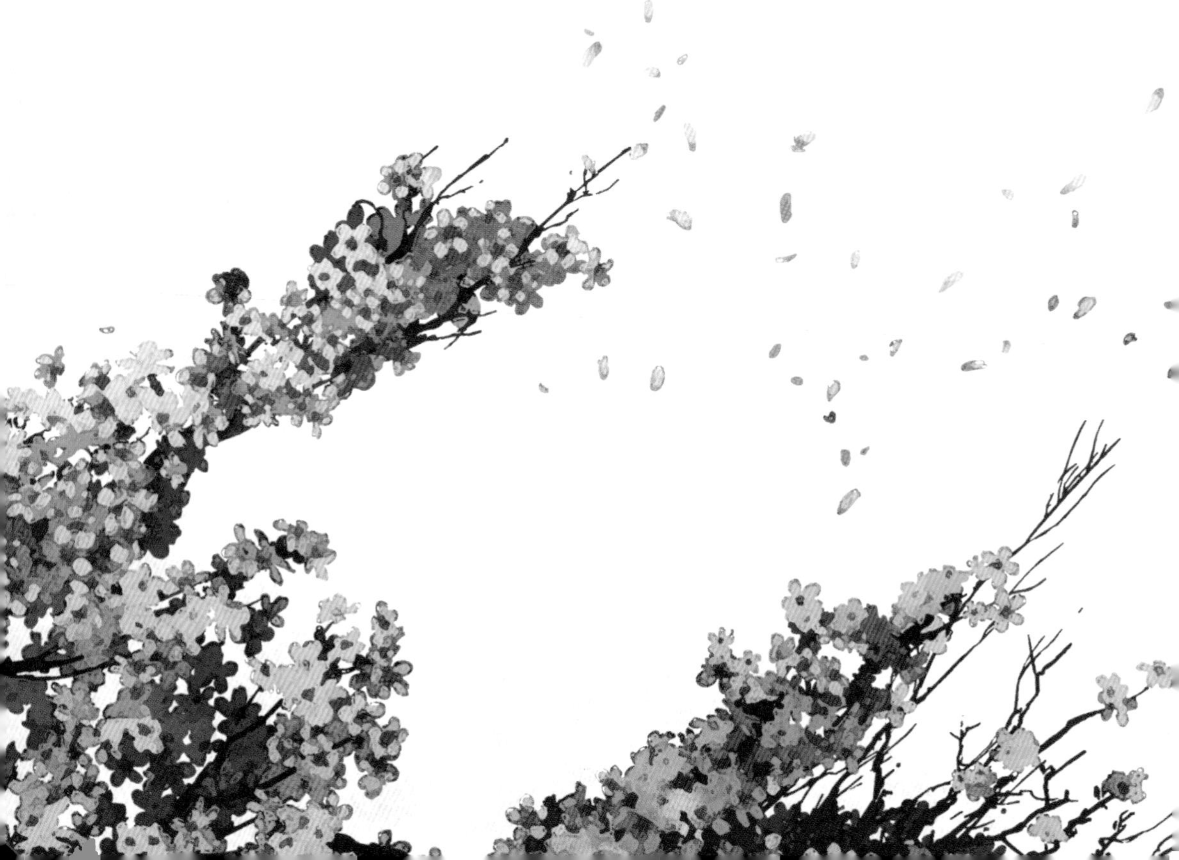

デディケヨン

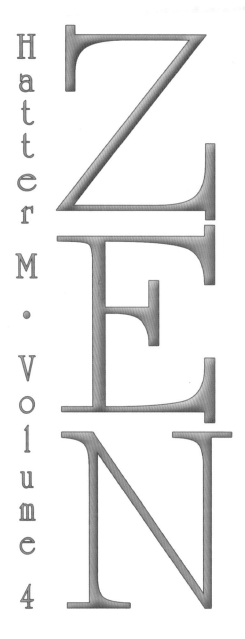

ZEN of WONDER

禅

Hatter M · Volume 4

Written by
**Frank Beddor &
Liz Cavalier**
Art by
Sami Makkonen

Automatic
Pictures
Publishing

Hatter M: Zen of Wonder
Volume 4

Writers
Frank Beddor
Liz Cavalier

Art
Sami Makkonen

Cover Art
Bill Sienkiewicz

Letterer
Tom B. Long

Demonologist
Sonja Midthun

Logo Design by
Christina Craemer

Interiors Designed by
Tom B. Long

www.lookingglasswars.com

The Looking Glass Wars ® is a trademark of Automatic Pictures, Inc.
Copyright © 2013 Automatic Pictures, Inc.
All rights reserved.

Printed in Korea.

ISBN: 978-0-9818737-9-4

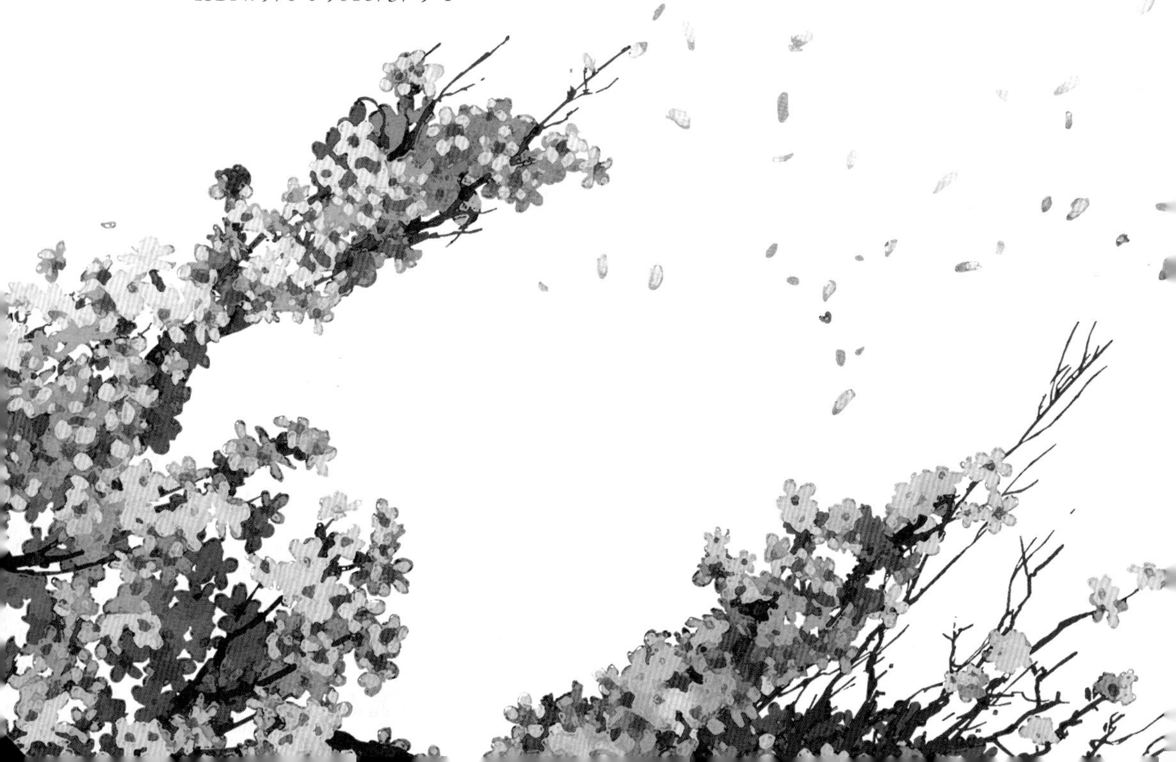

This is not the story of a Mad Hatter.

内容

THANK YOU

Masters, Sages and Mad Monks
who lit the path we travel.

序文

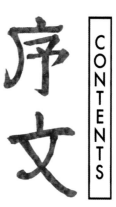

CONTENTS

Who Are We?

The Hatter M Institute for Paranormal Travel is a devout assemblage of radical historians, cartographers and geo-graphic theorists pledged to uncovering and documenting through the medium of sequential art the full spectrum journey of Hatter Madigan as he traversed our world from 1859-1872 searching for Princess Alyss of Wonderland.

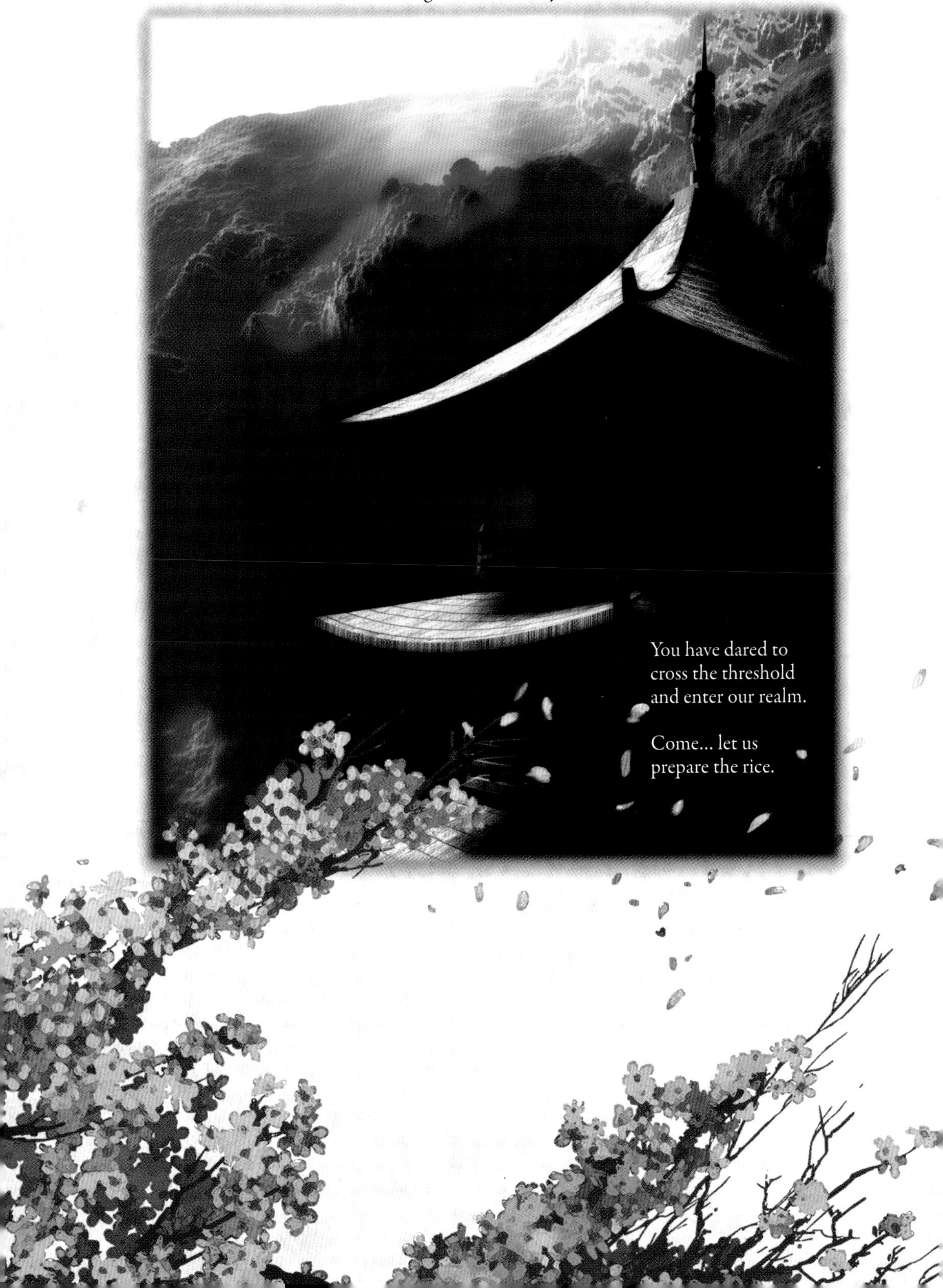
You have dared to cross the threshold and enter our realm.
Come... let us prepare the rice.

GONG

Some say it is the journey not the destination that matters, but there is also much to celebrate when a destination is reached. The presentation of the *Zen of Wonder* to our fellow seekers is great cause for celebration and we hope you find value in what you are about to discover. In the course of tracking this adventure we moved our headquarters to a Japanese Zen monastery where icy cold morning meditations, bowls of rice and temple cats helped us travel the same Zen path that Hatter Madigan experienced in 1871. In following his maps and journal entries we tracked not only Hatter's exterior movements, but his interior struggle as well. In order to find Alyss, Hatter must stop desiring to find Alyss. As the Zen proverb states: When you seek it you cannot find it. Sometimes one must remain still in order to advance and even loyal bodyguards need a vacation.

Will Nekko's Zen guidance free Hatter from his rational mind and set him on the proper path to finding the lost Princess of Wonderland? As the lessons unfold, riddles, jokes and spontaneous laughter lead Hatter on the search of his life for answers to questions he never knew existed. In maddening Zen fashion, the answers only raise more questions. Will Hatter reach satori before his head explodes? Is it really all a joke? Zen can only hint and beckon. The goal is experience, not understanding.

Read this book for the experience.
Do not attempt to understand.

See you on the other side, if there is one.

-Hatter M Institute

Keep cool but care.
    -Thomas Pynchon

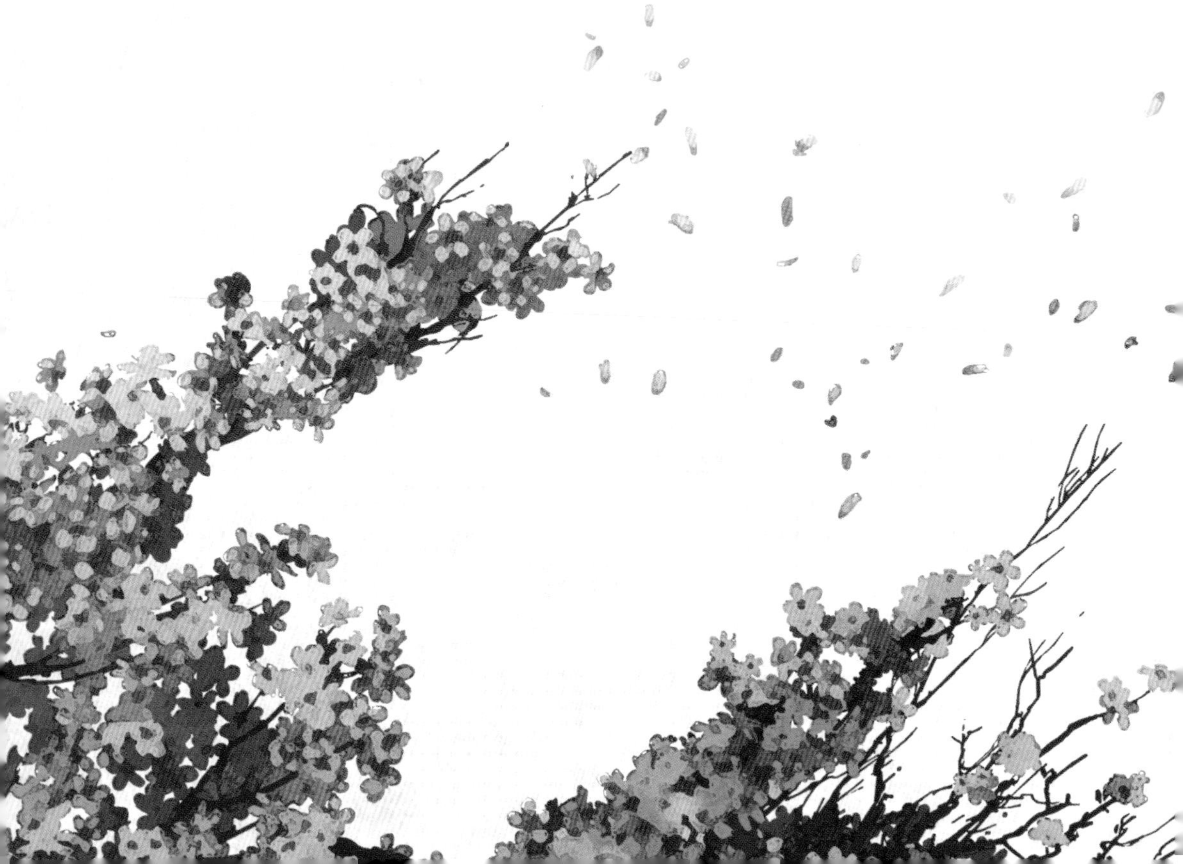

序章 PROLOGUE

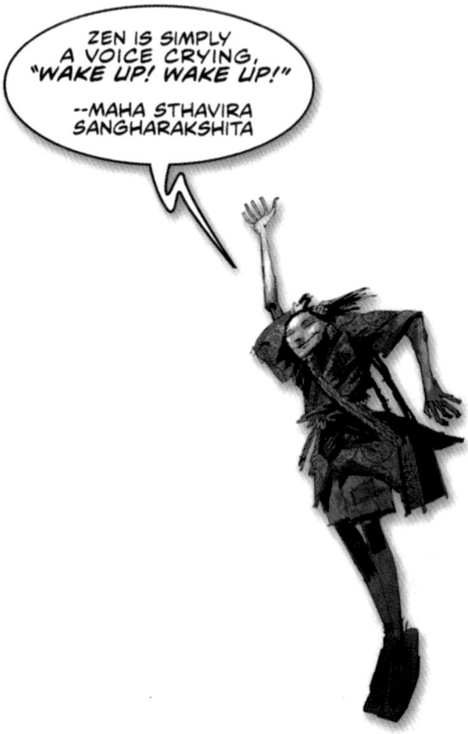
ZEN IS SIMPLY A VOICE CRYING, "WAKE UP! WAKE UP!"
--MAHA STHAVIRA SANGHARAKSHITA

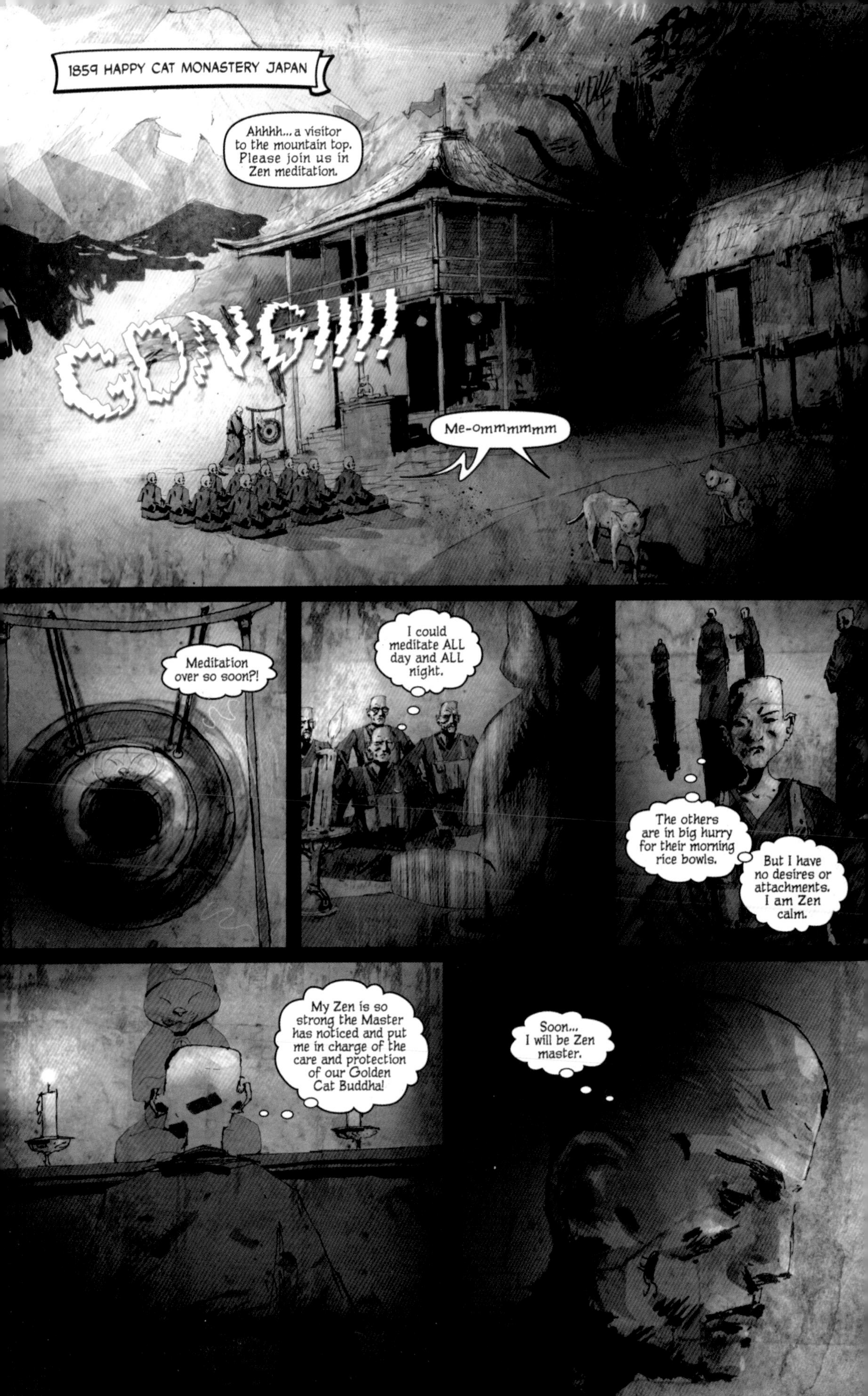
1859 HAPPY CAT MONASTERY JAPAN
Ahhhh... a visitor to the mountain top. Please join us in Zen meditation.
GONG!!!!
Me-ommmmmm
Meditation over so soon?!
I could meditate ALL day and ALL night.
The others are in big hurry for their morning rice bowls.
But I have no desires or attachments. I am Zen calm.
My Zen is so strong the Master has noticed and put me in charge of the care and protection of our Golden Cat Buddha!
Soon... I will be Zen master.

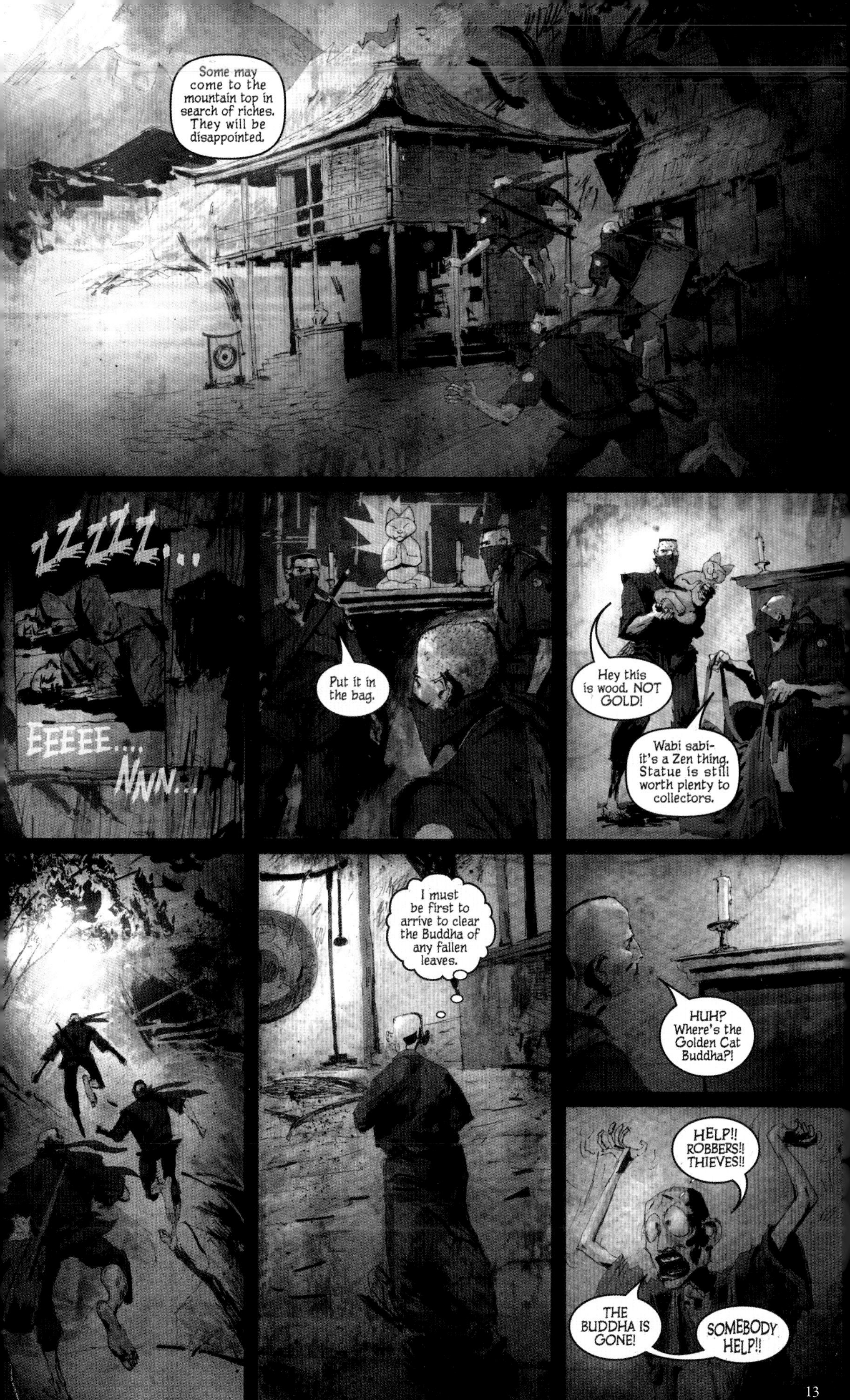
Some may come to the mountain top in search of riches. They will be disappointed.
ZZZZZ...
EEEEE....
NNN...
Put it in the bag.
Hey this is wood. NOT GOLD!
Wabi sabi- it's a Zen thing. Statue is still worth plenty to collectors.
I must be first to arrive to clear the Buddha of any fallen leaves.
HUH? Where's the Golden Cat Buddha?!
HELP!! ROBBERS!! THIEVES!!
THE BUDDHA IS GONE!
SOMEBODY HELP!!

The art of the tea Way consists
simply of boiling water,
preparing tea and drinking it.
         -Rikyu

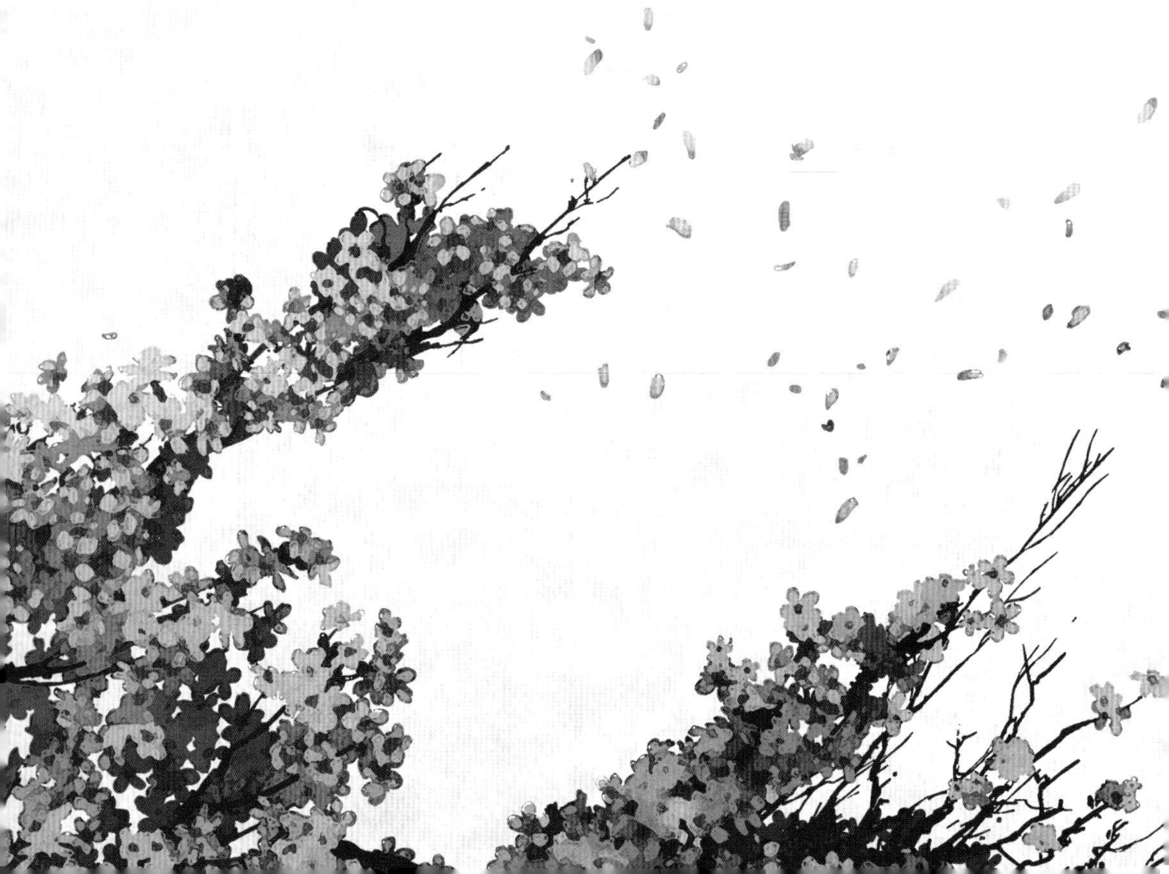

endless seasons pass
the lost sun eludes contact
until it explodes

探求者

CHAPTER 1
THE SEEKER

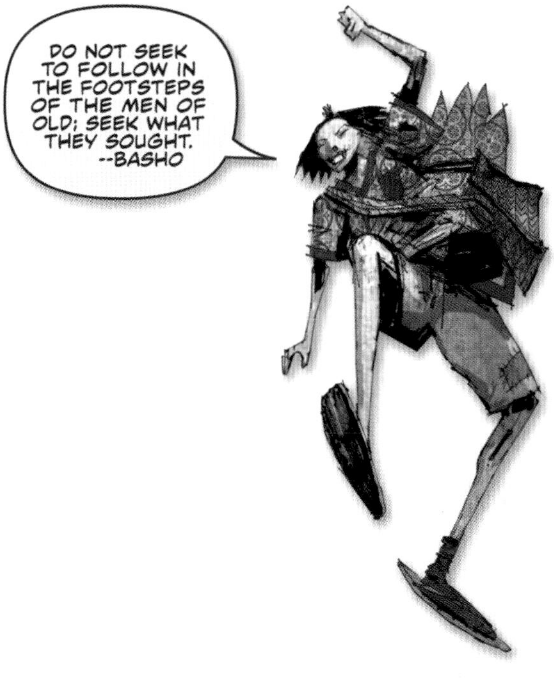
DO NOT SEEK TO FOLLOW IN THE FOOTSTEPS OF THE MEN OF OLD; SEEK WHAT THEY SOUGHT. --BASHO

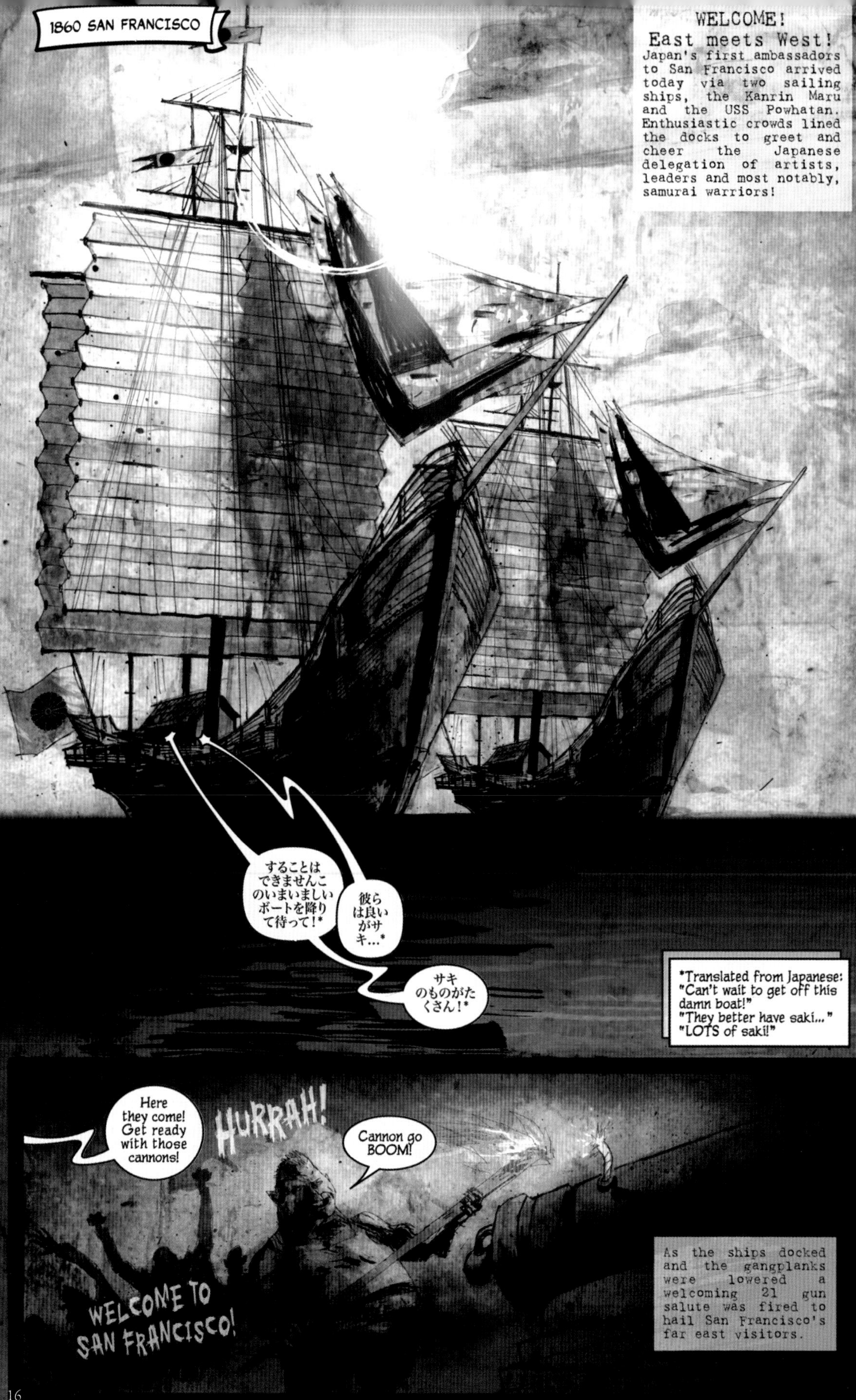
1860 SAN FRANCISCO
WELCOME!
East meets West!
Japan's first ambassadors to San Francisco arrived today via two sailing ships, the Kanrin Maru and the USS Powhatan. Enthusiastic crowds lined the docks to greet and cheer the Japanese delegation of artists, leaders and most notably, samurai warriors!
することはできませんこのいまいましいボートを降りて待って！*
彼らは良いがサキ…*
サキのものがたくさん！*
*Translated from Japanese: "Can't wait to get off this damn boat!" "They better have saki..." "LOTS of saki!"
Here they come! Get ready with those cannons!
HURRAH!
Cannon go BOOM!
WELCOME TO SAN FRANCISCO!
As the ships docked and the gangplanks were lowered a welcoming 21 gun salute was fired to hail San Francisco's far east visitors.

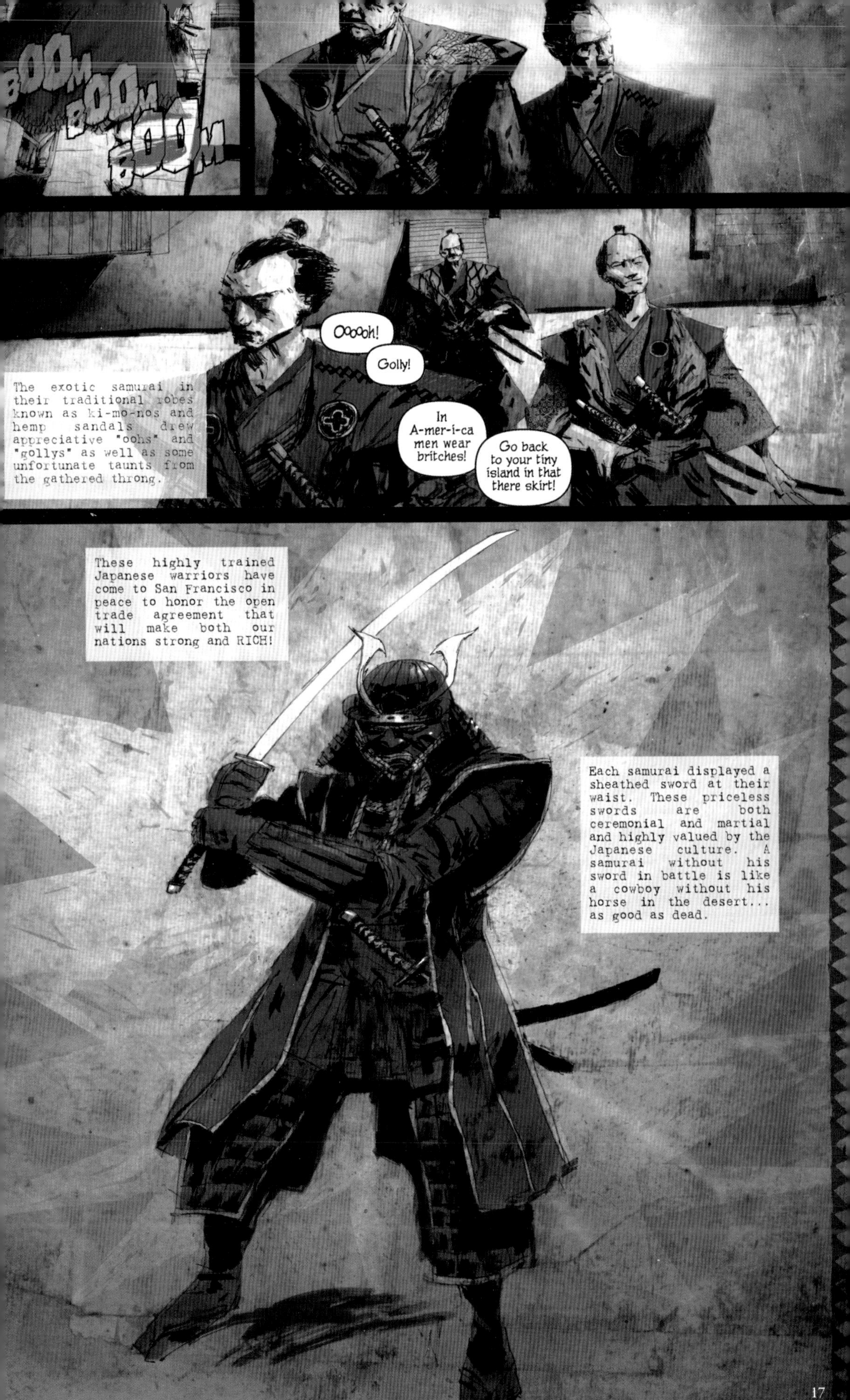
BOOM BOOM BOOM
The exotic samurai in their traditional robes known as ki-mo-nos and hemp sandals drew appreciative "oohs" and "gollys" as well as some unfortunate taunts from the gathered throng.
Oooooh!
Golly!
In A-mer-i-ca men wear britches!
Go back to your tiny island in that there skirt!
These highly trained Japanese warriors have come to San Francisco in peace to honor the open trade agreement that will make both our nations strong and RICH!
Each samurai displayed a sheathed sword at their waist. These priceless swords are both ceremonial and martial and highly valued by the Japanese culture. A samurai without his sword in battle is like a cowboy without his horse in the desert... as good as dead.

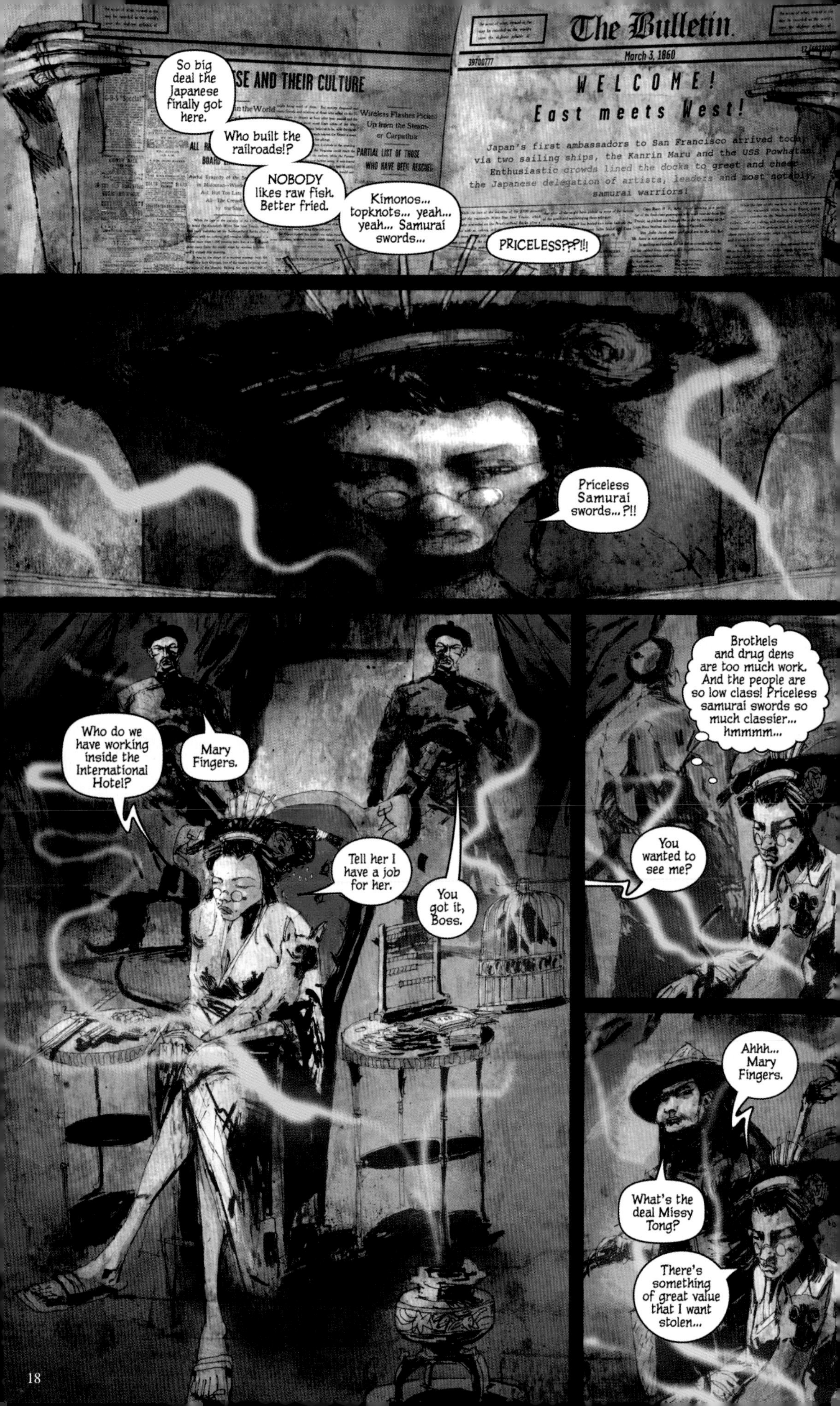
The Bulletin
March 3, 1860
WELCOME!
East meets West!
Japan's first ambassadors to San Francisco arrived today via two sailing ships, the Kanrin Maru and the USS Powhatan. Enthusiastic crowds lined the docks to greet and cheer the Japanese delegation of artists, leaders and most notably, samurai warriors!
SE AND THEIR CULTURE
Wireless Flashes Picked Up from the Steamer Carpathia
PARTIAL LIST OF THOSE WHO HAVE BEEN RESCUED
So big deal the Japanese finally got here.
Who built the railroads!?
NOBODY likes raw fish. Better fried.
Kimonos... topknots... yeah... yeah... Samurai swords...
PRICELESS???!!
Priceless Samurai swords...?!!
Who do we have working inside the International Hotel?
Mary Fingers.
Tell her I have a job for her.
You got it, Boss.
Brothels and drug dens are too much work. And the people are so low class! Priceless samurai swords so much classier... hmmmm...
You wanted to see me?
Ahhh... Mary Fingers.
What's the deal Missy Tong?
There's something of great value that I want stolen...

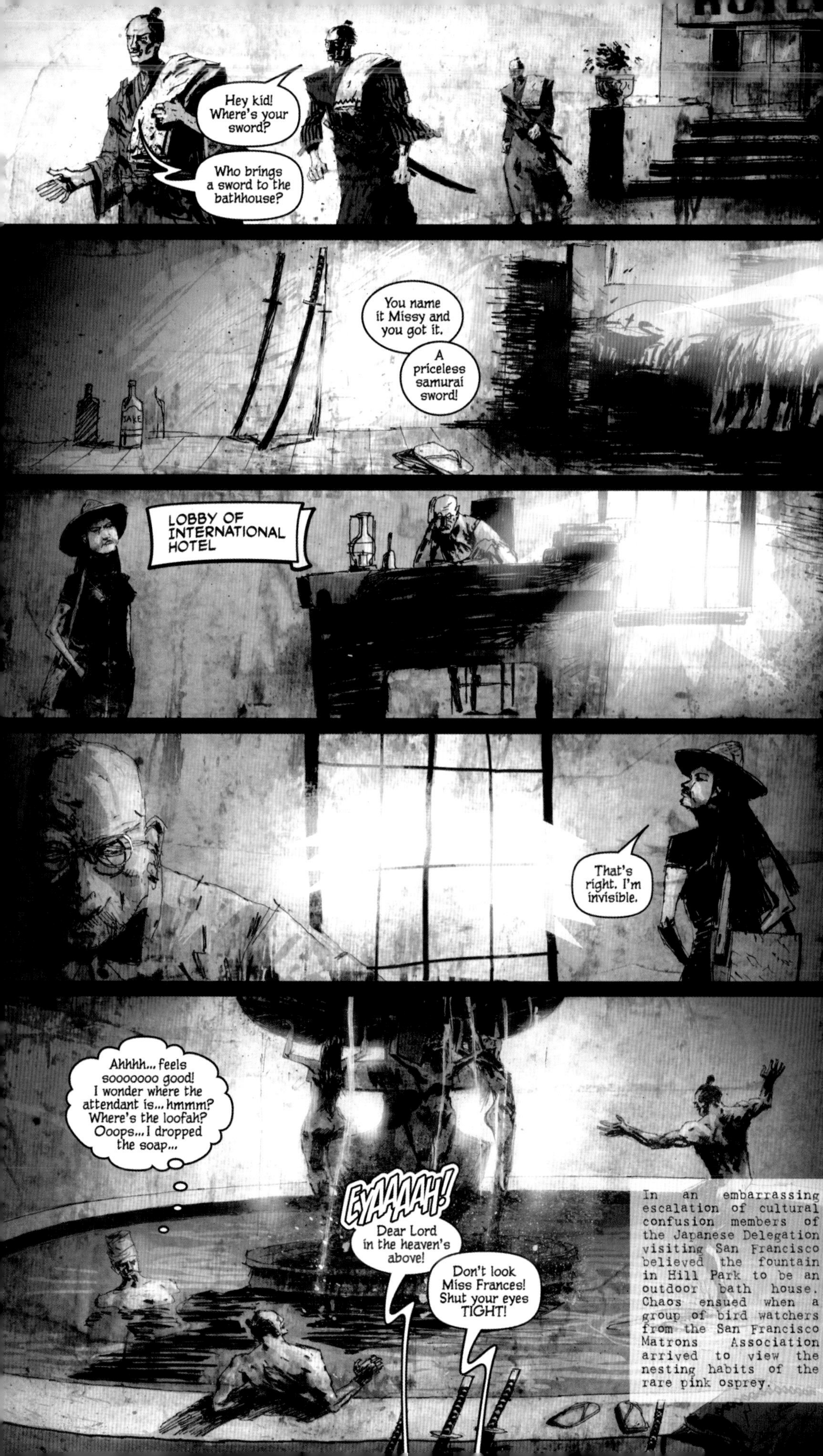

Hey kid! Where's your sword?
Who brings a sword to the bathhouse?
You name it Missy and you got it.
A priceless samurai sword!
SAKE
LOBBY OF INTERNATIONAL HOTEL
That's right. I'm invisible.
Ahhhh... feels soooooo good! I wonder where the attendant is... hmmm? Where's the loofah? Ooops... I dropped the soap...
EYAAAAH!
Dear Lord in the heaven's above!
Don't look Miss Frances! Shut your eyes TIGHT!
In an embarrassing escalation of cultural confusion members of the Japanese Delegation visiting San Francisco believed the fountain in Hill Park to be an outdoor bath house. Chaos ensued when a group of bird watchers from the San Francisco Matrons Association arrived to view the nesting habits of the rare pink osprey.

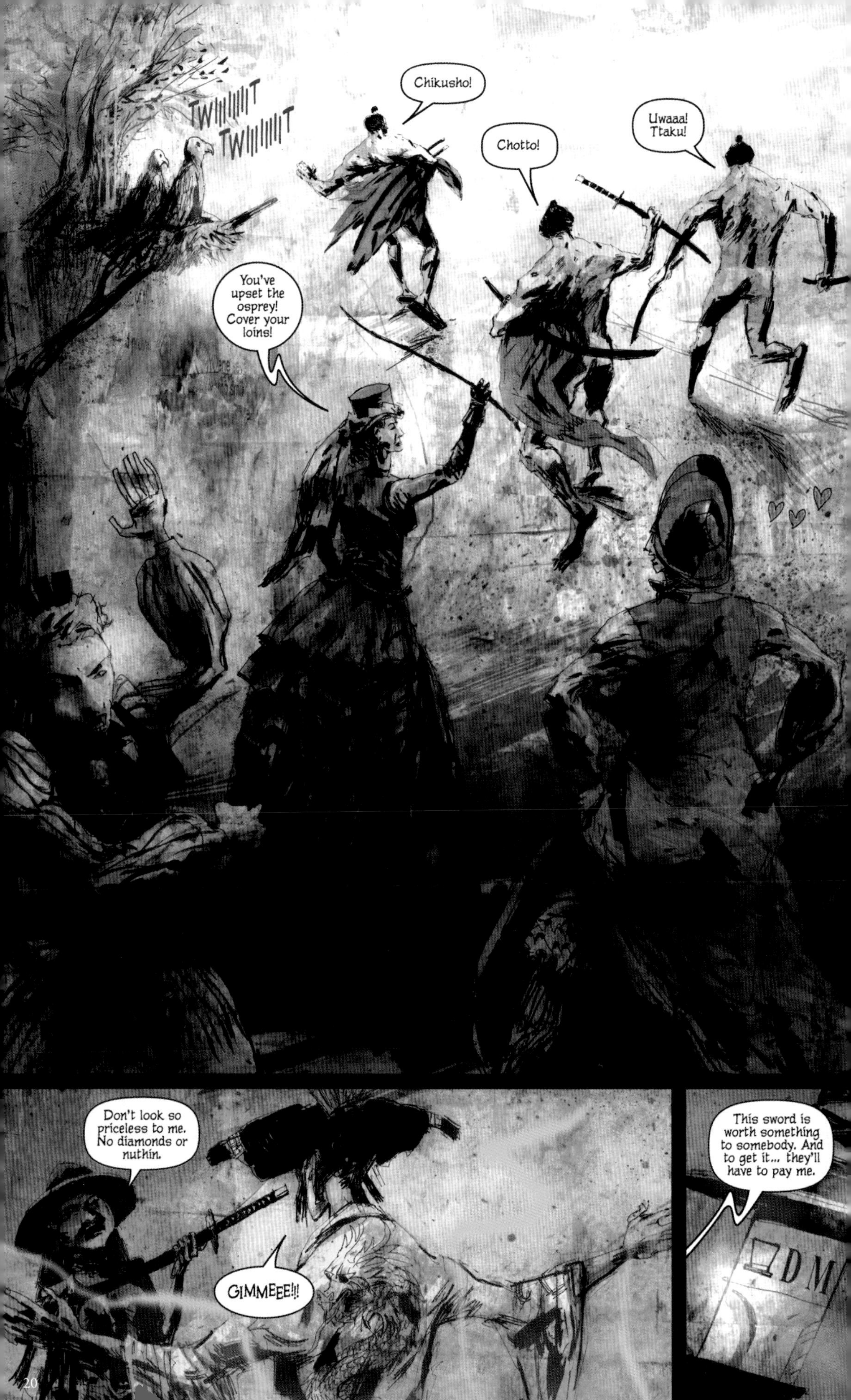
Chikusho!
Chotto!
Uwaaa! Ttaku!
You've upset the osprey! Cover your loins!
Don't look so priceless to me. No diamonds or nuthin.
GIMMEEE!!!
This sword is worth something to somebody. And to get it... they'll have to pay me.
DM

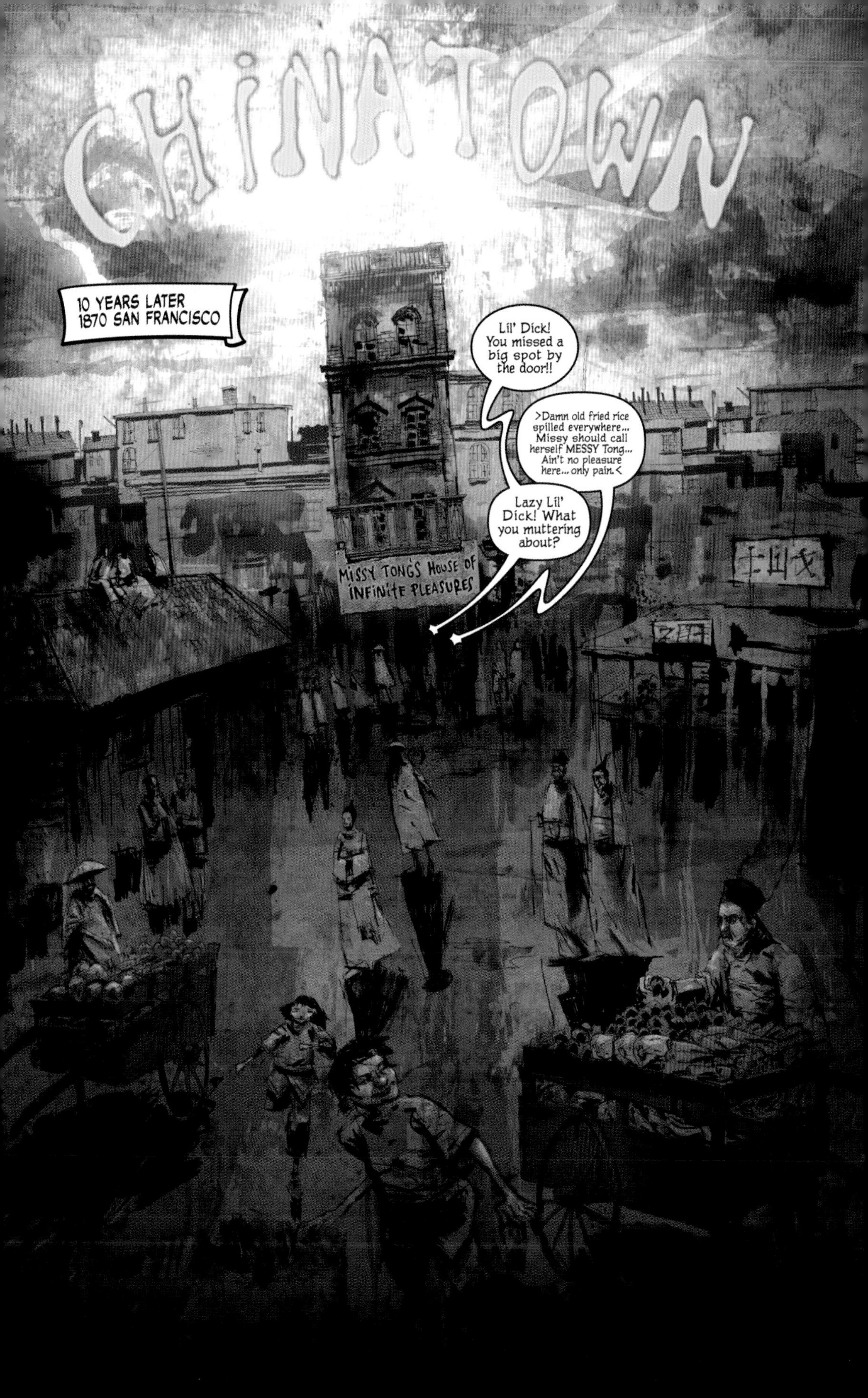
CHINATOWN
10 YEARS LATER 1870 SAN FRANCISCO
Lil' Dick! You missed a big spot by the door!!
>Damn old fried rice spilled everywhere... Missy should call herself MESSY Tong... Ain't no pleasure here... only pain.<
Lazy Lil' Dick! What you muttering about?
MISSY TONG'S HOUSE OF INFINITE PLEASURES

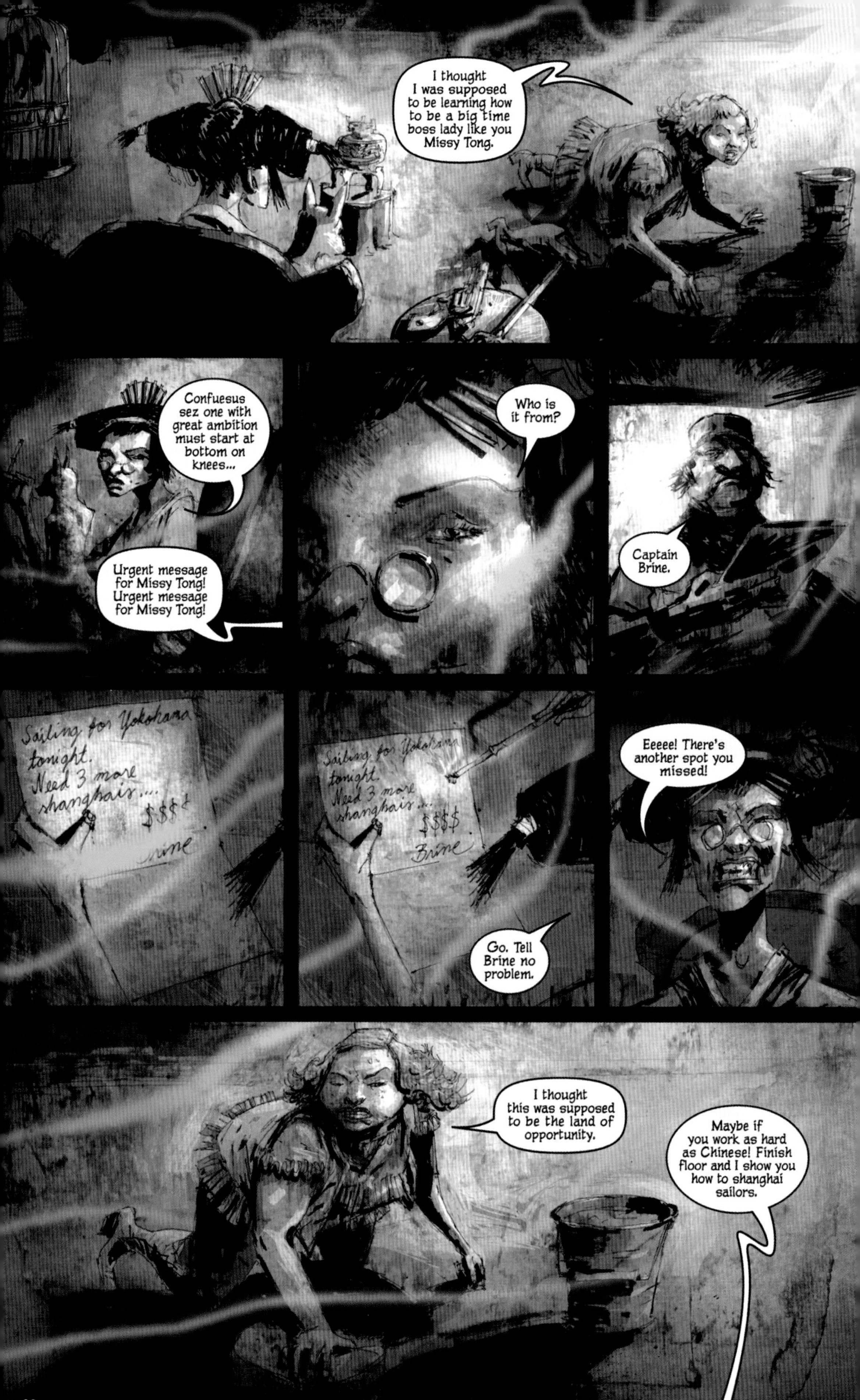
I thought I was supposed to be learning how to be a big time boss lady like you Missy Tong.
Confuesus sez one with great ambition must start at bottom on knees...
Urgent message for Missy Tong! Urgent message for Missy Tong!
Who is it from?
Captain Brine.
Sailing for Yokohama tonight. Need 3 more shanghais.... $$$
Sailing for Yokohama tonight. Need 3 more shanghais.... $$$$ Brine
Go. Tell Brine no problem.
Eeeee! There's another spot you missed!
I thought this was supposed to be the land of opportunity.
Maybe if you work as hard as Chinese! Finish floor and I show you how to shanghai sailors.

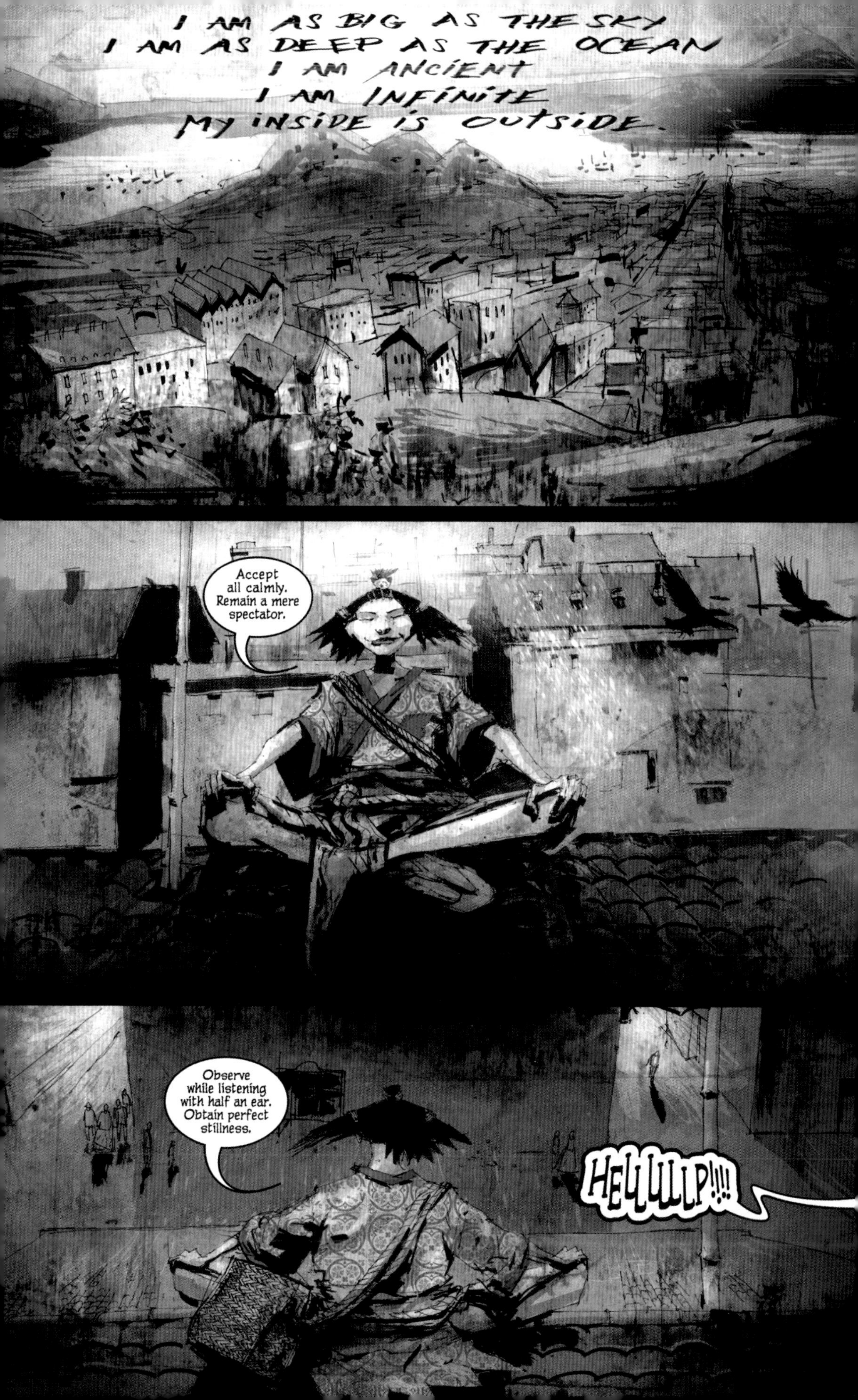
I AM AS BIG AS THE SKY
I AM AS DEEP AS THE OCEAN
I AM ANCIENT
I AM INFINITE
MY INSIDE IS OUTSIDE.
Accept all calmly. Remain a mere spectator.
Observe while listening with half an ear. Obtain perfect stillness.
HELLLLLP!!!!

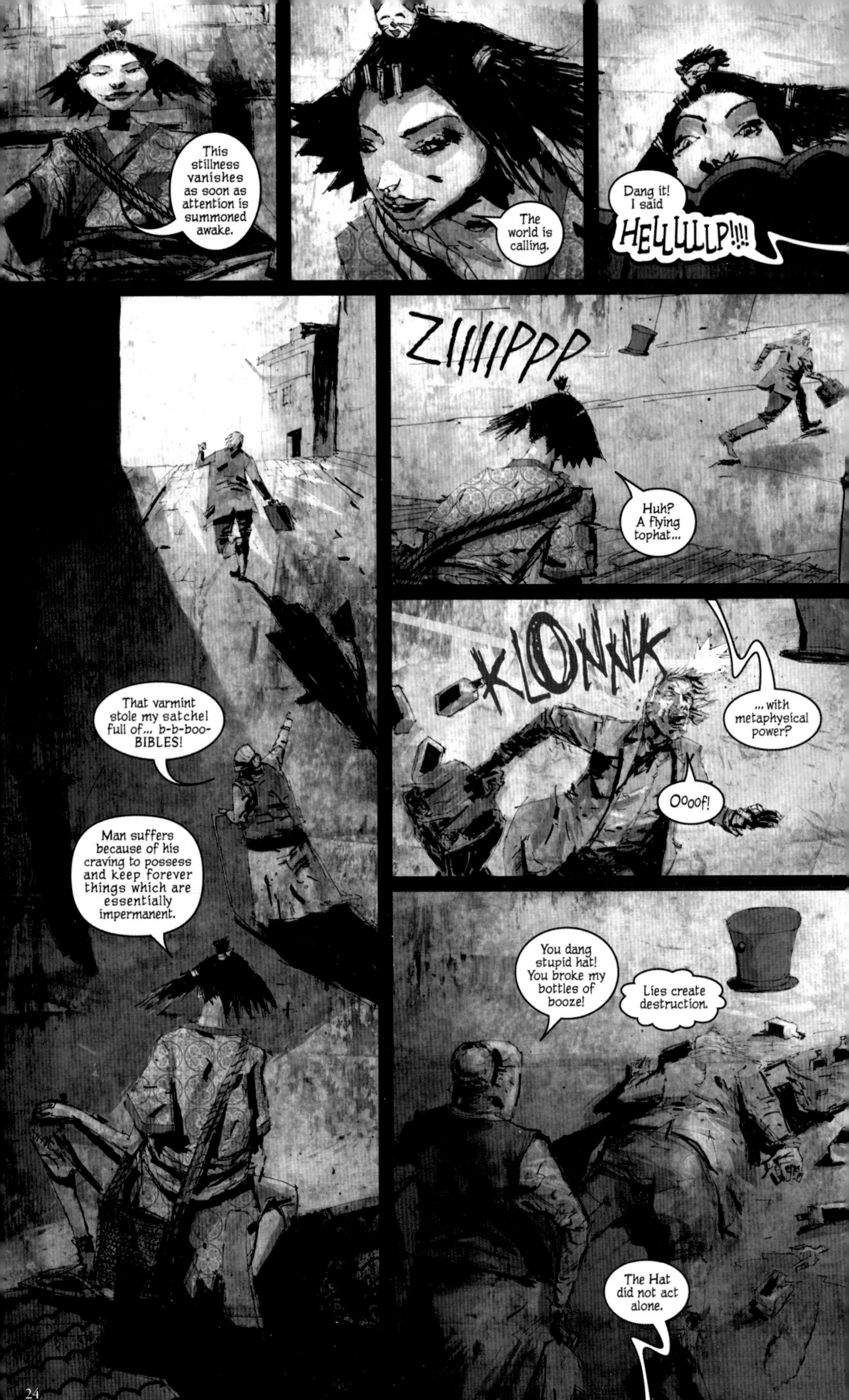
This stillness vanishes as soon as attention is summoned awake.
The world is calling.
Dang it! I said HELLLLLP!!!!
ZIIIIPPP
Huh? A flying tophat...
That varmint stole my satchel full of... b-b-boo-BIBLES!
Man suffers because of his craving to possess and keep forever things which are essentially impermanent.
KLONNK
...with metaphysical power?
Oooof!
You dang stupid hat! You broke my bottles of booze!
Lies create destruction.
The Hat did not act alone.

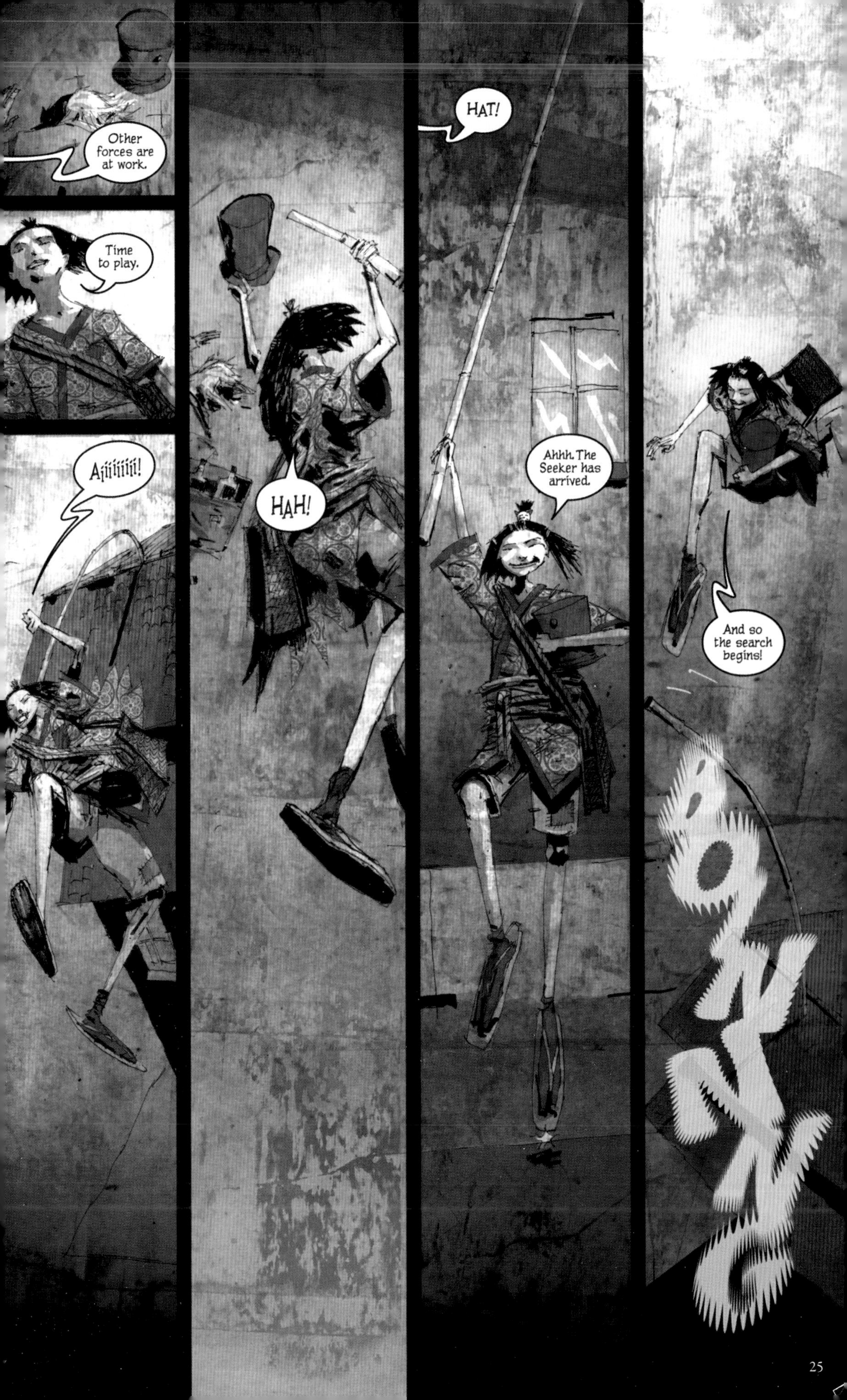
Other forces are at work.
Time to play.
Aiiiiiii!
HAH!
HAT!
Ahhh. The Seeker has arrived.
And so the search begins!

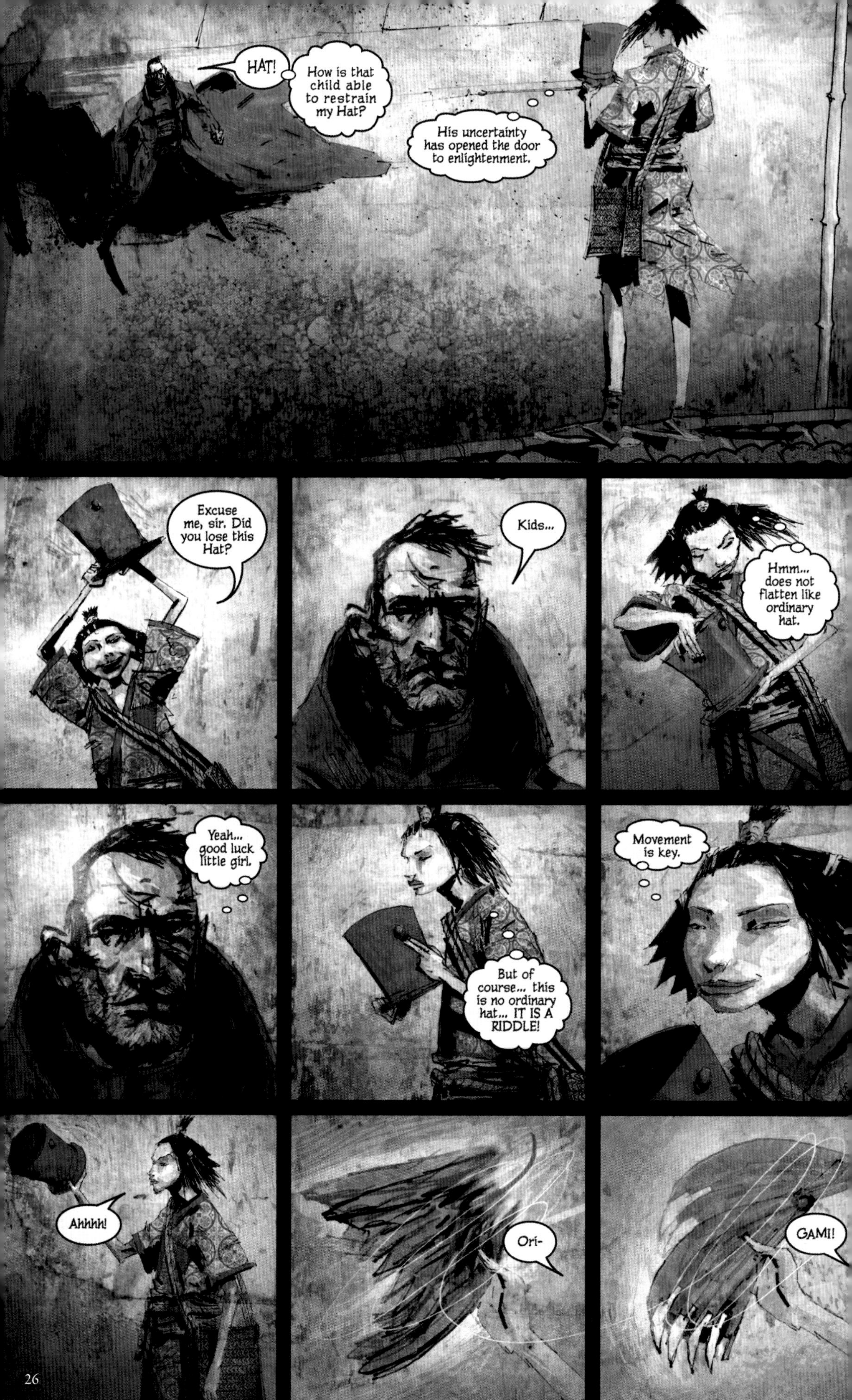
HAT!
How is that child able to restrain my Hat?
His uncertainty has opened the door to enlightenment.
Excuse me, sir. Did you lose this Hat?
Kids...
Hmm... does not flatten like ordinary hat.
Yeah... good luck little girl.
But of course... this is no ordinary hat... IT IS A RIDDLE!
Movement is key.
Ahhhh!
Ori-
GAMI!

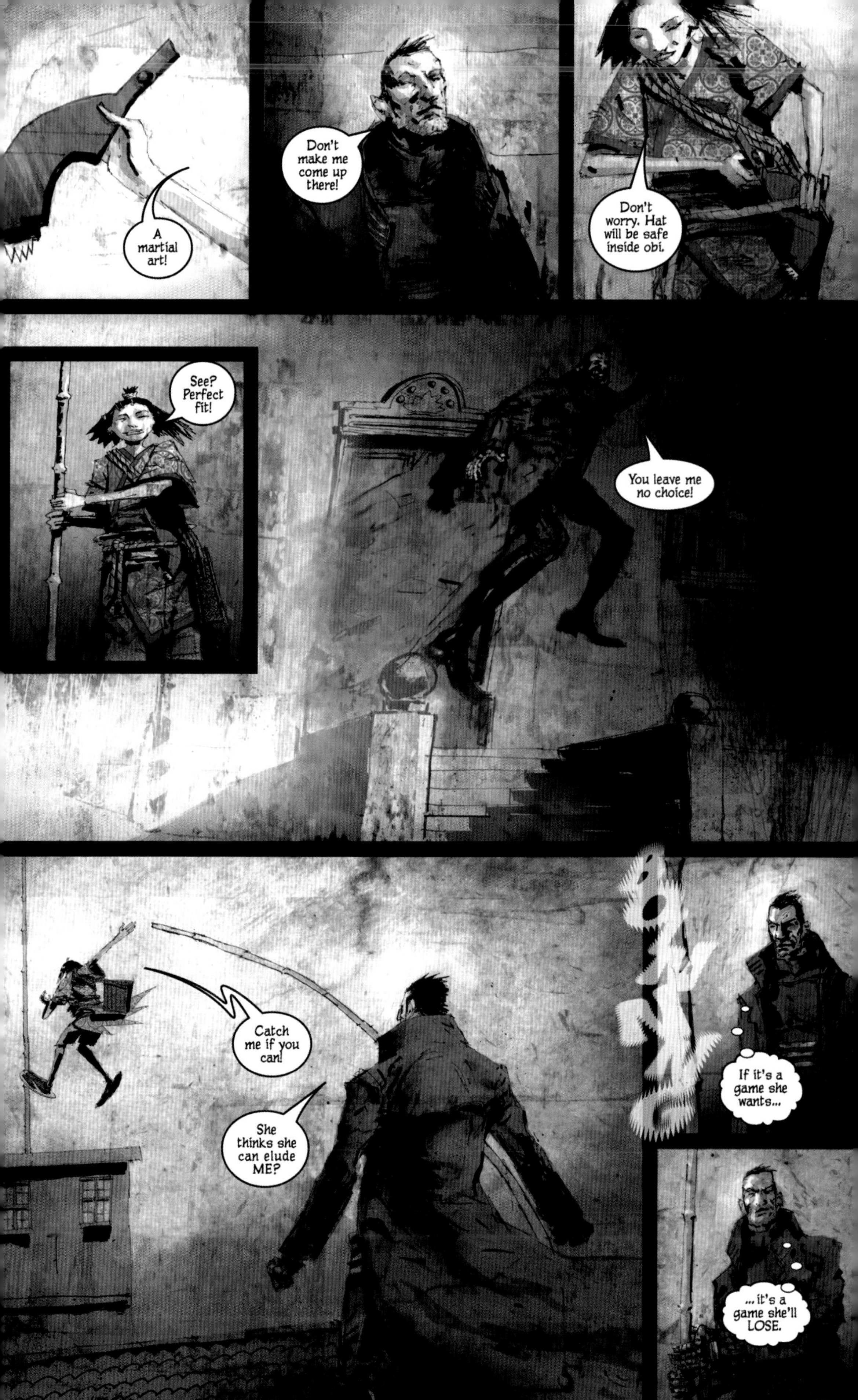
A martial art!
Don't make me come up there!
Don't worry. Hat will be safe inside obi.
See? Perfect fit!
You leave me no choice!
Catch me if you can!
She thinks she can elude ME?
If it's a game she wants...
...it's a game she'll LOSE.

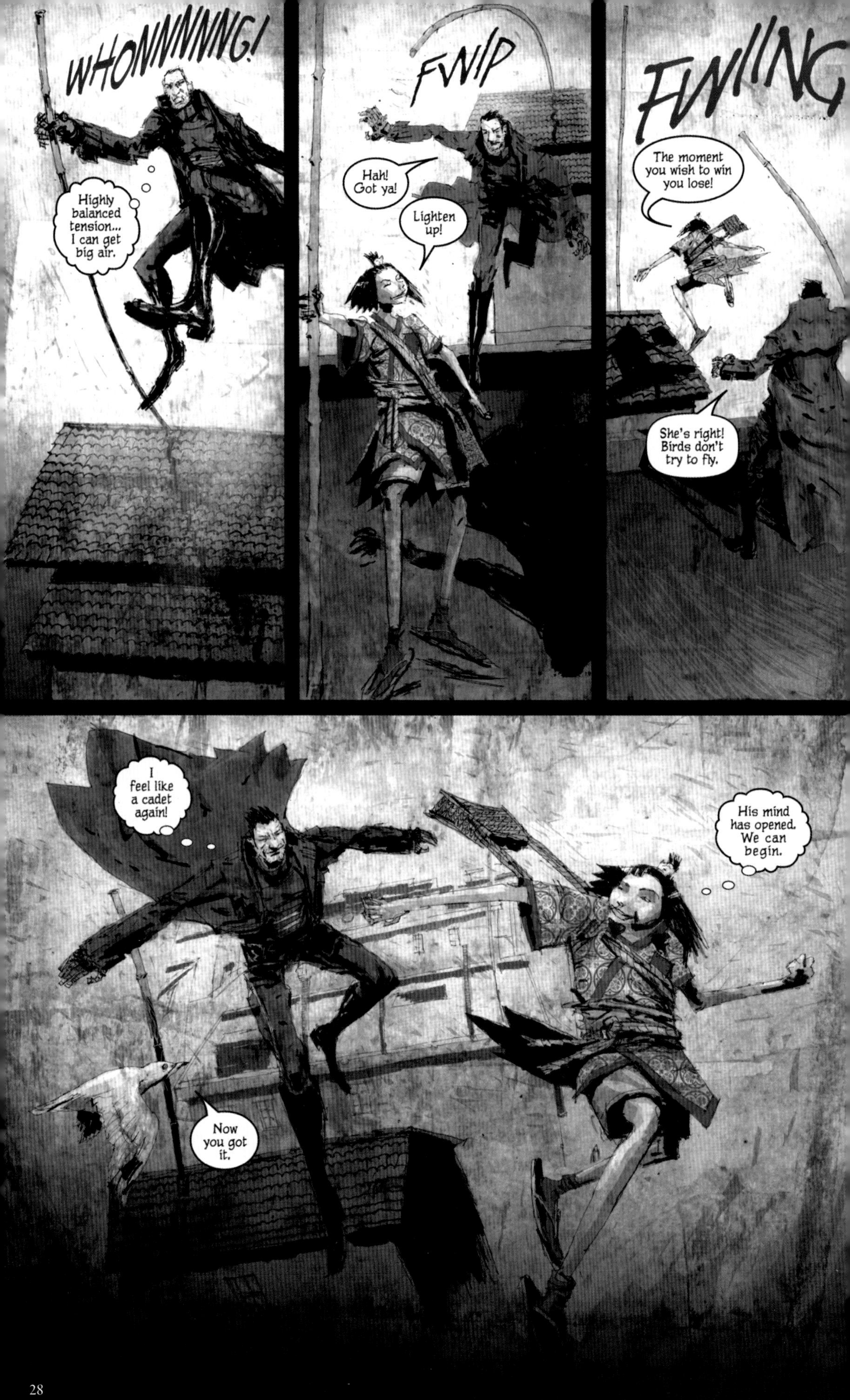
WHONNNNNG!
Highly balanced tension... I can get big air.
FWIP
Hah! Got ya!
Lighten up!
FWIING
The moment you wish to win you lose!
She's right! Birds don't try to fly.
I feel like a cadet again!
Now you got it.
His mind has opened. We can begin.

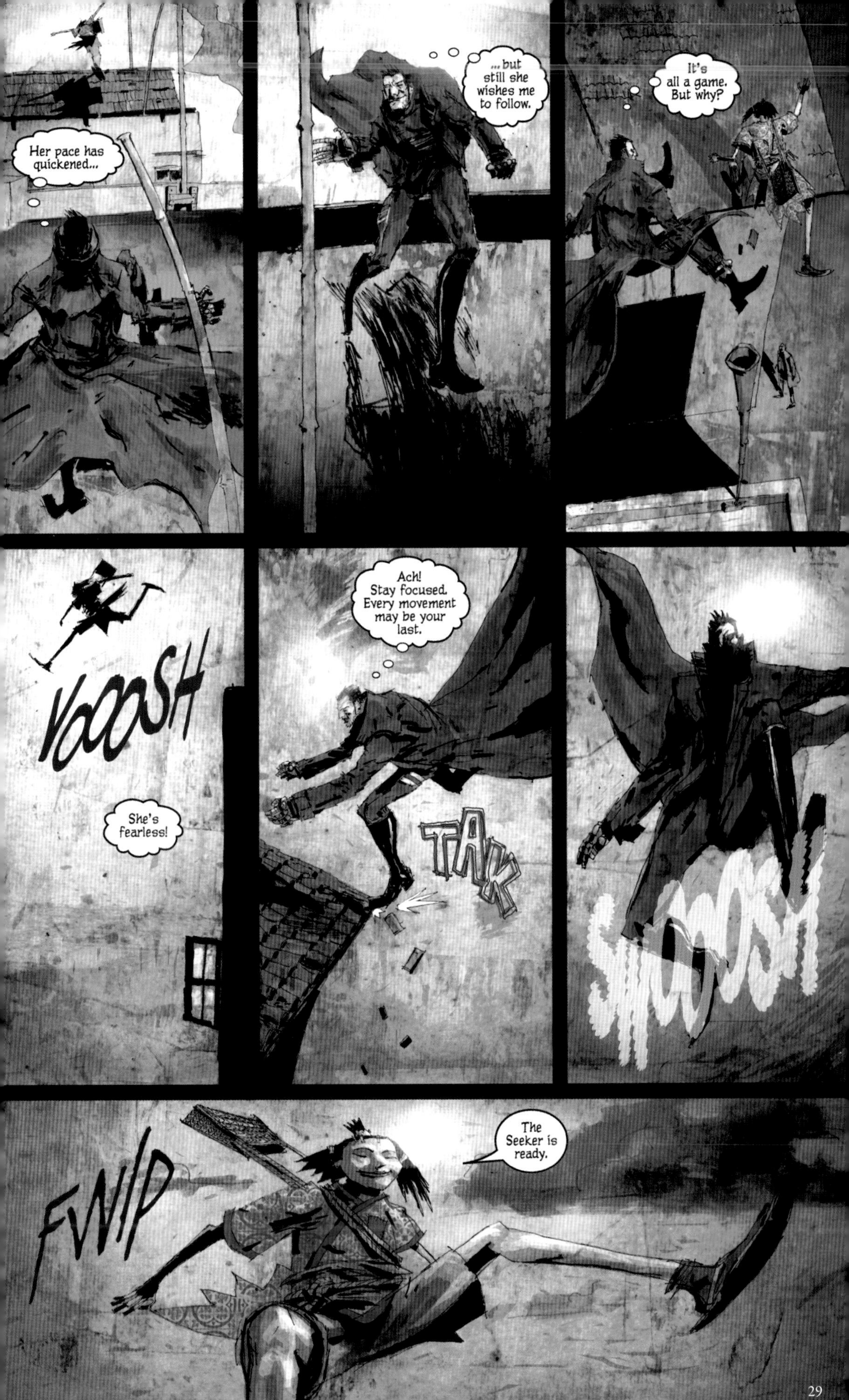
Her pace has quickened...
...but still she wishes me to follow.
It's all a game. But why?
VOOOSH
She's fearless!
Ach! Stay focused. Every movement may be your last.
TAK
SWOOSH
FWIP
The Seeker is ready.

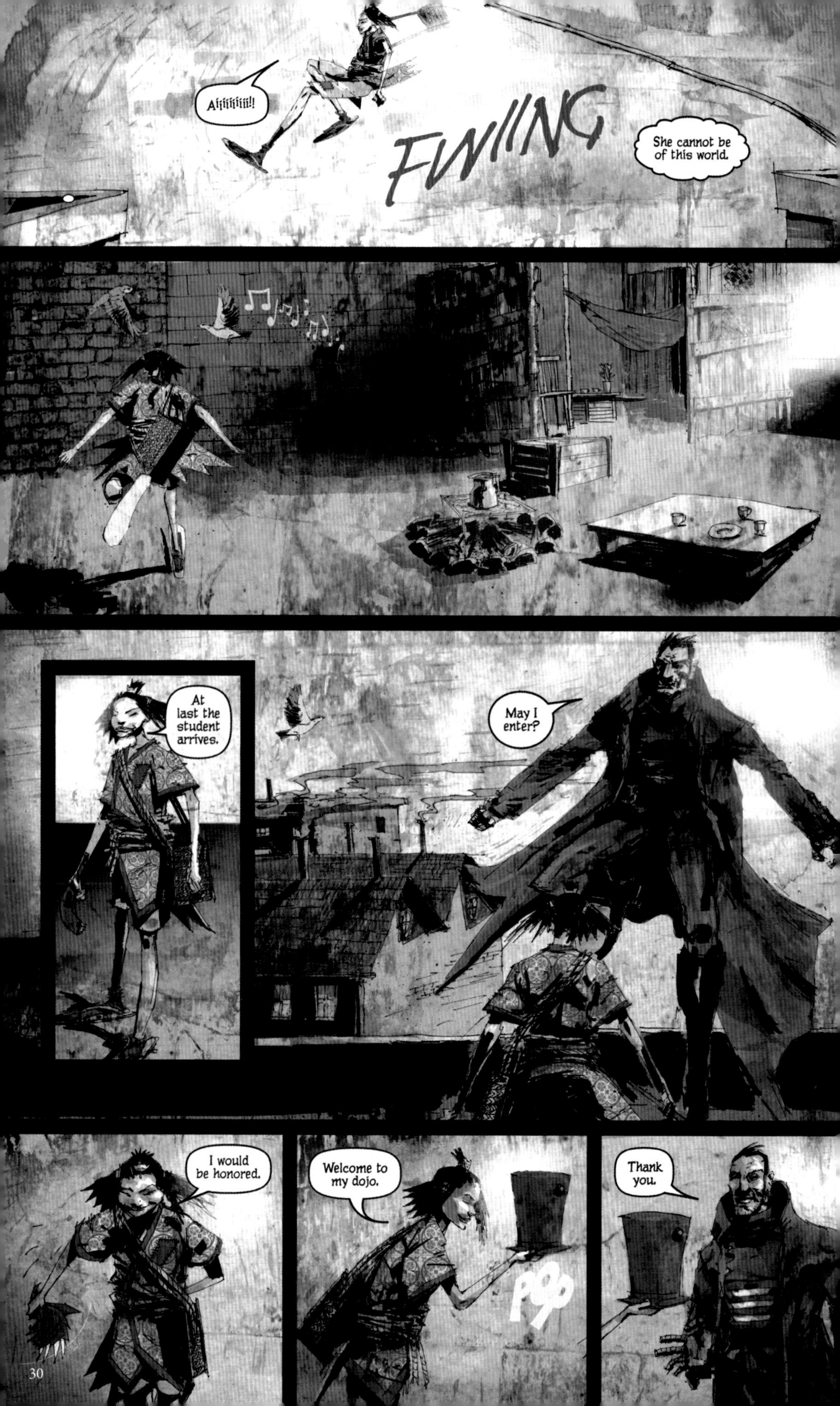
Aiiiiiiii!!
FWIING
She cannot be of this world.
At last the student arrives.
May I enter?
I would be honored.
Welcome to my dojo.
POP
Thank you.

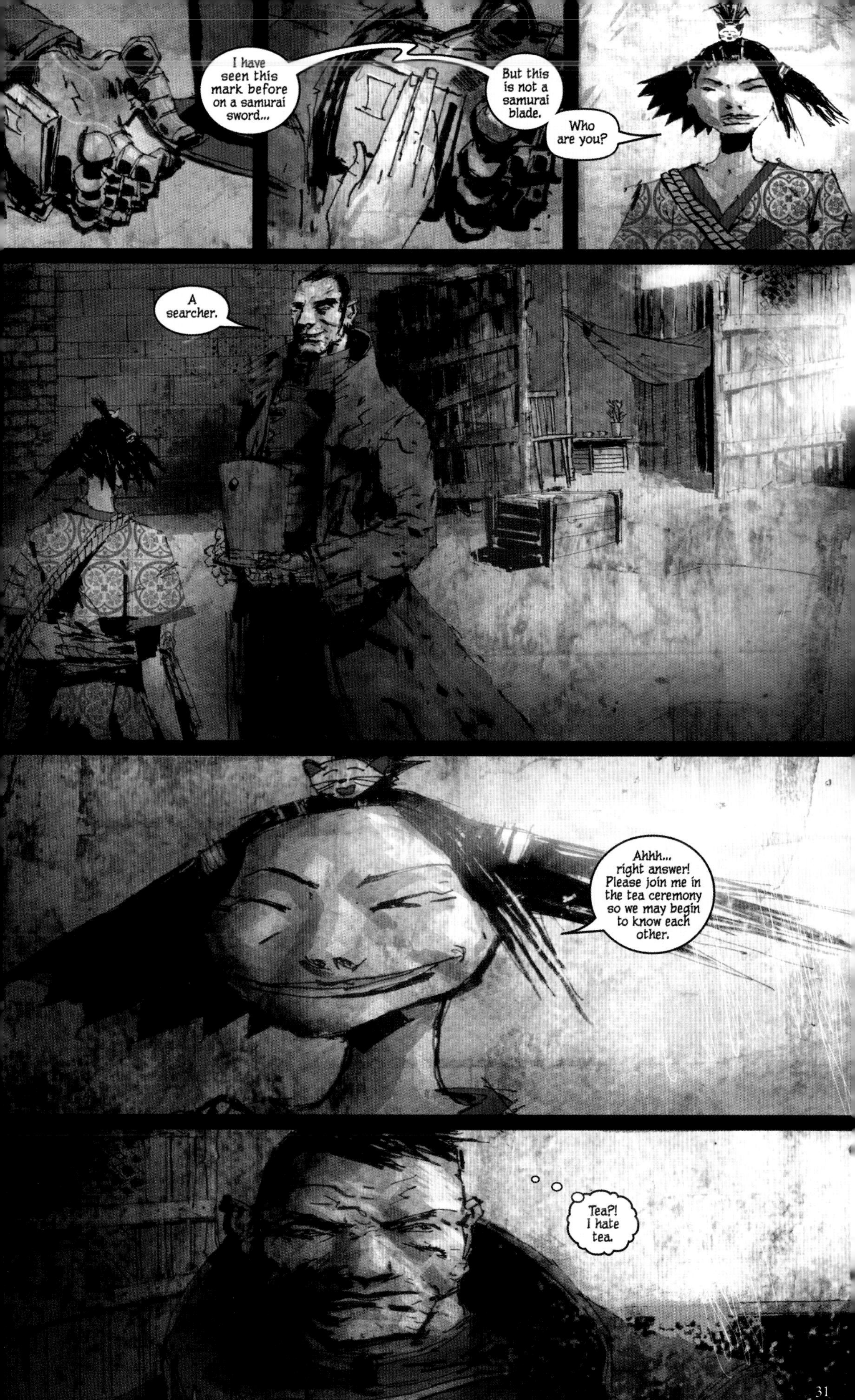
I have seen this mark before on a samurai sword...
But this is not a samurai blade.
Who are you?
A searcher.
Ahhh... right answer! Please join me in the tea ceremony so we may begin to know each other.
Tea?! I hate tea.

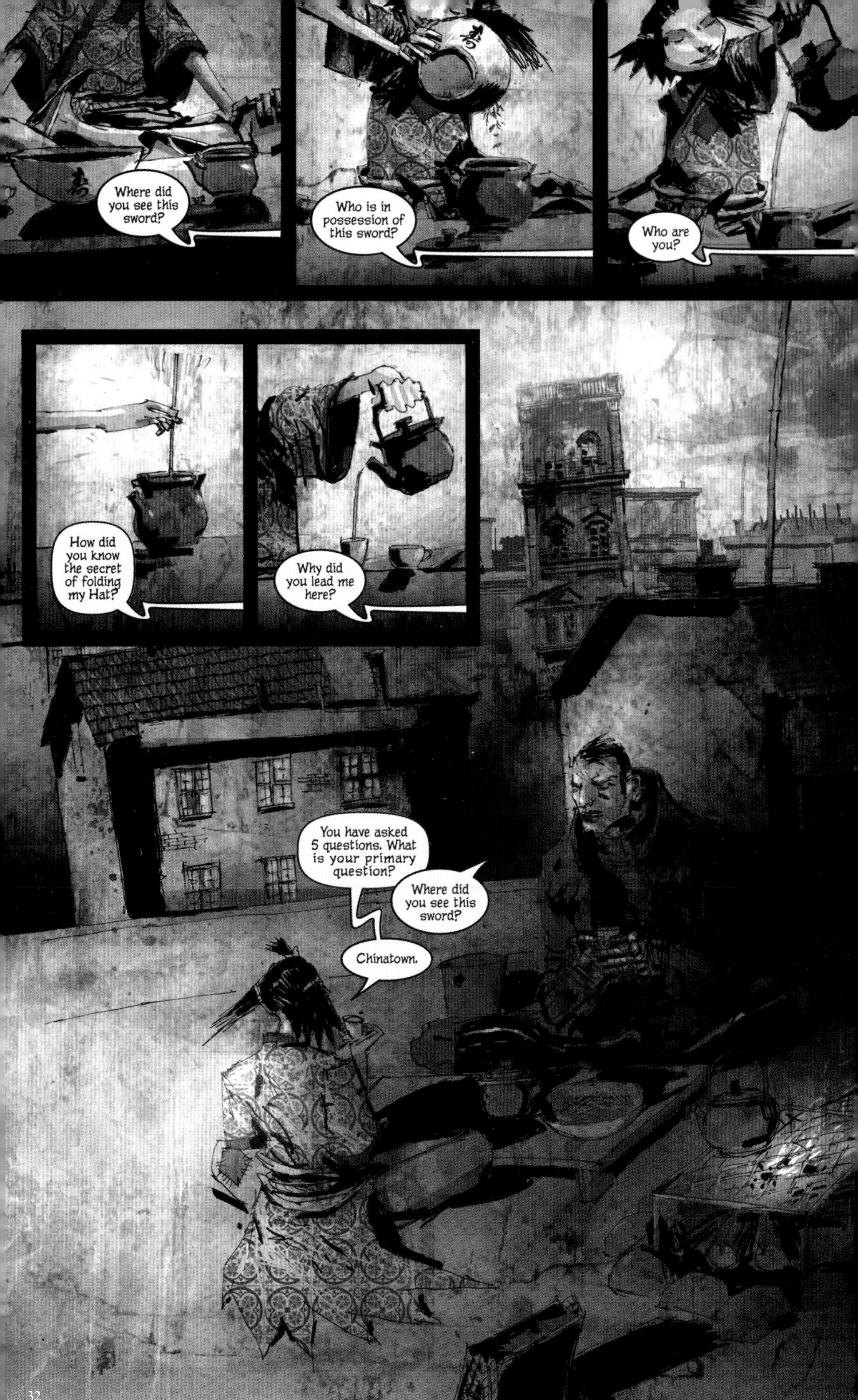
Where did you see this sword?
Who is in possession of this sword?
Who are you?
How did you know the secret of folding my Hat?
Why did you lead me here?
You have asked 5 questions. What is your primary question?
Where did you see this sword?
Chinatown.

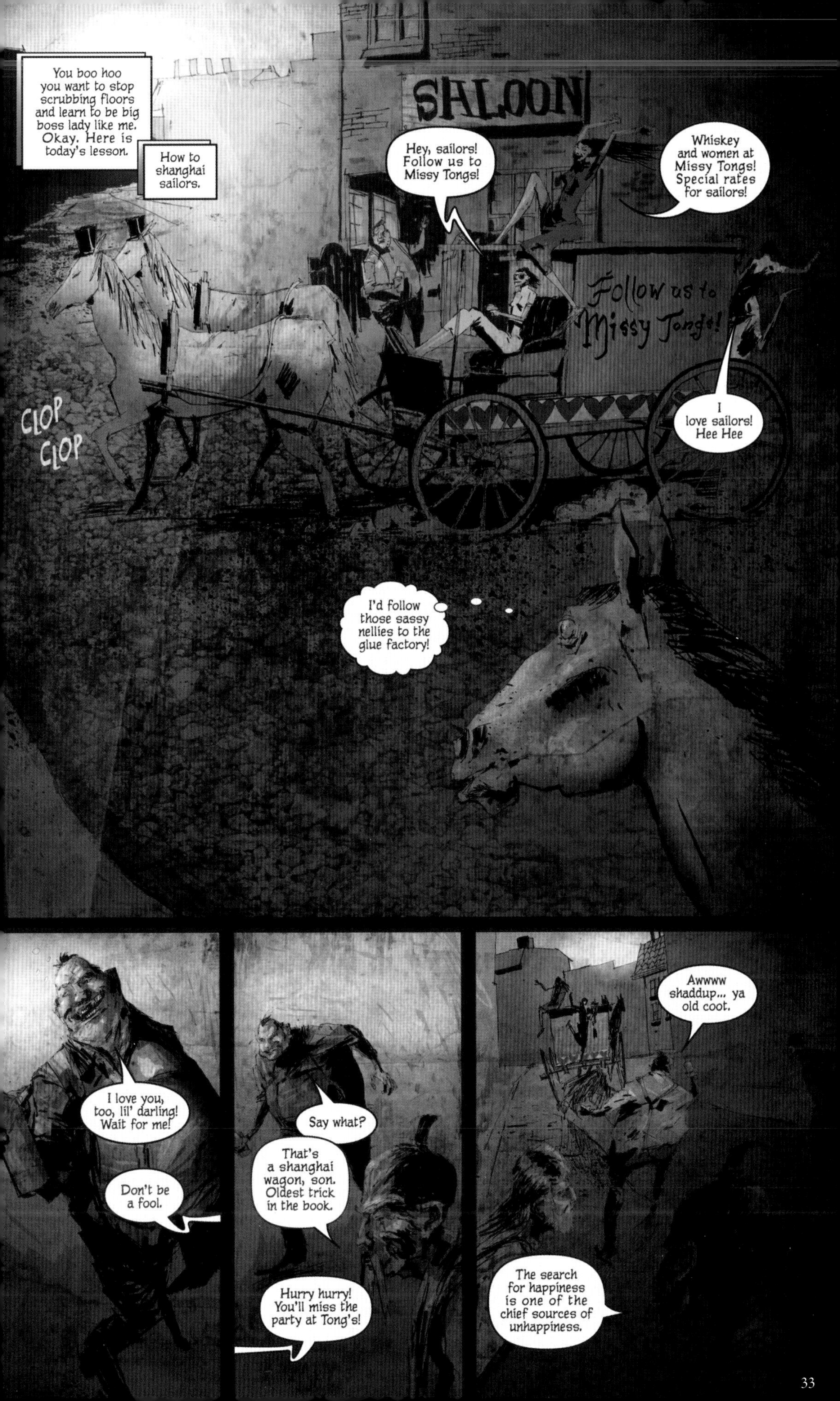

You boo hoo you want to stop scrubbing floors and learn to be big boss lady like me. Okay. Here is today's lesson.
How to shanghai sailors.
SALOON
Hey, sailors! Follow us to Missy Tongs!
Whiskey and women at Missy Tongs! Special rates for sailors!
Follow us to Missy Tongs!
I love sailors! Hee Hee
CLOP
CLOP
I'd follow those sassy nellies to the glue factory!
I love you, too, lil' darling! Wait for me!
Don't be a fool.
Say what?
That's a shanghai wagon, son. Oldest trick in the book.
Hurry hurry! You'll miss the party at Tong's!
Awwww shaddup... ya old coot.
The search for happiness is one of the chief sources of unhappiness.

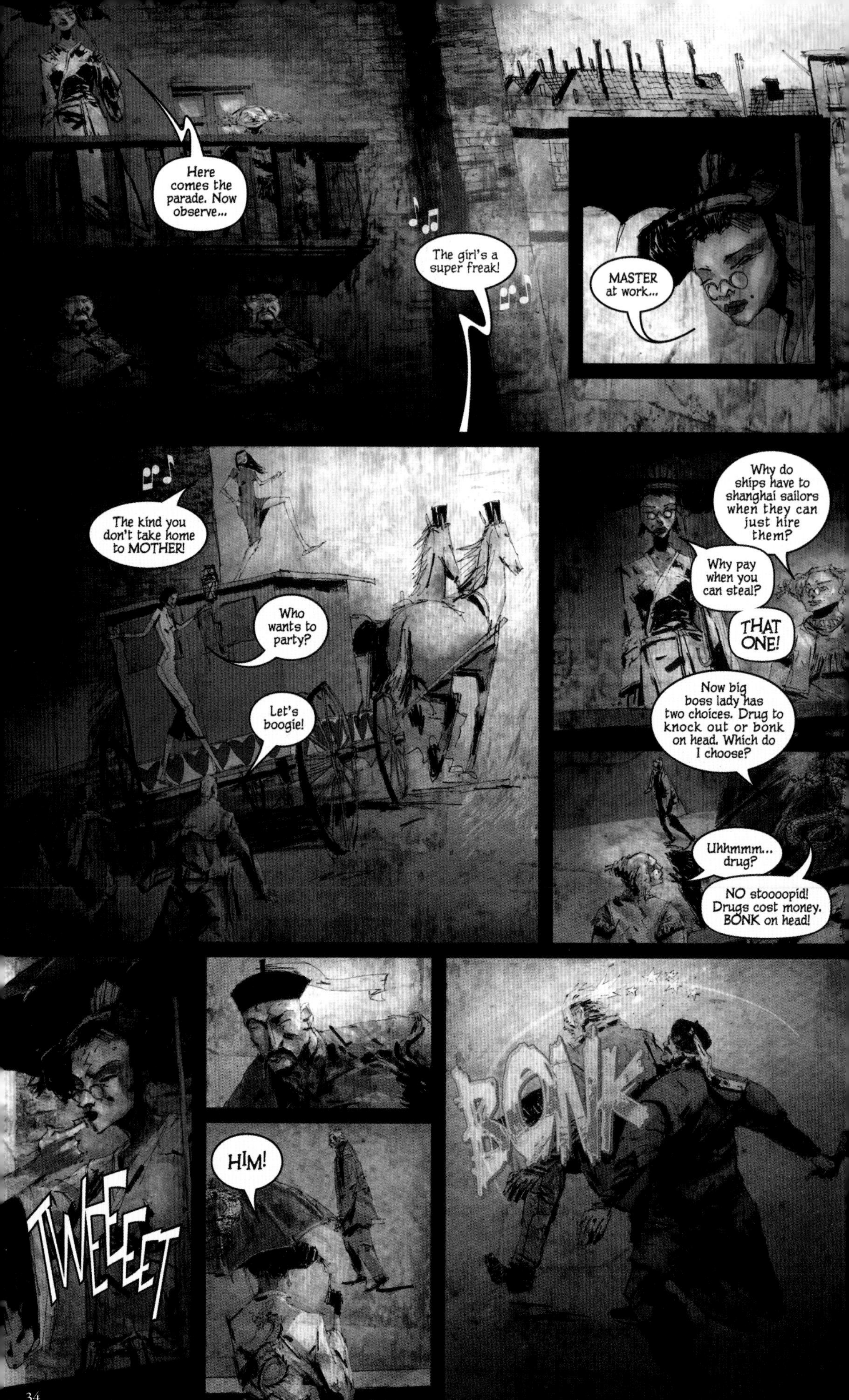
Here comes the parade. Now observe...
The girl's a super freak!
MASTER at work...
The kind you don't take home to MOTHER!
Who wants to party?
Let's boogie!
Why do ships have to shanghai sailors when they can just hire them?
Why pay when you can steal?
THAT ONE!
Now big boss lady has two choices. Drug to knock out or bonk on head. Which do I choose?
Uhhmmm... drug?
NO stoooopid! Drugs cost money. BONK on head!
TWEEEET
HIM!
BONK

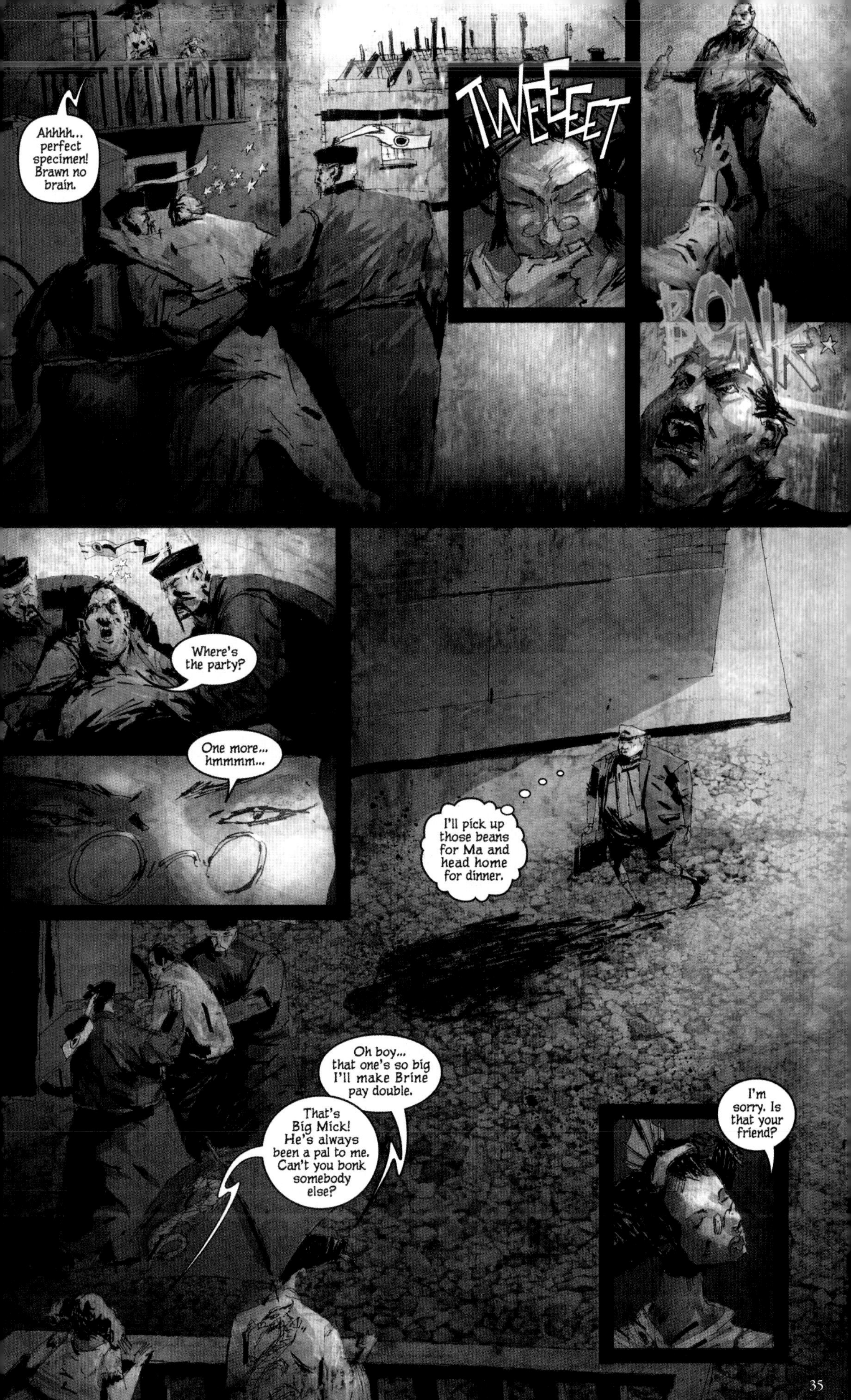

Ahhhh... perfect specimen! Brawn no brain.
TWEEEEET
BONK
Where's the party?
One more... hmmmm...
I'll pick up those beans for Ma and head home for dinner.
Oh boy... that one's so big I'll make Brine pay double.
That's Big Mick! He's always been a pal to me. Can't you bonk somebody else?
I'm sorry. Is that your friend?

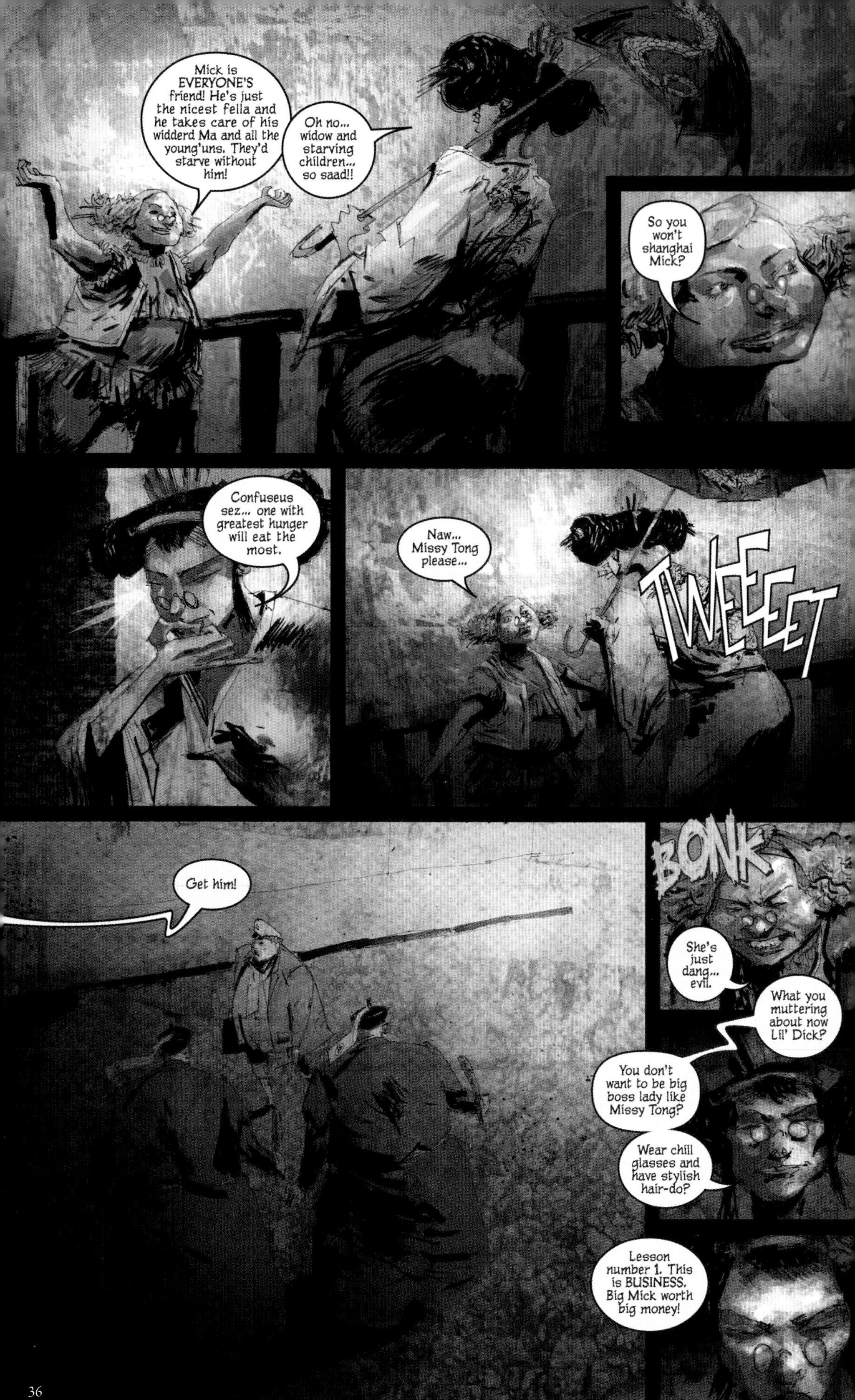
Mick is EVERYONE'S friend! He's just the nicest fella and he takes care of his widderd Ma and all the young'uns. They'd starve without him!
Oh no... widow and starving children... so saad!!
So you won't shanghai Mick?
Confuseus sez... one with greatest hunger will eat the most.
Naw... Missy Tong please...
TWEEEEET
Get him!
BONK
She's just dang... evil.
What you muttering about now Lil' Dick?
You don't want to be big boss lady like Missy Tong?
Wear chill glasses and have stylish hair-do?
Lesson number 1. This is BUSINESS. Big Mick worth big money!

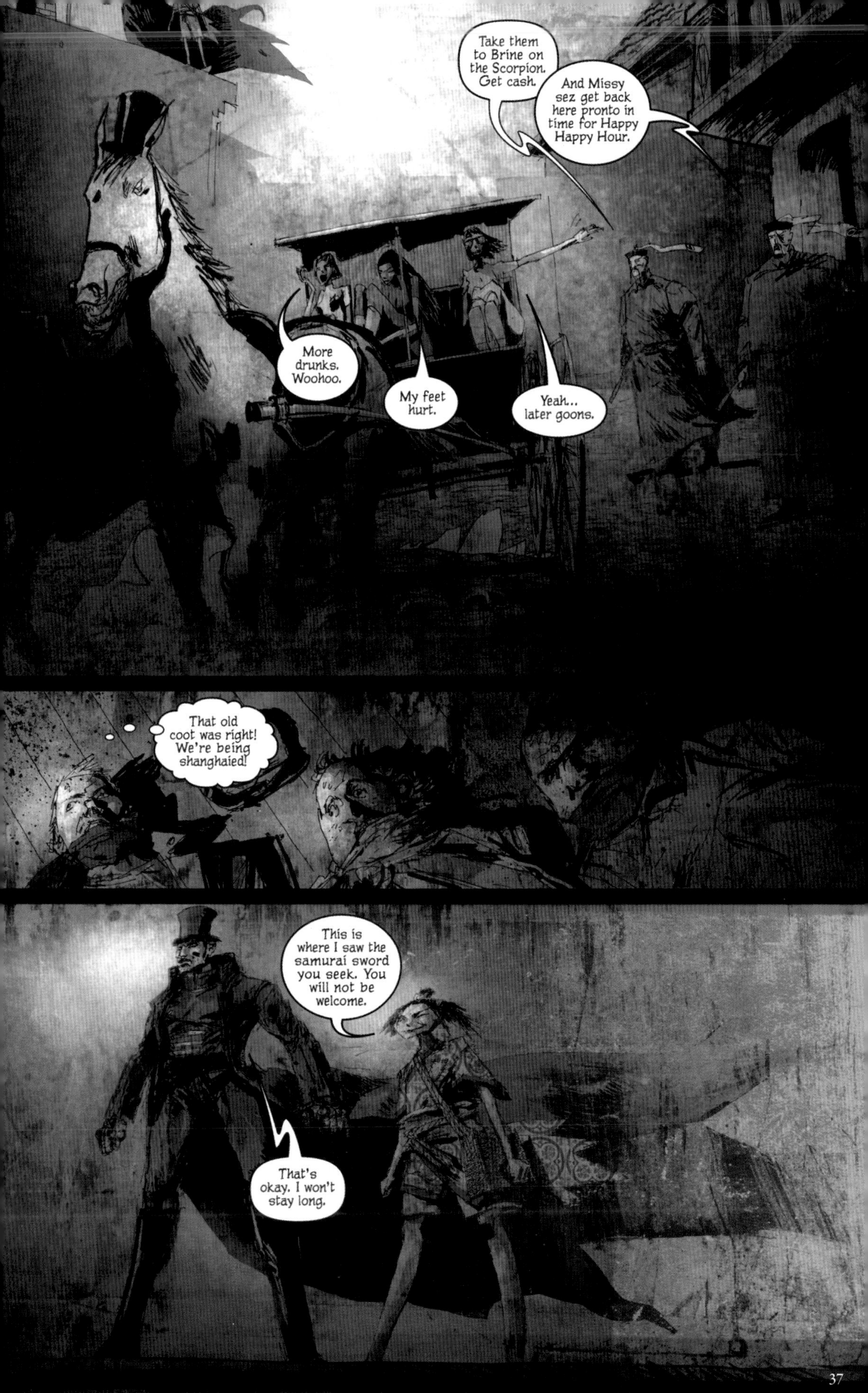

Take them to Brine on the Scorpion. Get cash.
And Missy sez get back here pronto in time for Happy Happy Hour.
More drunks. Woohoo.
My feet hurt.
Yeah... later goons.
That old coot was right! We're being shanghaied!
This is where I saw the samurai sword you seek. You will not be welcome.
That's okay. I won't stay long.

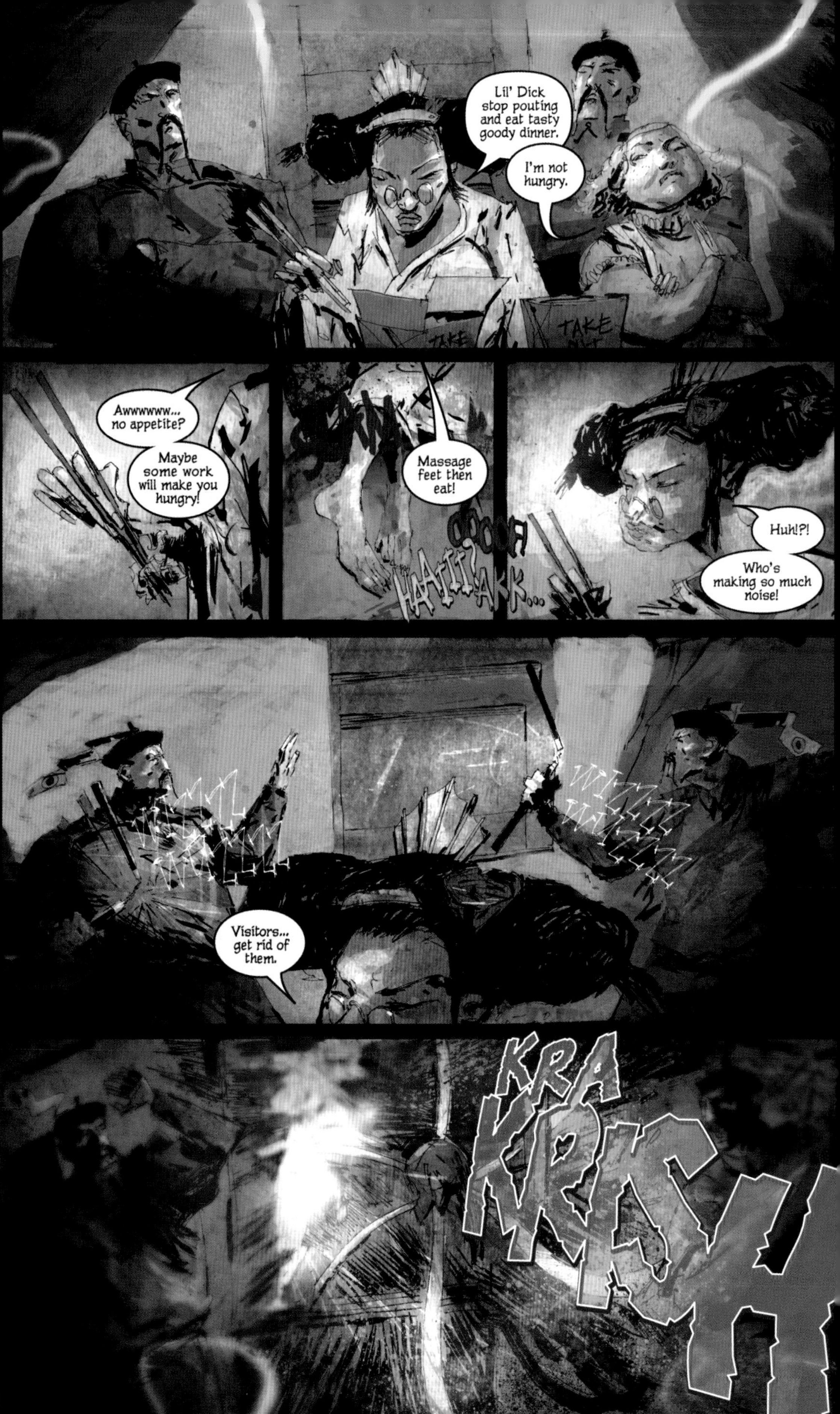
Lil' Dick stop pouting and eat tasty goody dinner.
I'm not hungry.
Awwwwww... no appetite?
Maybe some work will make you hungry!
Massage feet then eat!
OOOOF
HAAII!?AKK...
Huh!?!
Who's making so much noise!
Visitors... get rid of them.
KRA
KRASH

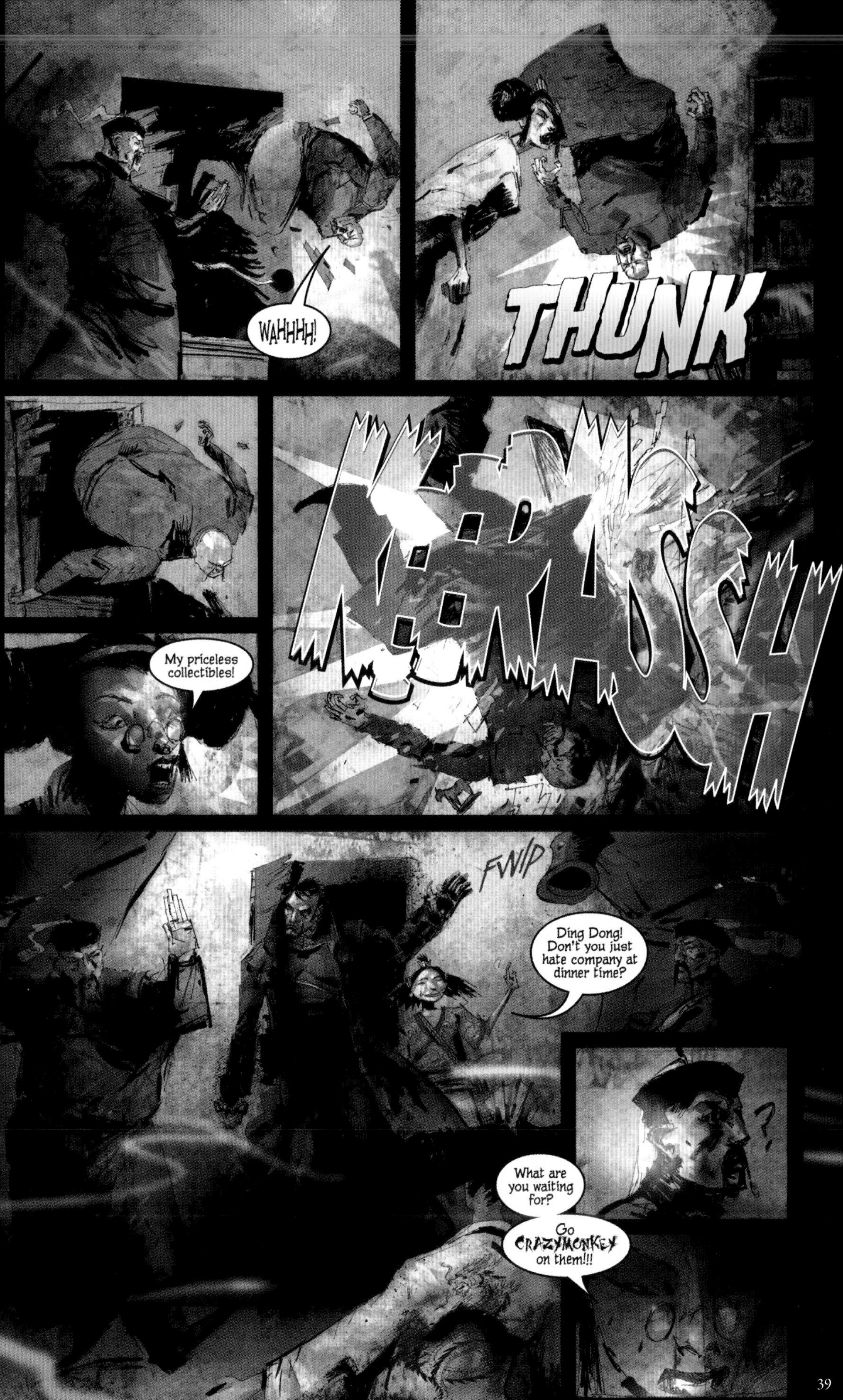
WAHHHH!
THUNK
My priceless collectibles!
FWIP
Ding Dong! Don't you just hate company at dinner time?
What are you waiting for?
Go CRAZYMONKEY on them!!!

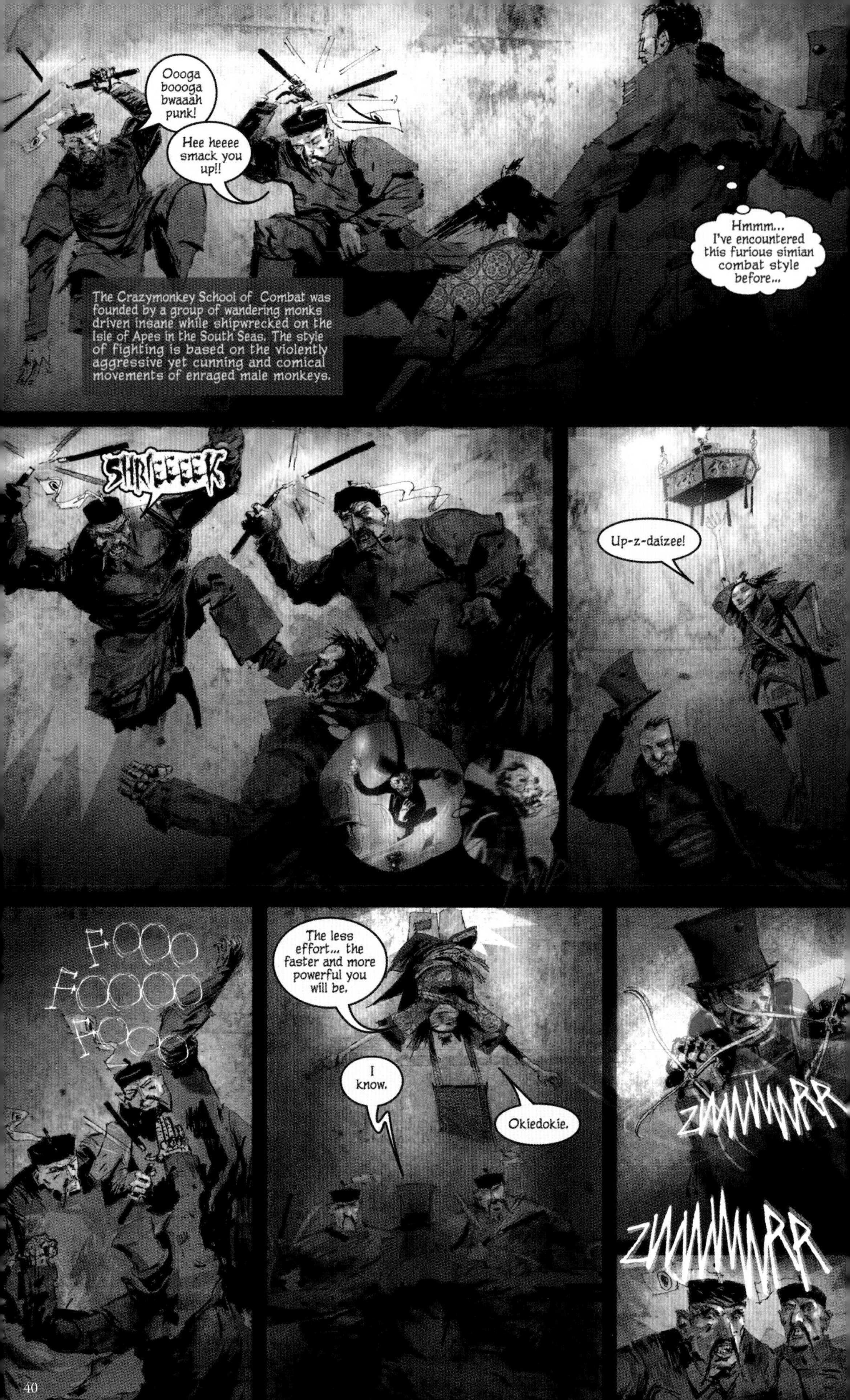
Oooga boooga bwaaah punk!
Hee heeee smack you up!!
Hmmm... I've encountered this furious simian combat style before...
The Crazymonkey School of Combat was founded by a group of wandering monks driven insane while shipwrecked on the Isle of Apes in the South Seas. The style of fighting is based on the violently aggressive yet cunning and comical movements of enraged male monkeys.
SHRIEEEEK
Up-z-daizee!
FOOO
FOOOOO
FOOO
The less effort... the faster and more powerful you will be.
I know.
Okiedokie.
ZWWWWRR
ZWWWWRR

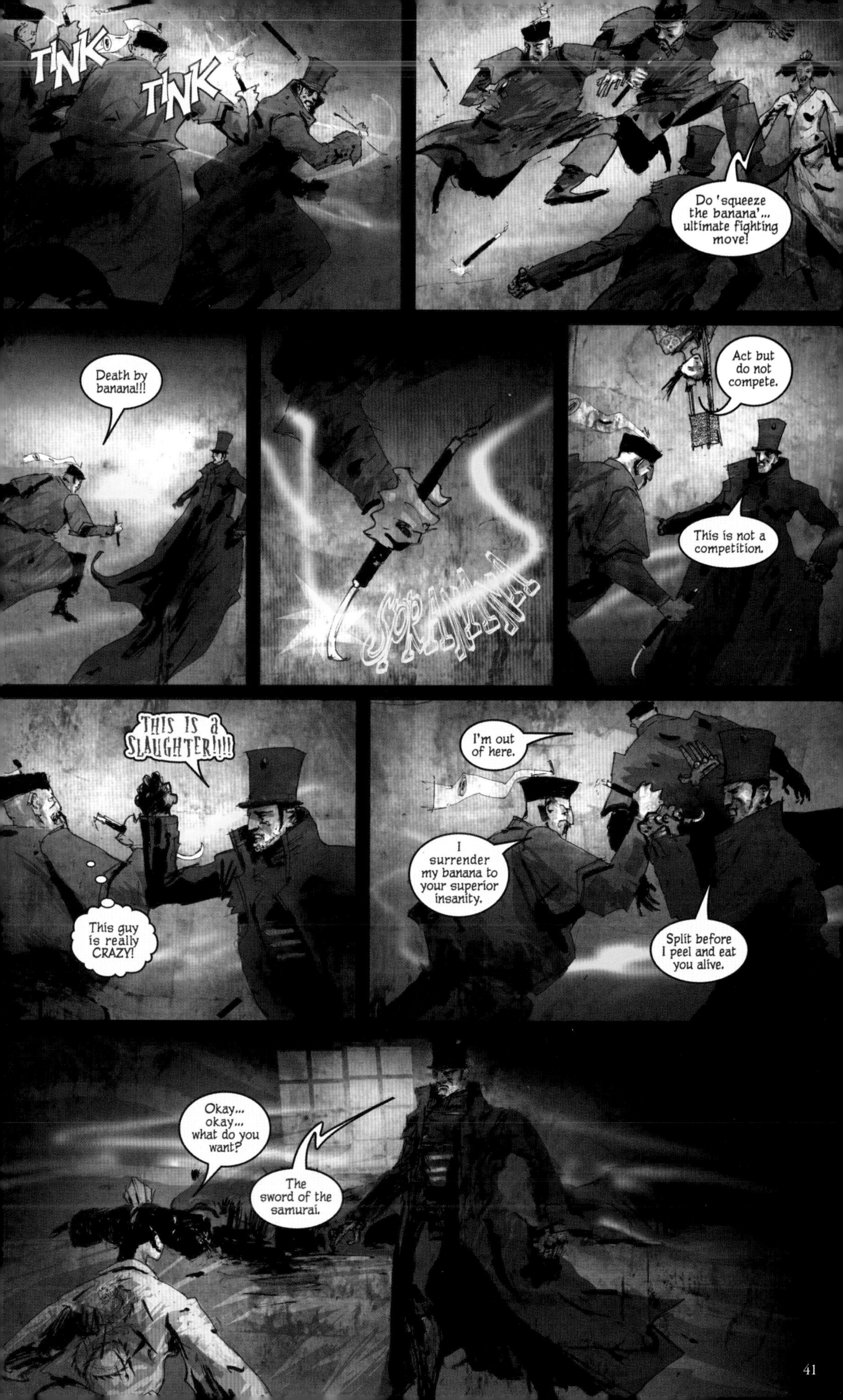
TINK
TINK
Do 'squeeze the banana'... ultimate fighting move!
Death by banana!!!
Act but do not compete.
This is not a competition.
THIS IS a SLAUGHTER!!!!
This guy is really CRAZY!
I'm out of here.
I surrender my banana to your superior insanity.
Split before I peel and eat you alive.
Okay... okay... what do you want?
The sword of the samurai.

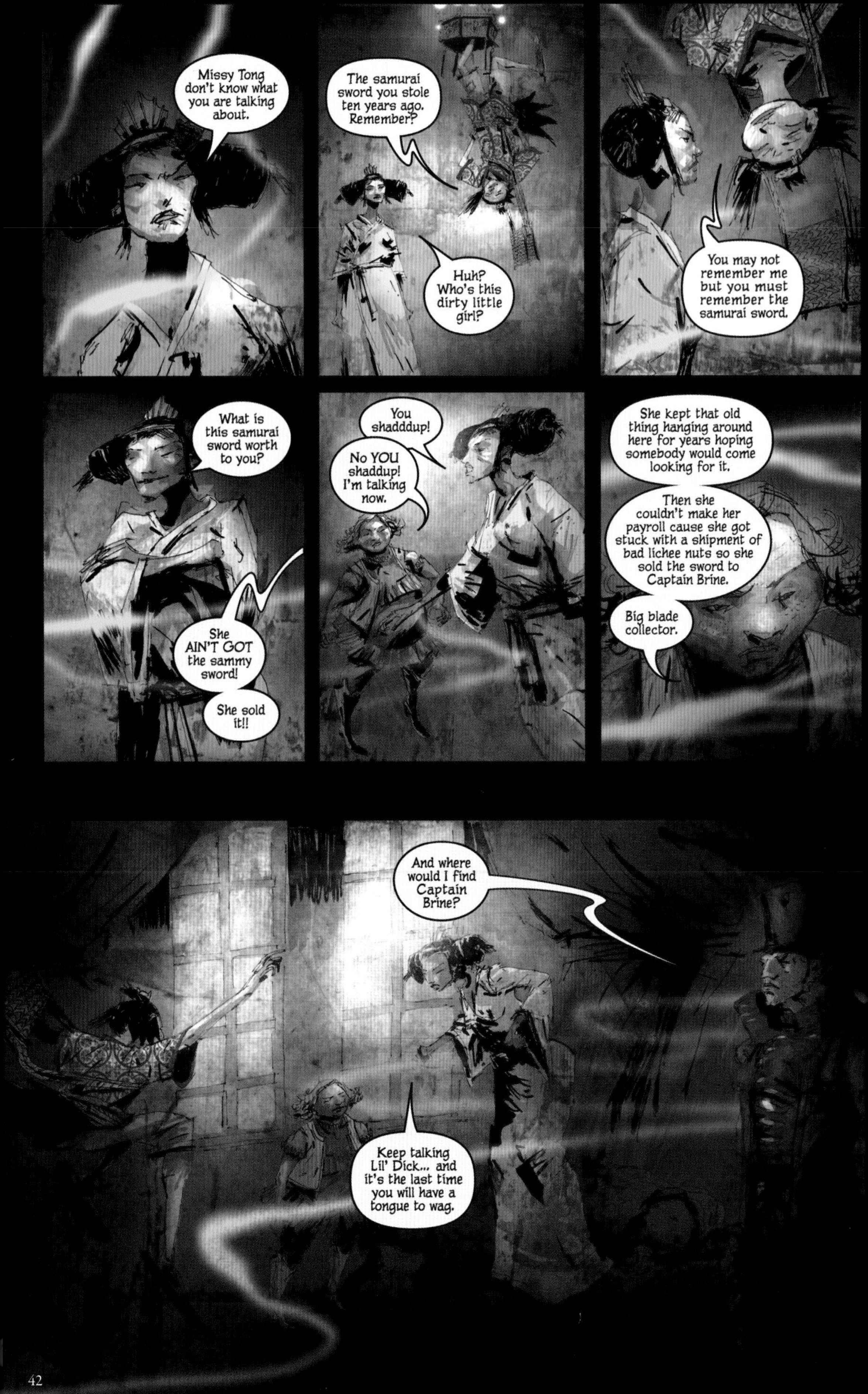
Missy Tong don't know what you are talking about.
The samurai sword you stole ten years ago. Remember?
Huh? Who's this dirty little girl?
You may not remember me but you must remember the samurai sword.
What is this samurai sword worth to you?
She AIN'T GOT the sammy sword!
She sold it!!
You shadddup!
No YOU shaddup! I'm talking now.
She kept that old thing hanging around here for years hoping somebody would come looking for it.
Then she couldn't make her payroll cause she got stuck with a shipment of bad lichee nuts so she sold the sword to Captain Brine.
Big blade collector.
And where would I find Captain Brine?
Keep talking Lil' Dick... and it's the last time you will have a tongue to wag.

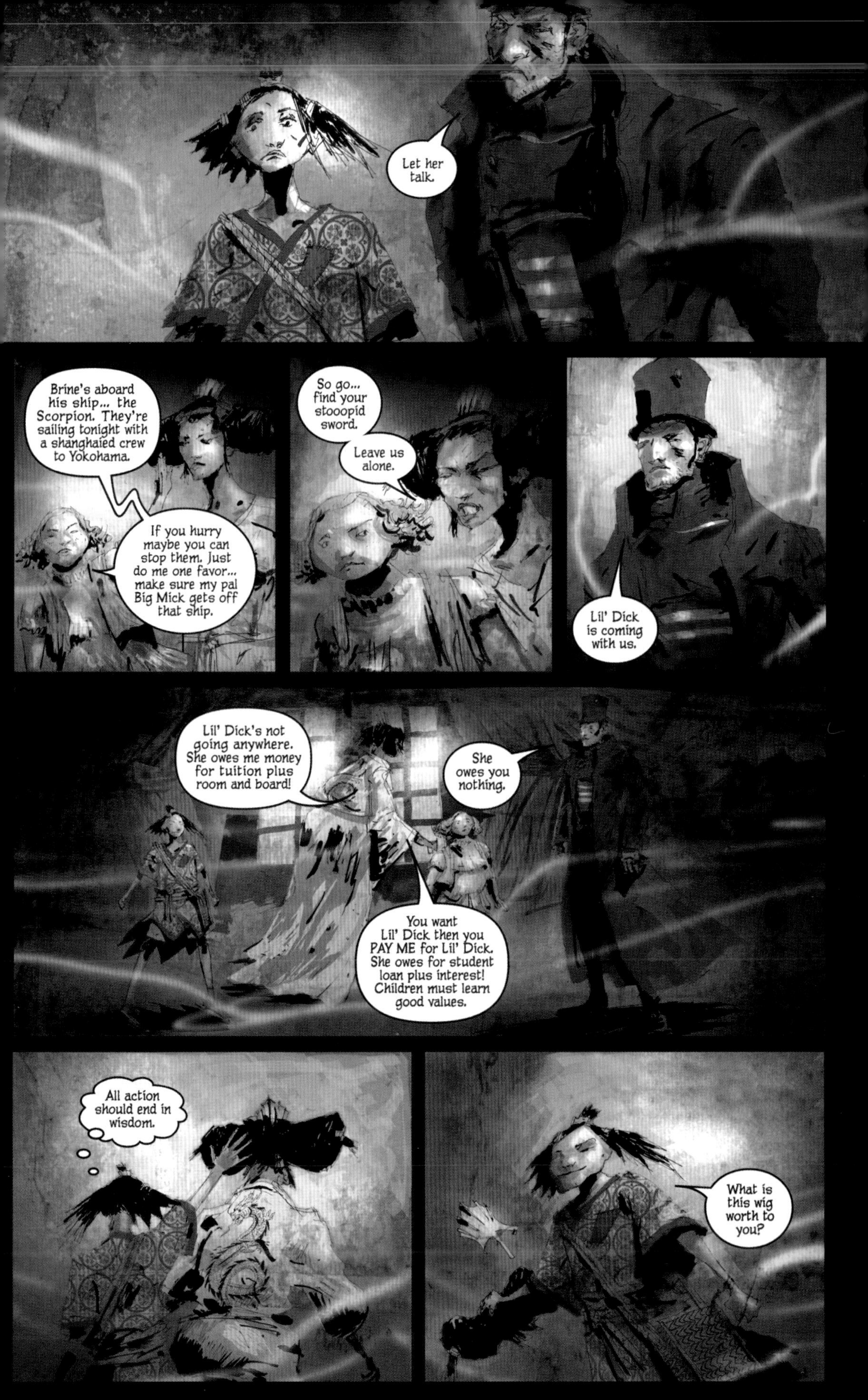
Let her talk.
Brine's aboard his ship... the Scorpion. They're sailing tonight with a shanghaied crew to Yokohama.
If you hurry maybe you can stop them. Just do me one favor... make sure my pal Big Mick gets off that ship.
So go... find your stooopid sword.
Leave us alone.
Lil' Dick is coming with us.
Lil' Dick's not going anywhere. She owes me money for tuition plus room and board!
She owes you nothing.
You want Lil' Dick then you PAY ME for Lil' Dick. She owes for student loan plus interest! Children must learn good values.
All action should end in wisdom.
What is this wig worth to you?

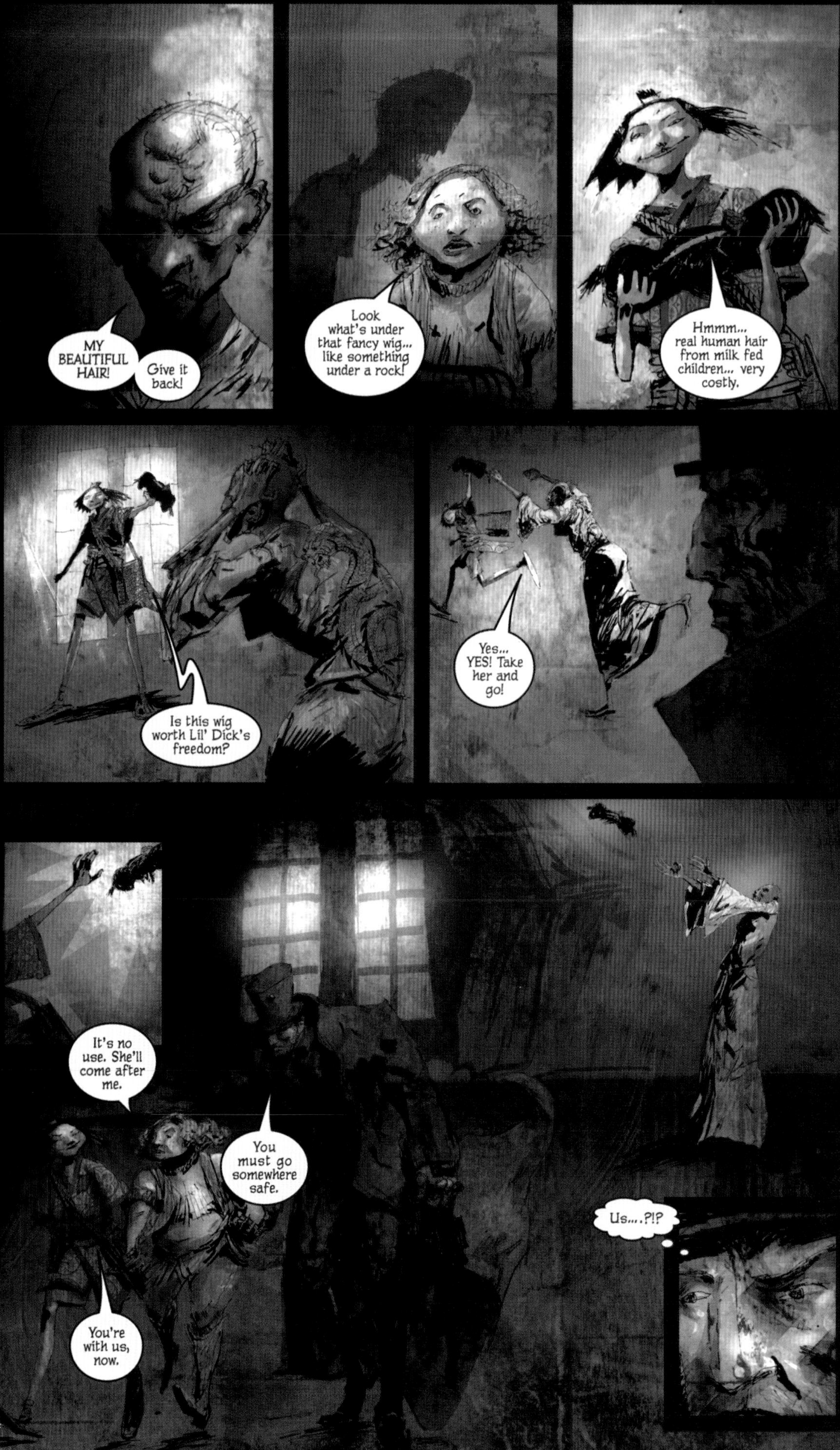

MY BEAUTIFUL HAIR!
Give it back!
Look what's under that fancy wig... like something under a rock!
Hmmm... real human hair from milk fed children... very costly.
Is this wig worth Lil' Dick's freedom?
Yes... YES! Take her and go!
It's no use. She'll come after me.
You must go somewhere safe.
You're with us, now.
Us... ?!?

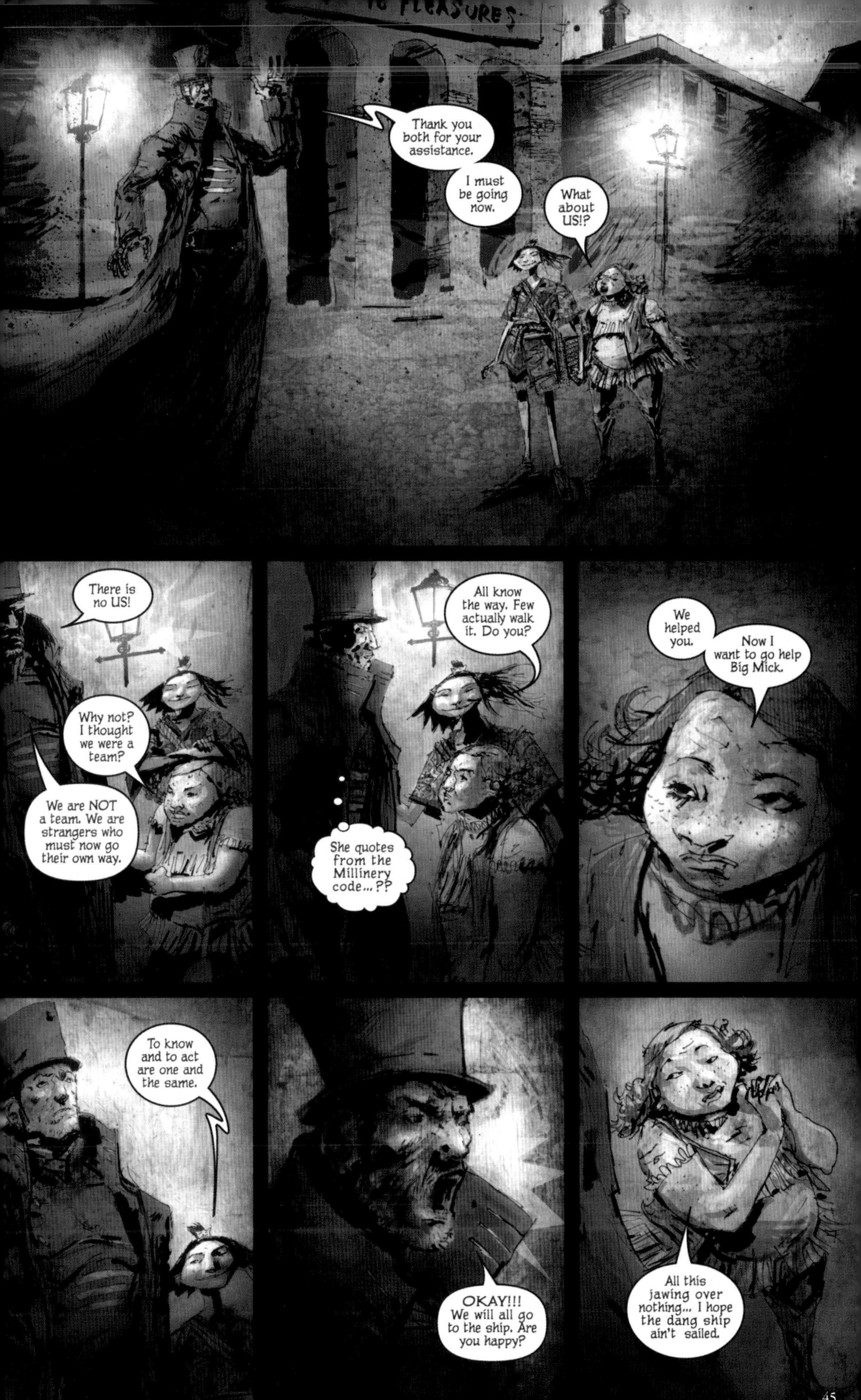
TO PLEASURES
Thank you both for your assistance.
I must be going now.
What about US!?
There is no US!
Why not? I thought we were a team?
We are NOT a team. We are strangers who must now go their own way.
All know the way. Few actually walk it. Do you?
She quotes from the Millinery code...??
We helped you.
Now I want to go help Big Mick.
To know and to act are one and the same.
OKAY!!! We will all go to the ship. Are you happy?
All this jawing over nothing... I hope the dang ship ain't sailed.

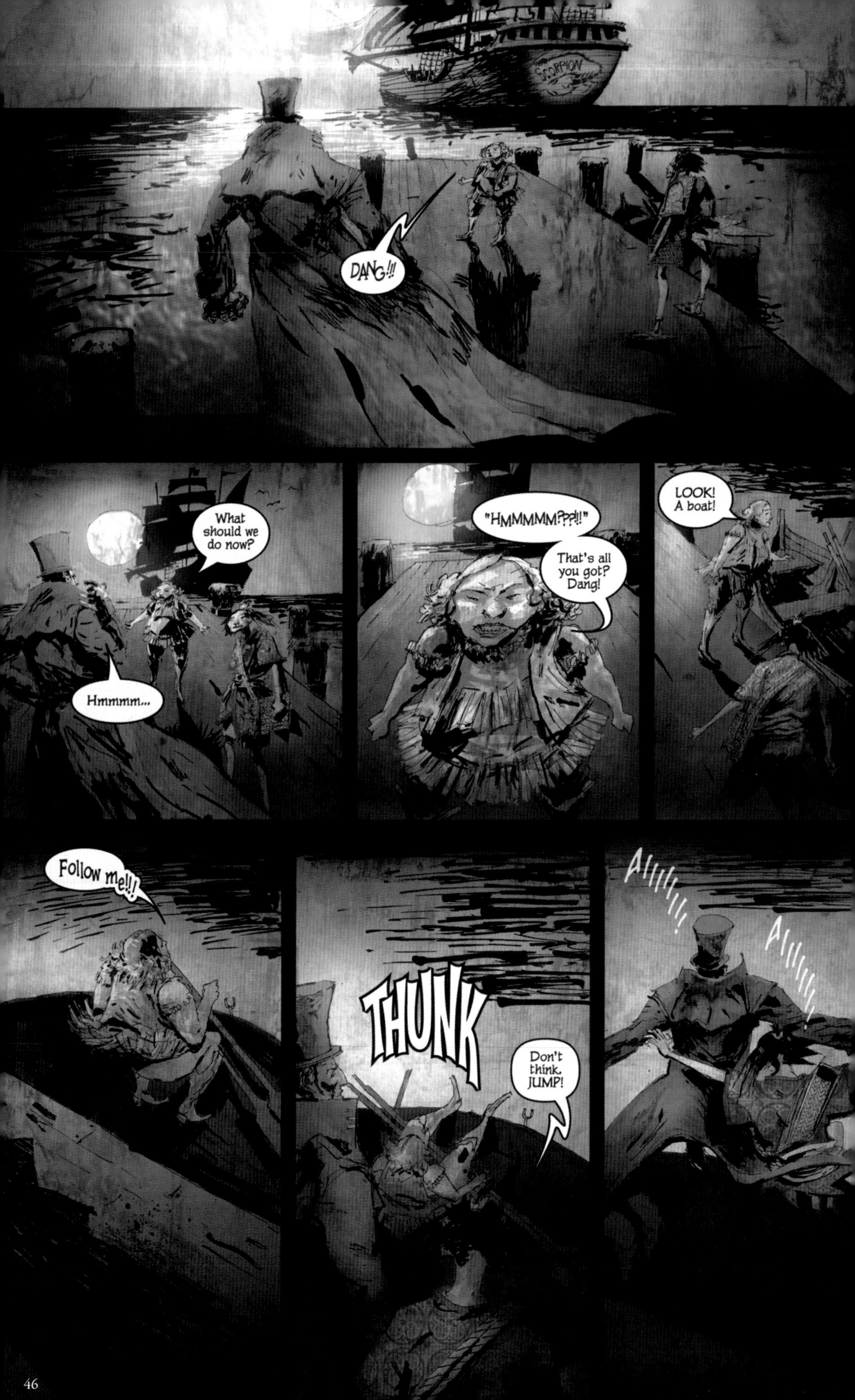
SCORPION
DANG!!!
What should we do now?
Hmmmm...
"HMMMMM???!!"
That's all you got? Dang!
LOOK! A boat!
Follow me!!!
THUNK
Don't think. JUMP!
Aiiiiiii!
Aiiiiiii!

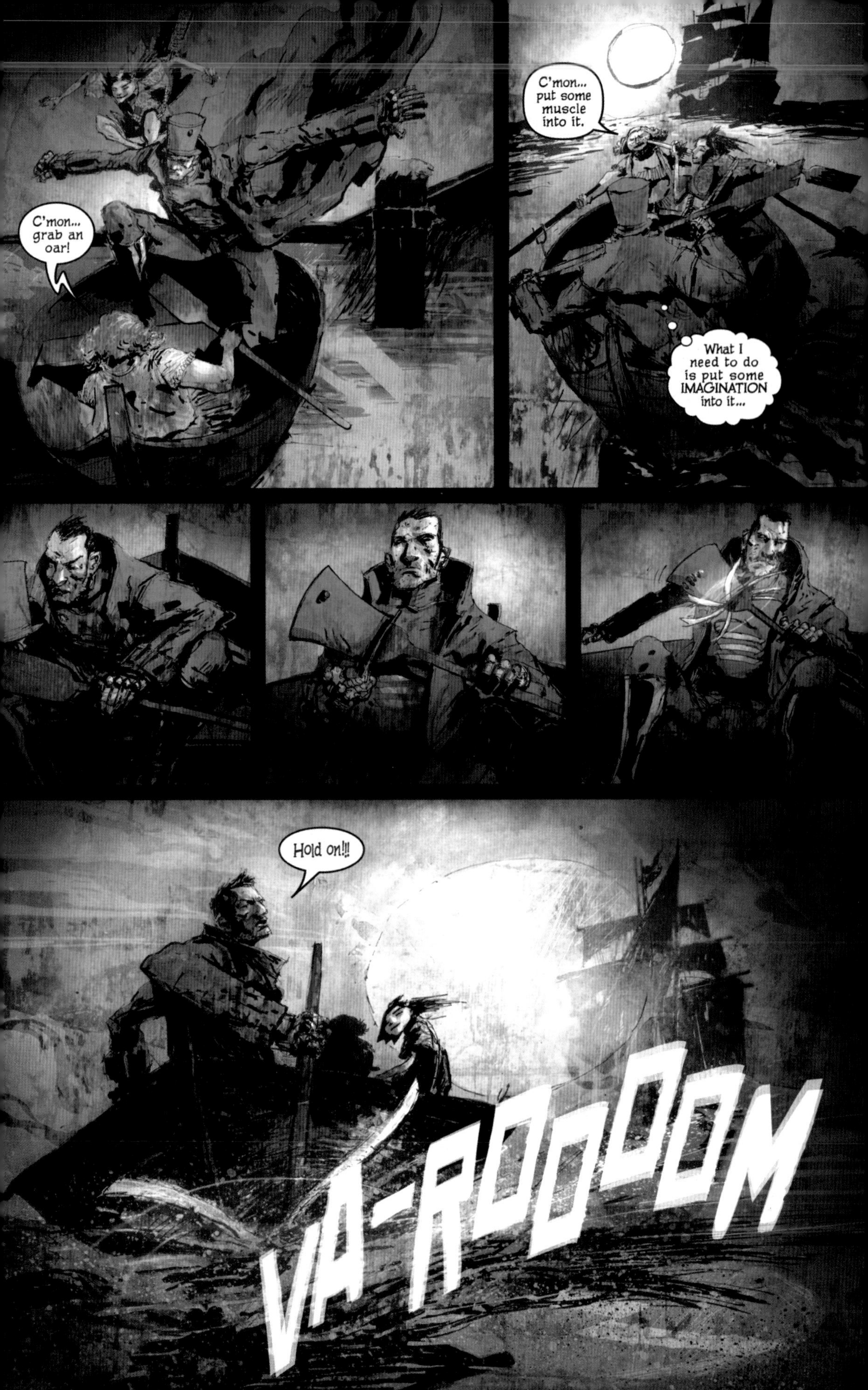
C'mon... grab an oar!
C'mon... put some muscle into it.
What I need to do is put some IMAGINATION into it...
Hold on!!!
VA-ROOOOOM

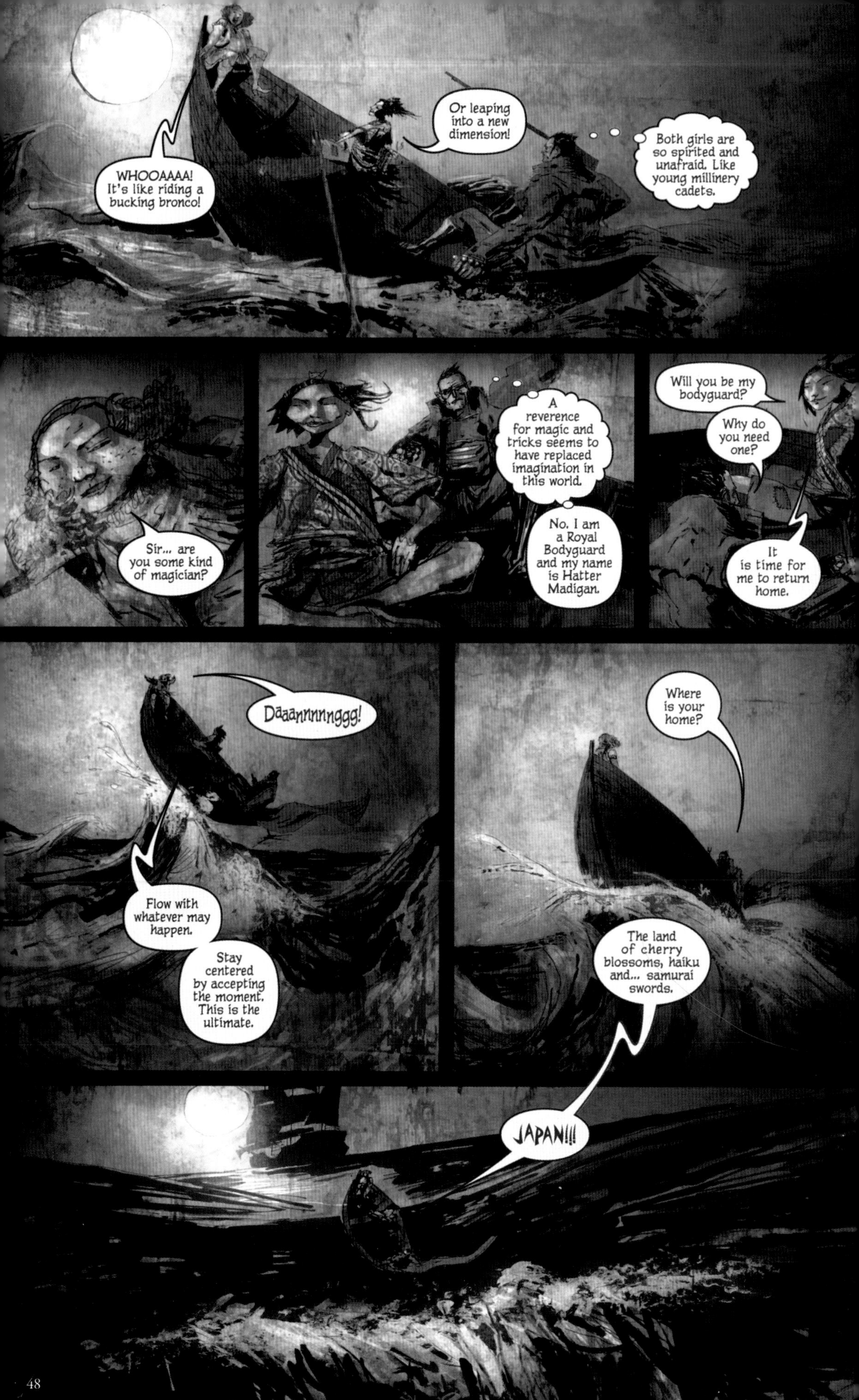
WHOOAAAA! It's like riding a bucking bronco!
Or leaping into a new dimension!
Both girls are so spirited and unafraid. Like young millinery cadets.
Sir... are you some kind of magician?
A reverence for magic and tricks seems to have replaced imagination in this world.
No. I am a Royal Bodyguard and my name is Hatter Madigan.
Will you be my bodyguard?
Why do you need one?
It is time for me to return home.
Daaannnnnggg!
Flow with whatever may happen.
Stay centered by accepting the moment. This is the ultimate.
Where is your home?
The land of cherry blossoms, haiku and... samurai swords.
JAPAN!!!

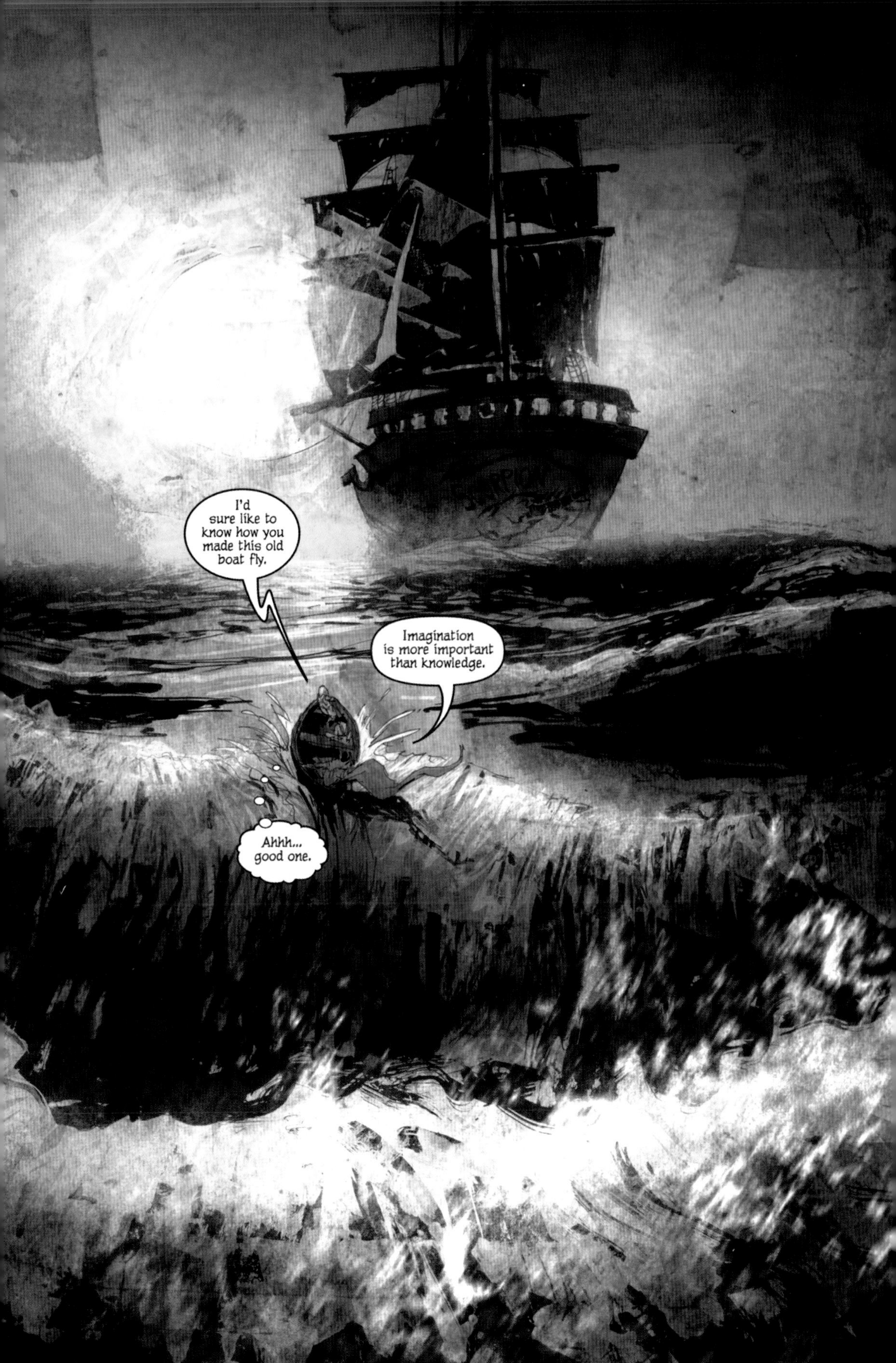
I'd sure like to know how you made this old boat fly.
Imagination is more important than knowledge.
Ahhh... good one.

Let go or be dragged.
			-Zen proverb

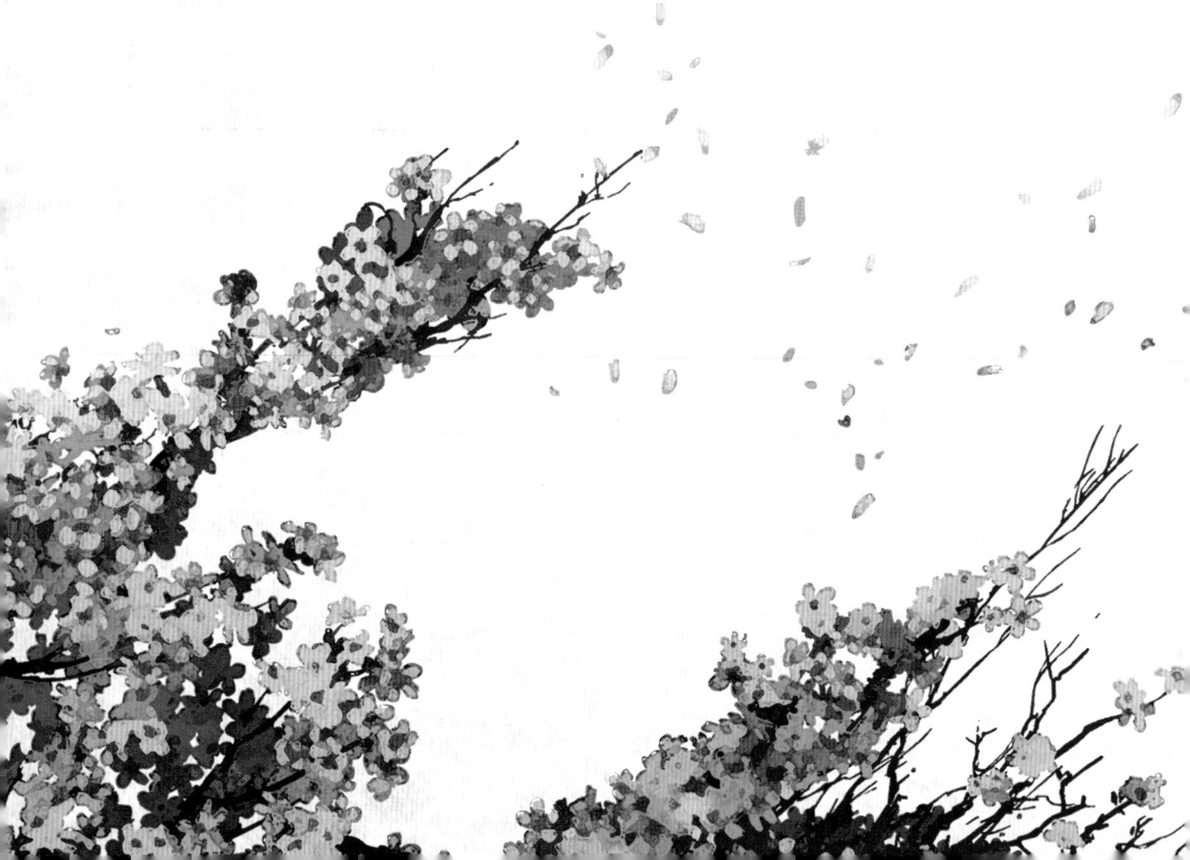

sky water sun waves
finding balance in the depths
as the world unfolds

水を度る

CHAPTER 2 CROSSING THE WATER

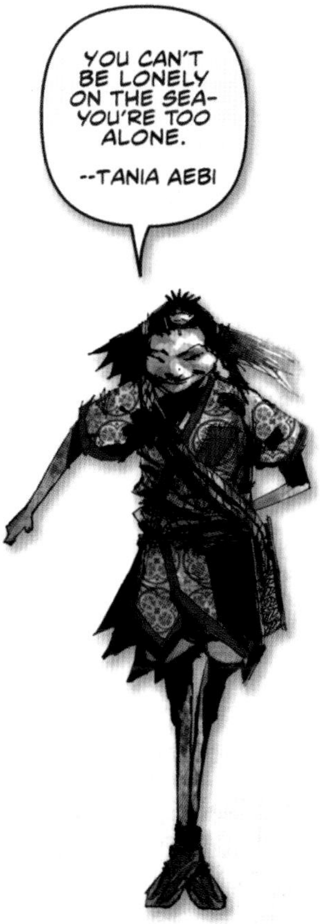
YOU CAN'T BE LONELY ON THE SEA- YOU'RE TOO ALONE.
--TANIA AEBI

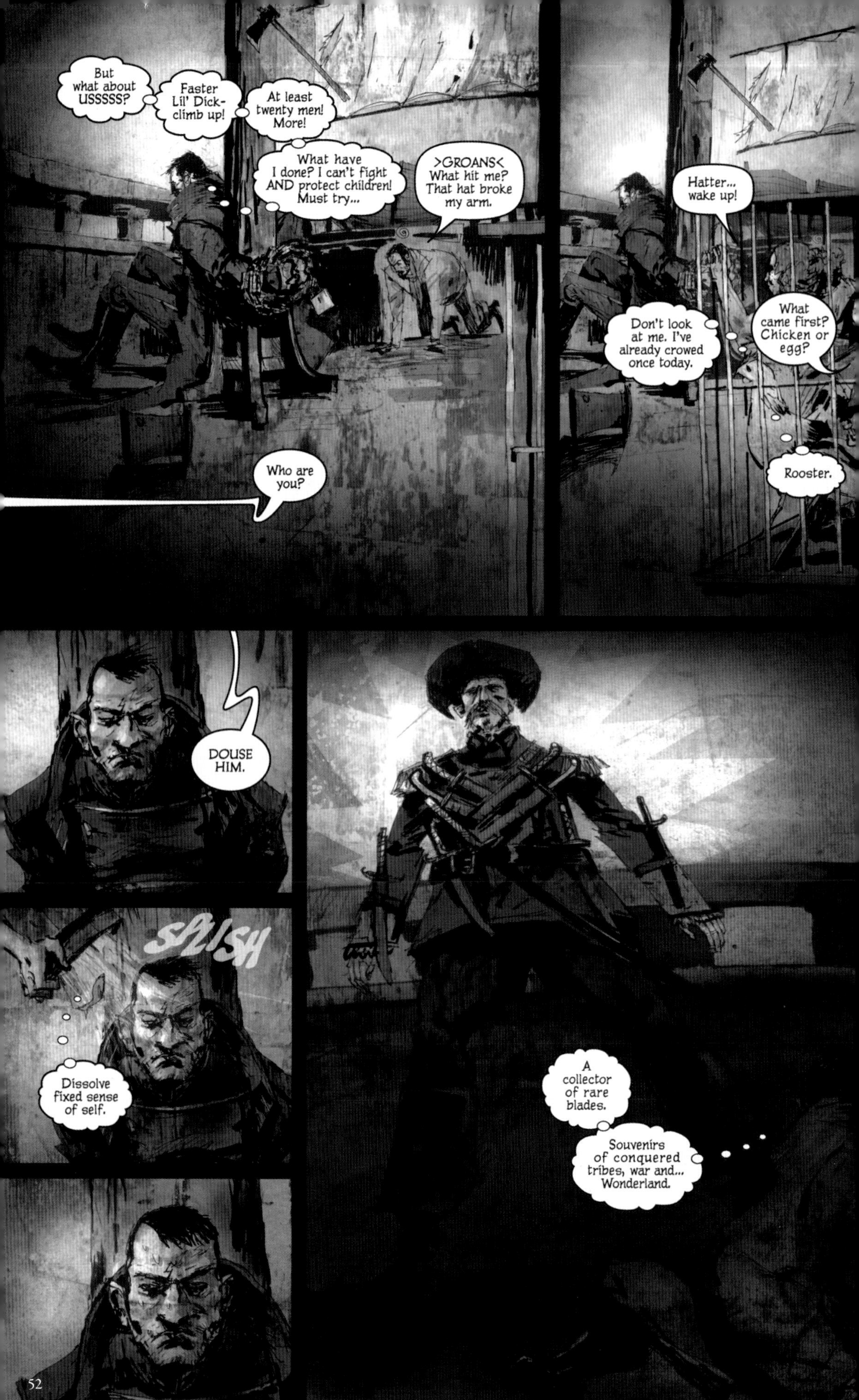
But what about USSSSS?
Faster Lil' Dick- climb up!
At least twenty men! More!
What have I done? I can't fight AND protect children! Must try...
>GROANS< What hit me? That hat broke my arm.
Who are you?
Hatter... wake up!
Don't look at me. I've already crowed once today.
What came first? Chicken or egg?
Rooster.
DOUSE HIM.
SPLISH
Dissolve fixed sense of self.
A collector of rare blades.
Souvenirs of conquered tribes, war and... Wonderland.

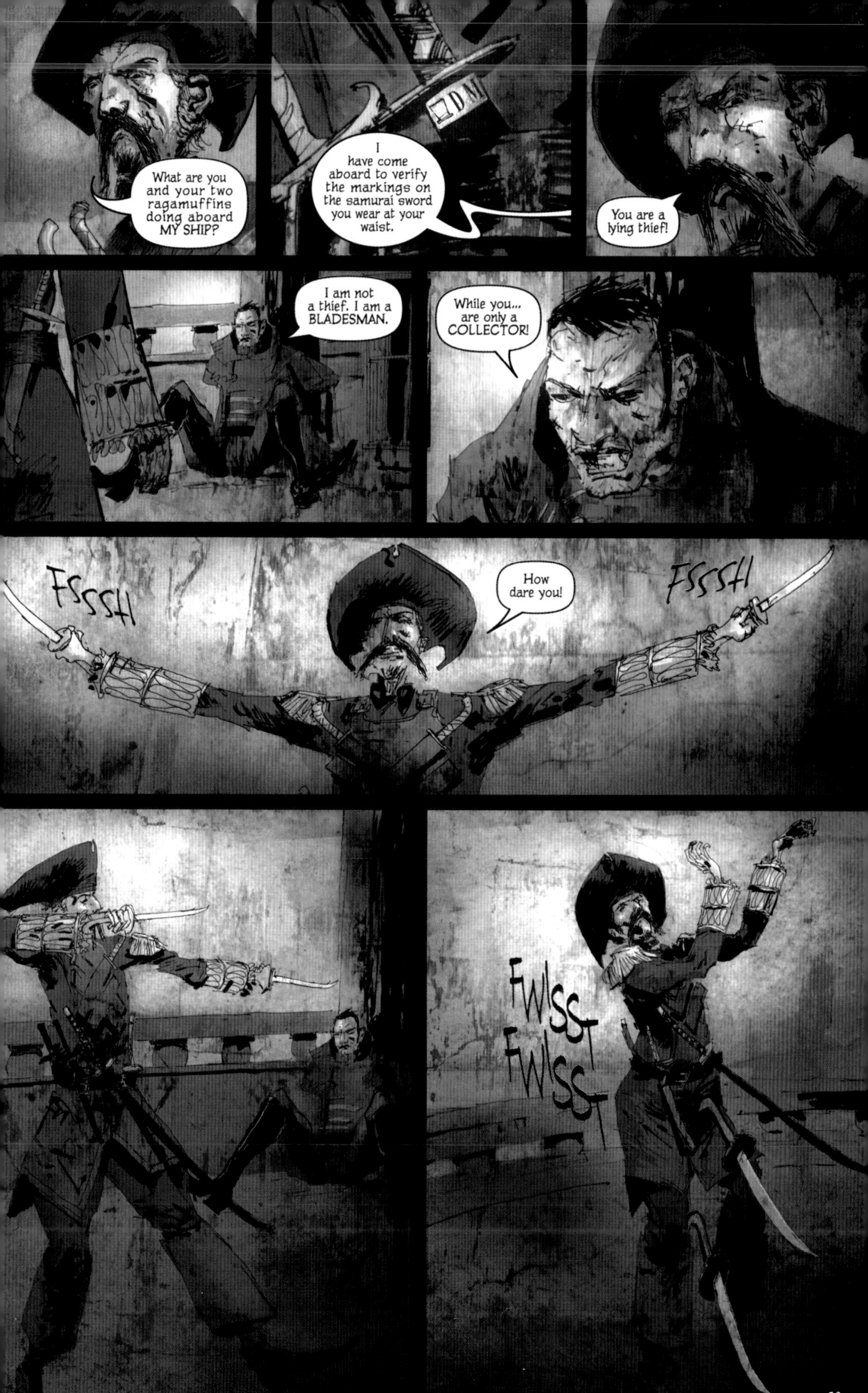
What are you and your two ragamuffins doing aboard MY SHIP?
I have come aboard to verify the markings on the samurai sword you wear at your waist.
You are a lying thief!
I am not a thief. I am a BLADESMAN.
While you... are only a COLLECTOR!
FSSSTI
How dare you!
FSSSTI
FWISST
FWISST

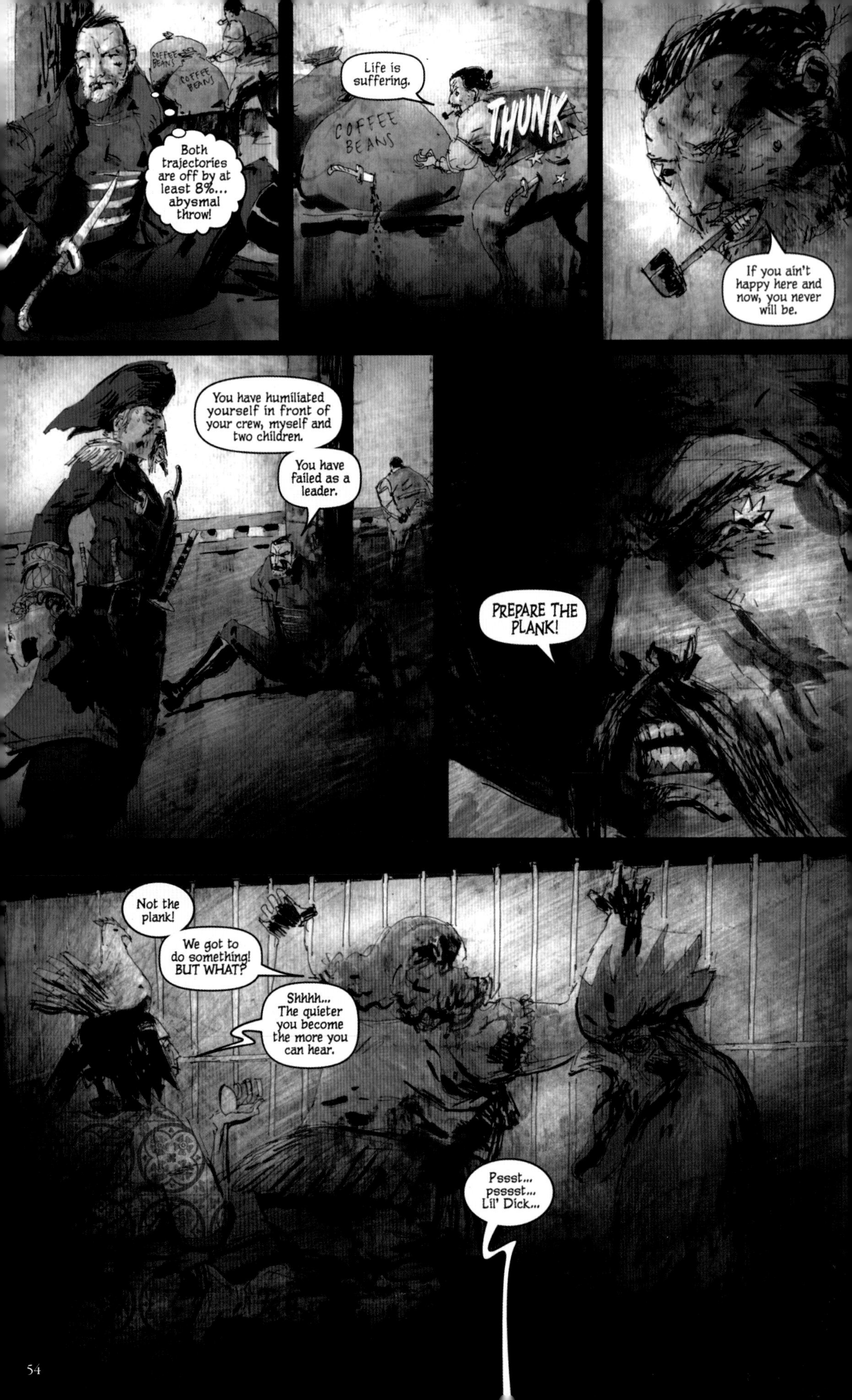
COFFEE BEANS
COFFEE BEANS
Both trajectories are off by at least 8%... abysmal throw!
Life is suffering.
COFFEE BEANS
THUNK
If you ain't happy here and now, you never will be.
You have humiliated yourself in front of your crew, myself and two children.
You have failed as a leader.
PREPARE THE PLANK!
Not the plank!
We got to do something! BUT WHAT?
Shhhh... The quieter you become the more you can hear.
Pssst... psssst... Lil' Dick...

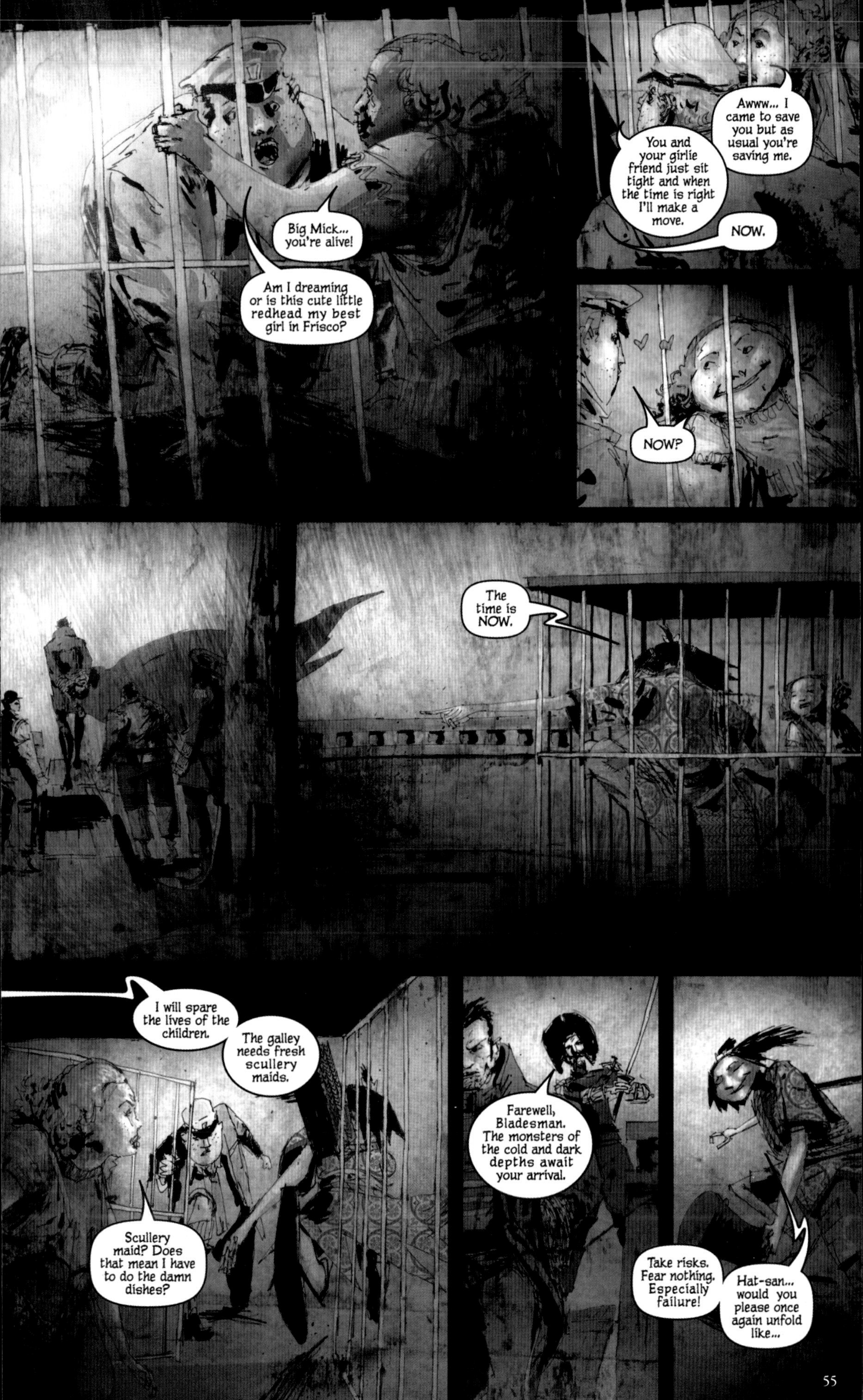
Big Mick... you're alive!
Am I dreaming or is this cute little redhead my best girl in Frisco?
Awww... I came to save you but as usual you're saving me.
You and your girlie friend just sit tight and when the time is right I'll make a move.
NOW.
NOW?
The time is NOW.
I will spare the lives of the children.
The galley needs fresh scullery maids.
Scullery maid? Does that mean I have to do the damn dishes?
Farewell, Bladesman. The monsters of the cold and dark depths await your arrival.
Take risks. Fear nothing. Especially failure!
Hat-san... would you please once again unfold like...

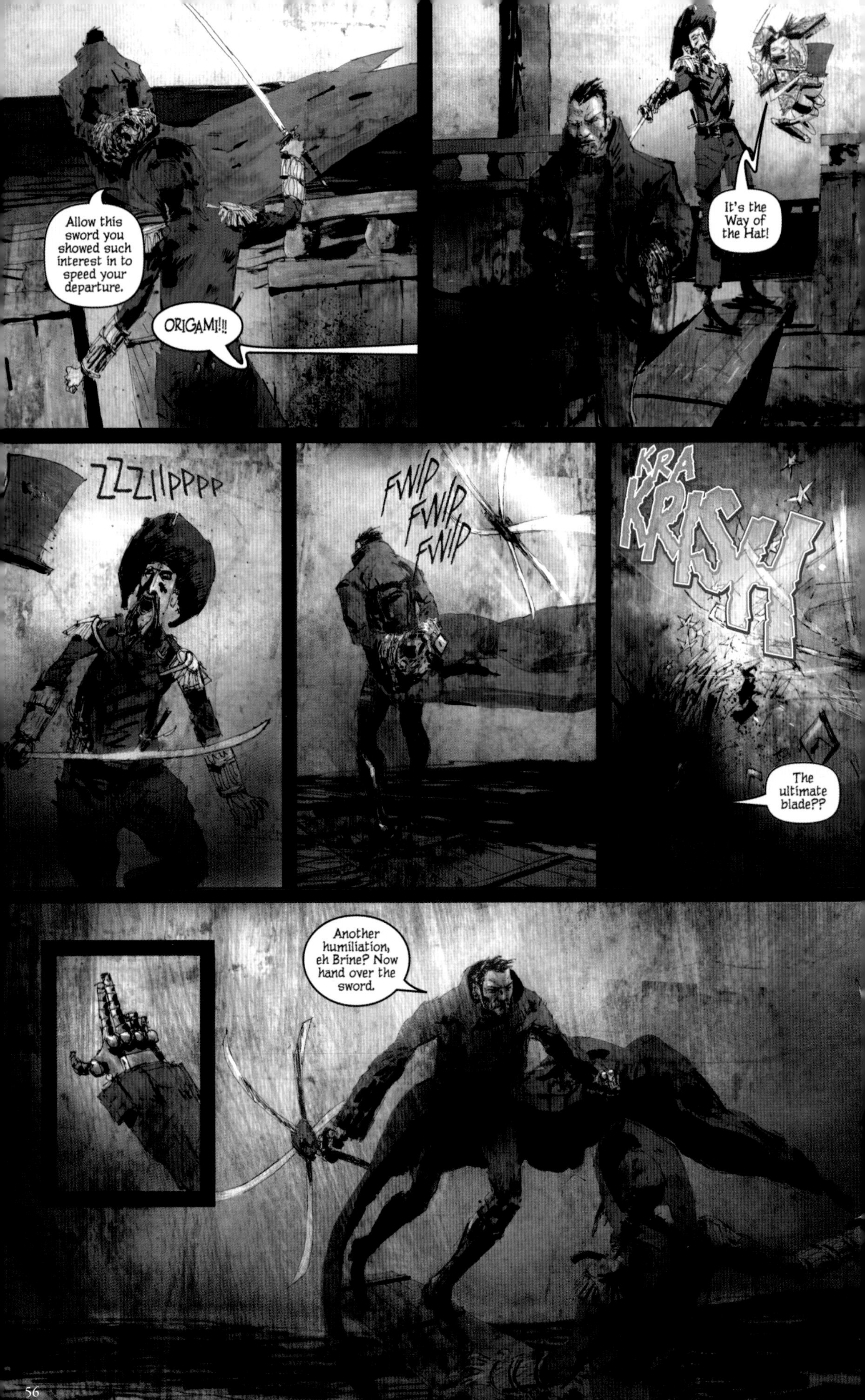

Allow this sword you showed such interest in to speed your departure.
ORIGAMI!!!
It's the Way of the Hat!
ZZZIIPPPP
FWIP FWIP FWIP
KRA KRASH
The ultimate blade??
Another humiliation, eh Brine? Now hand over the sword.

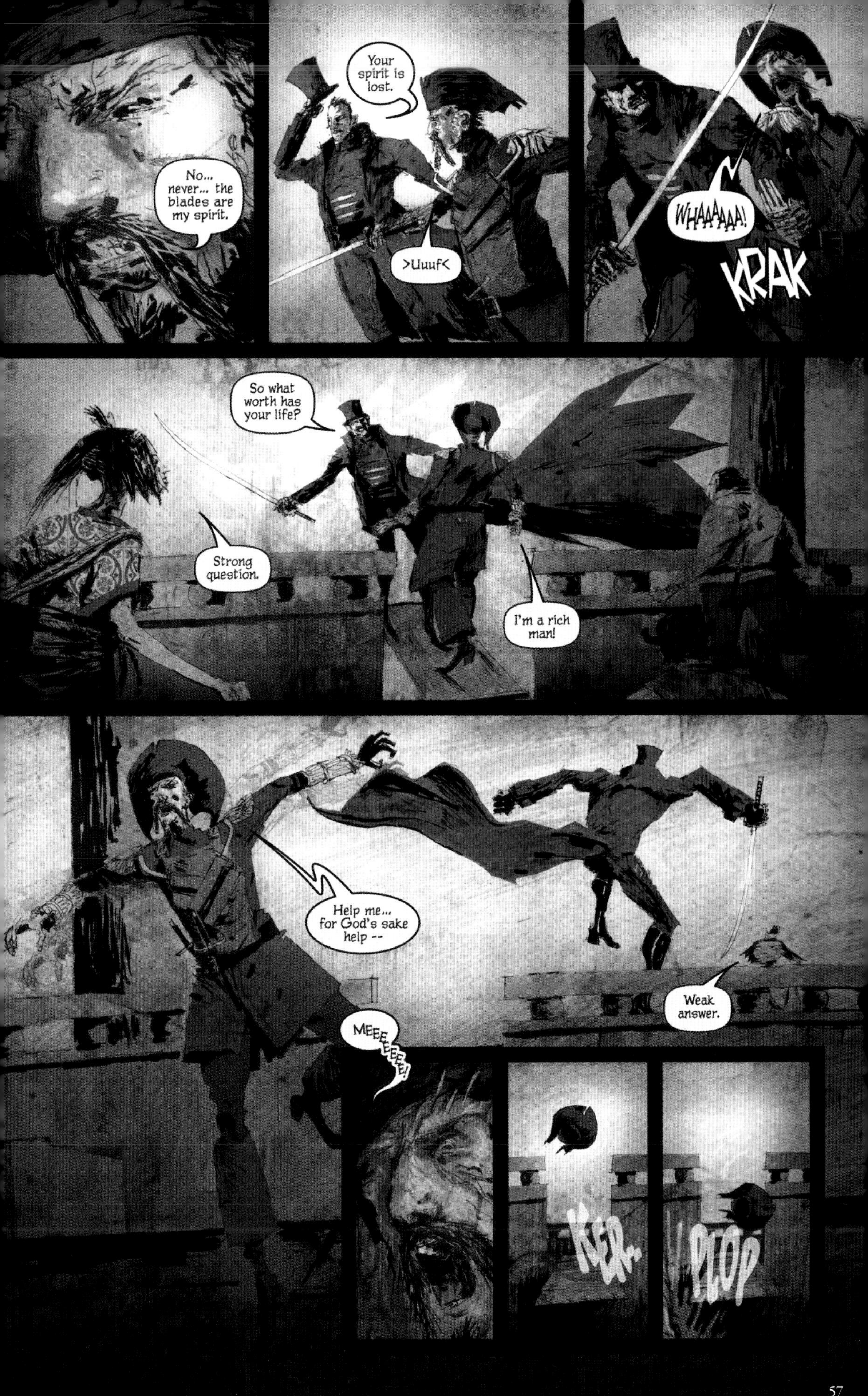
No... never... the blades are my spirit.
Your spirit is lost.
>Uuuf<
WHAAAAAA!
KRAK
So what worth has your life?
Strong question.
I'm a rich man!
Help me... for God's sake help --
Weak answer.
MEEEEEEE!
KER..
PLOP

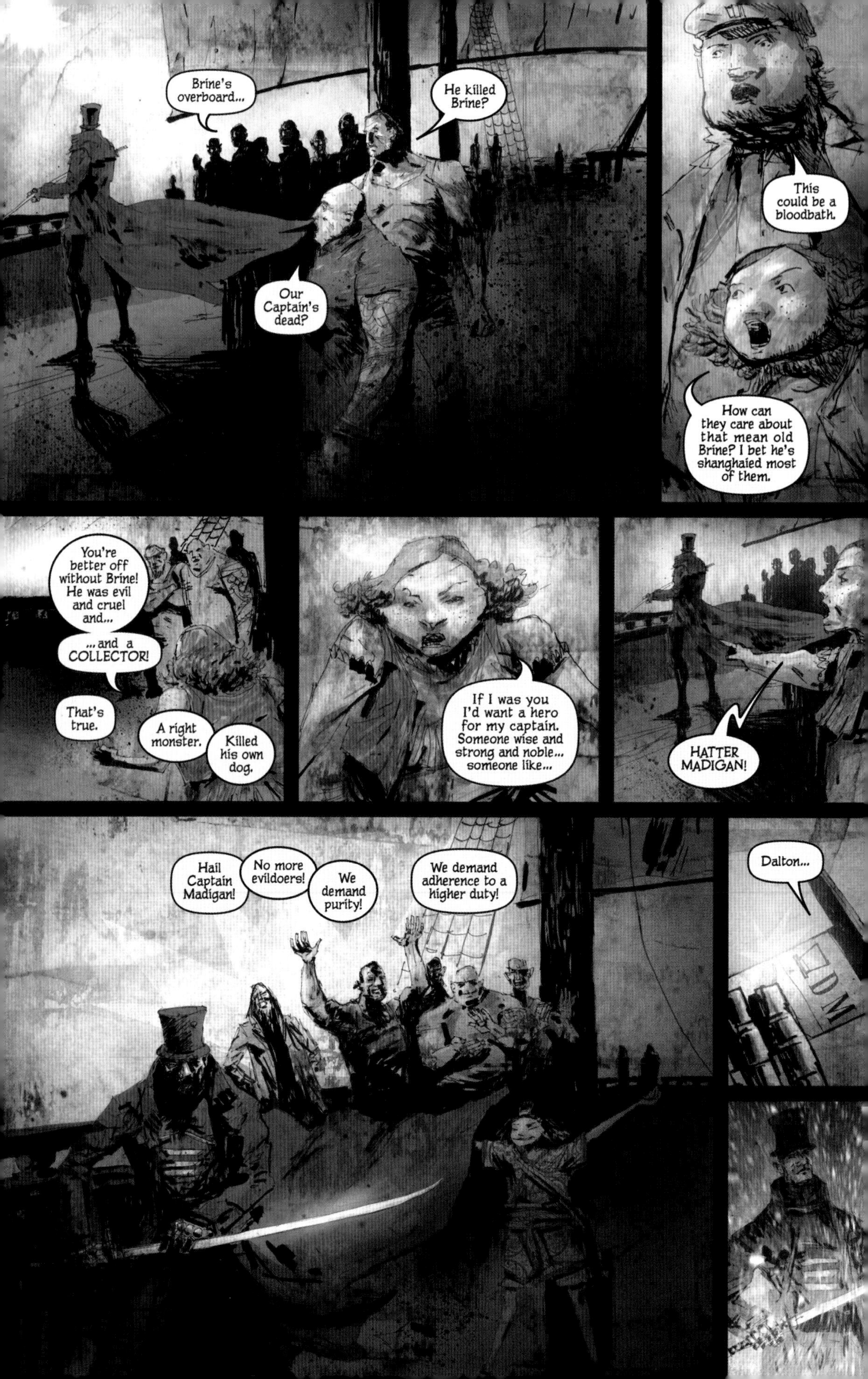
Brine's overboard...
He killed Brine?
Our Captain's dead?
This could be a bloodbath.
How can they care about that mean old Brine? I bet he's shanghaied most of them.
You're better off without Brine! He was evil and cruel and...
...and a COLLECTOR!
That's true.
A right monster.
Killed his own dog.
If I was you I'd want a hero for my captain. Someone wise and strong and noble... someone like...
HATTER MADIGAN!
Hail Captain Madigan!
No more evildoers!
We demand purity!
We demand adherence to a higher duty!
Dalton...

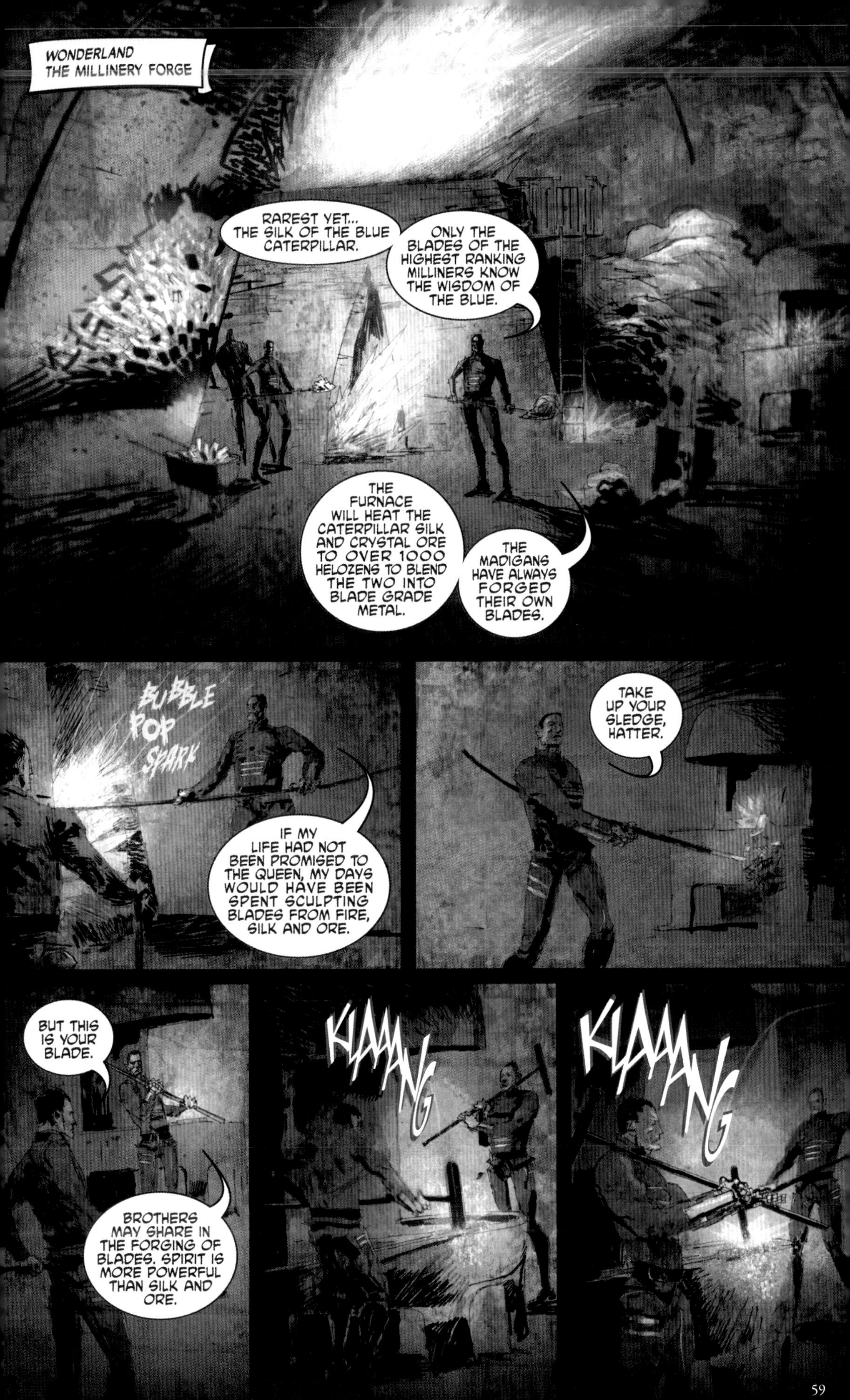
WONDERLAND
THE MILLINERY FORGE
RAREST YET... THE SILK OF THE BLUE CATERPILLAR.
ONLY THE BLADES OF THE HIGHEST RANKING MILLINERS KNOW THE WISDOM OF THE BLUE.
THE FURNACE WILL HEAT THE CATERPILLAR SILK AND CRYSTAL ORE TO OVER 1000 HELOZENS TO BLEND THE TWO INTO BLADE GRADE METAL.
THE MADIGANS HAVE ALWAYS FORGED THEIR OWN BLADES.
BUBBLE
POP
SPARK
IF MY LIFE HAD NOT BEEN PROMISED TO THE QUEEN, MY DAYS WOULD HAVE BEEN SPENT SCULPTING BLADES FROM FIRE, SILK AND ORE.
TAKE UP YOUR SLEDGE, HATTER.
BUT THIS IS YOUR BLADE.
BROTHERS MAY SHARE IN THE FORGING OF BLADES. SPIRIT IS MORE POWERFUL THAN SILK AND ORE.
KLAAANG
KLAAANG

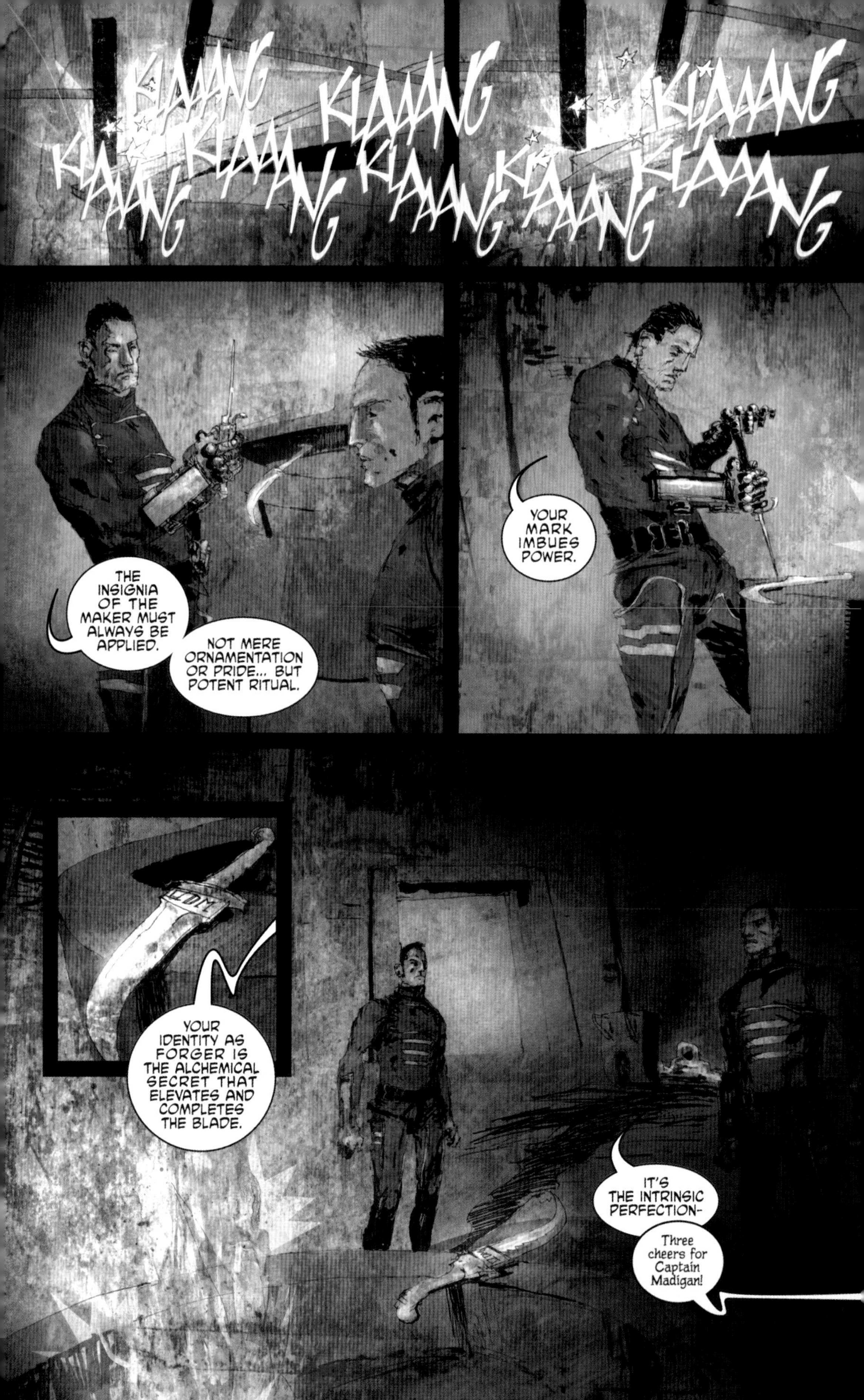
KLAAANG KLAAANG KLAAANG KLAAANG KLAAANG KLAAANG KLAAANG KLAAANG
THE INSIGNIA OF THE MAKER MUST ALWAYS BE APPLIED.
NOT MERE ORNAMENTATION OR PRIDE... BUT POTENT RITUAL.
YOUR MARK IMBUES POWER.
YOUR IDENTITY AS FORGER IS THE ALCHEMICAL SECRET THAT ELEVATES AND COMPLETES THE BLADE.
IT'S THE INTRINSIC PERFECTION-
Three cheers for Captain Madigan!

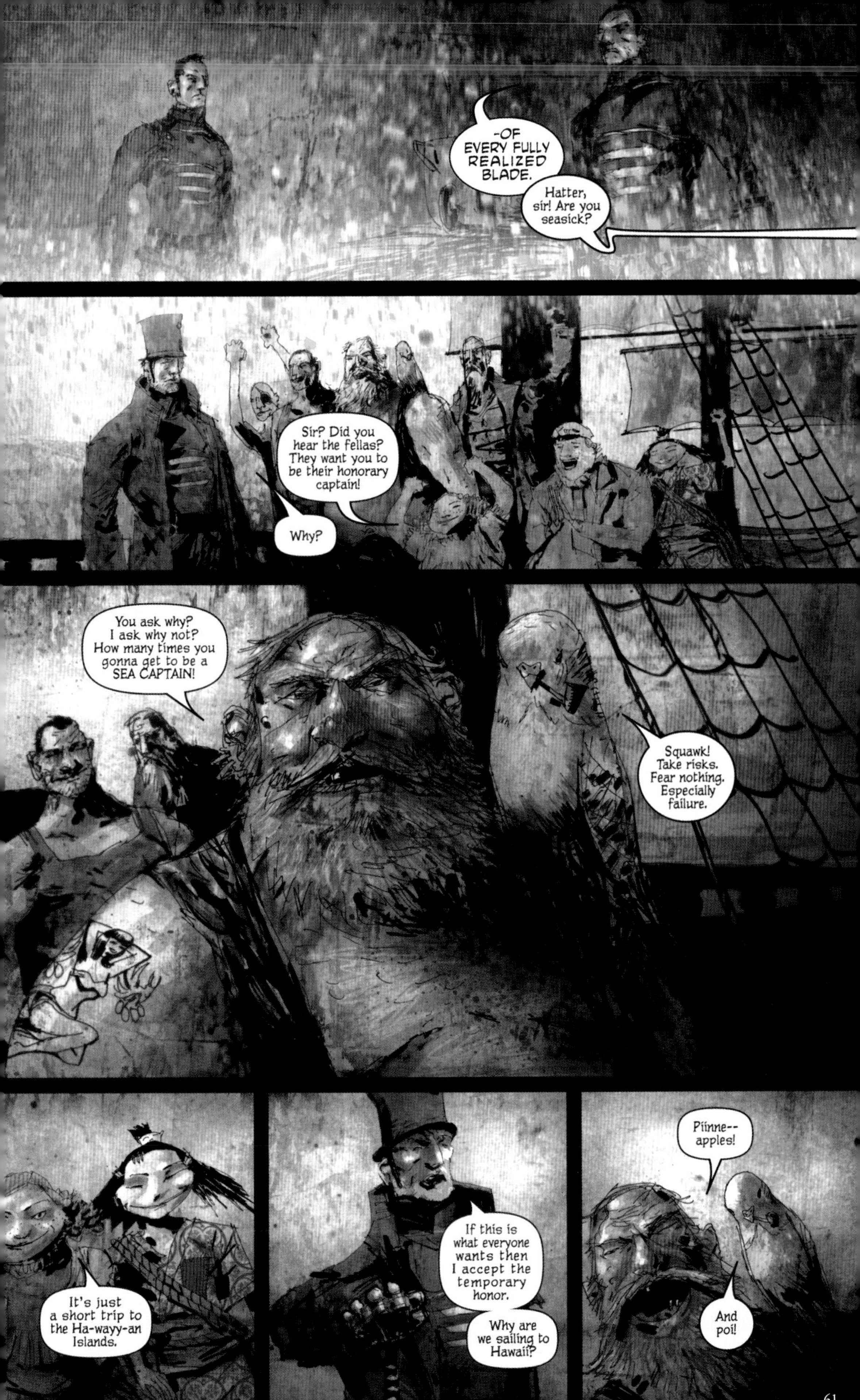
-OF EVERY FULLY REALIZED BLADE.
Hatter, sir! Are you seasick?
Sir? Did you hear the fellas? They want you to be their honorary captain!
Why?
You ask why? I ask why not? How many times you gonna get to be a SEA CAPTAIN!
Squawk! Take risks. Fear nothing. Especially failure.
It's just a short trip to the Ha-wayy-an Islands.
If this is what everyone wants then I accept the temporary honor.
Why are we sailing to Hawaii?
Piinne--apples!
And poi!

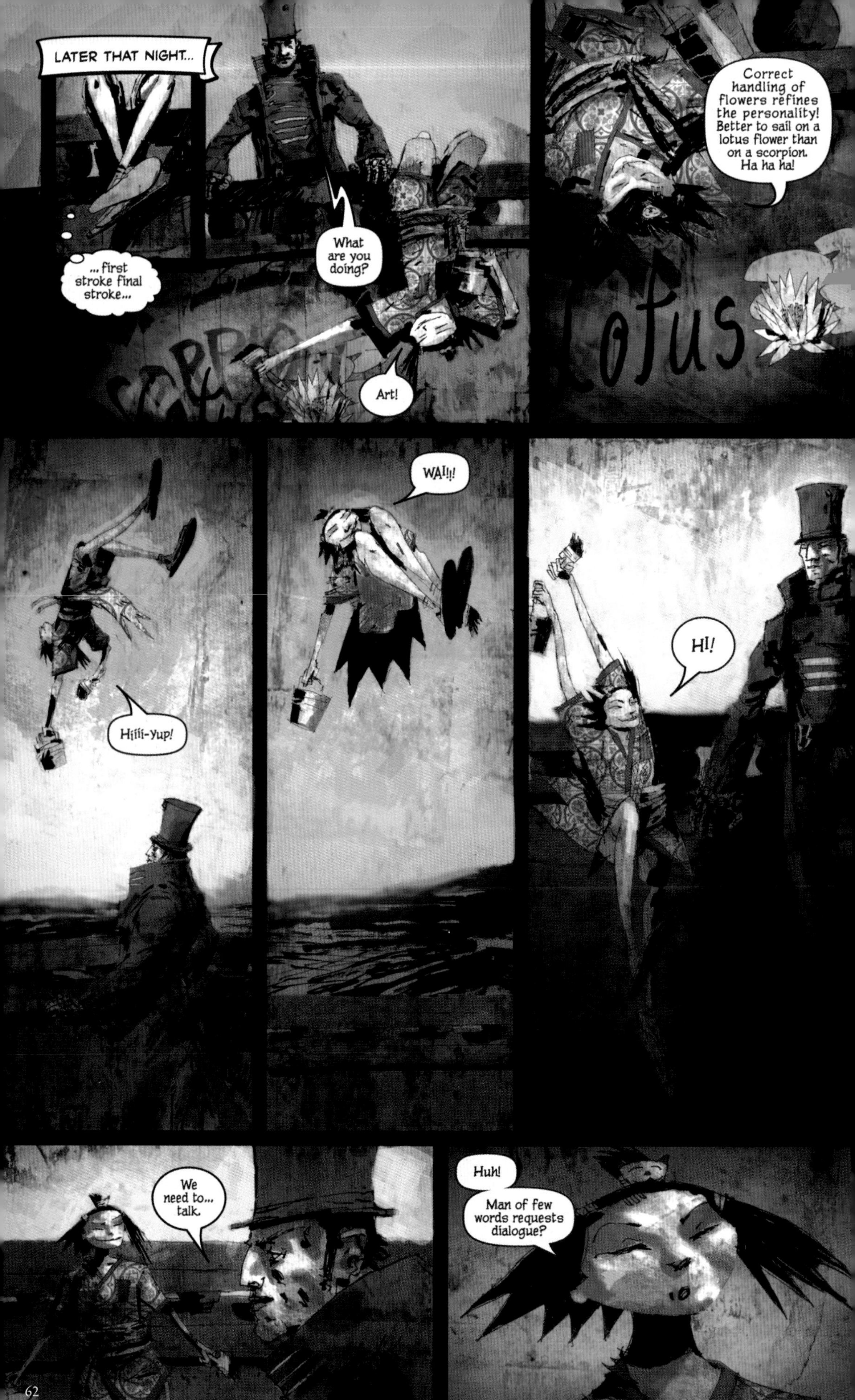
LATER THAT NIGHT...
...first stroke final stroke...
What are you doing?
Art!
Correct handling of flowers refines the personality! Better to sail on a lotus flower than on a scorpion. Ha ha ha!
Lotus
Hiiii-yup!
WAI!!!
HI!
We need to... talk.
Huh!
Man of few words requests dialogue?

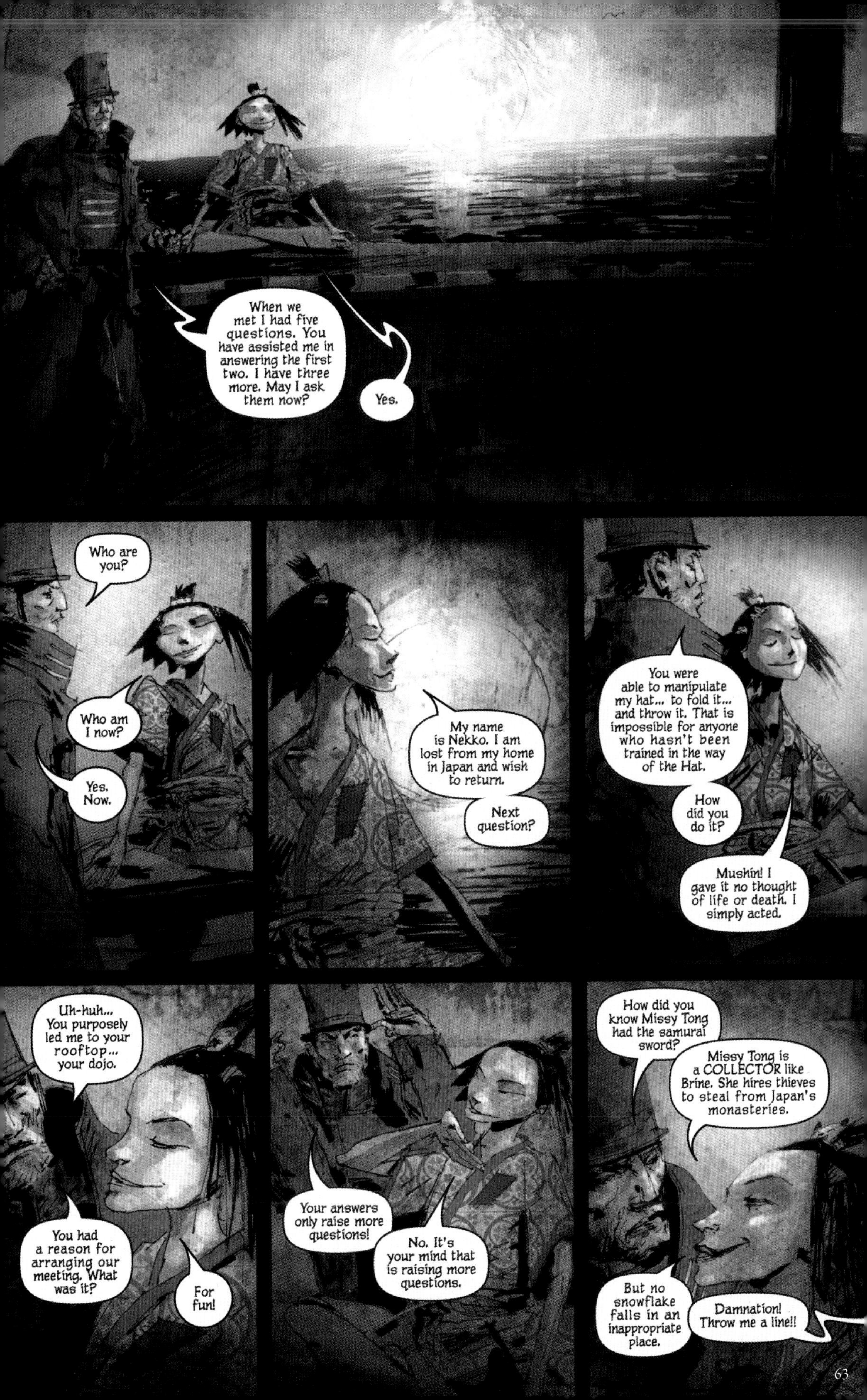
When we met I had five questions. You have assisted me in answering the first two. I have three more. May I ask them now?
Yes.
Who are you?
Who am I now?
Yes. Now.
My name is Nekko. I am lost from my home in Japan and wish to return.
Next question?
You were able to manipulate my hat... to fold it... and throw it. That is impossible for anyone who hasn't been trained in the way of the Hat.
How did you do it?
Mushin! I gave it no thought of life or death. I simply acted.
Uh-huh... You purposely led me to your rooftop... your dojo.
You had a reason for arranging our meeting. What was it?
For fun!
Your answers only raise more questions!
No. It's your mind that is raising more questions.
How did you know Missy Tong had the samurai sword?
Missy Tong is a COLLECTOR like Brine. She hires thieves to steal from Japan's monasteries.
But no snowflake falls in an inappropriate place.
Damnation! Throw me a line!!

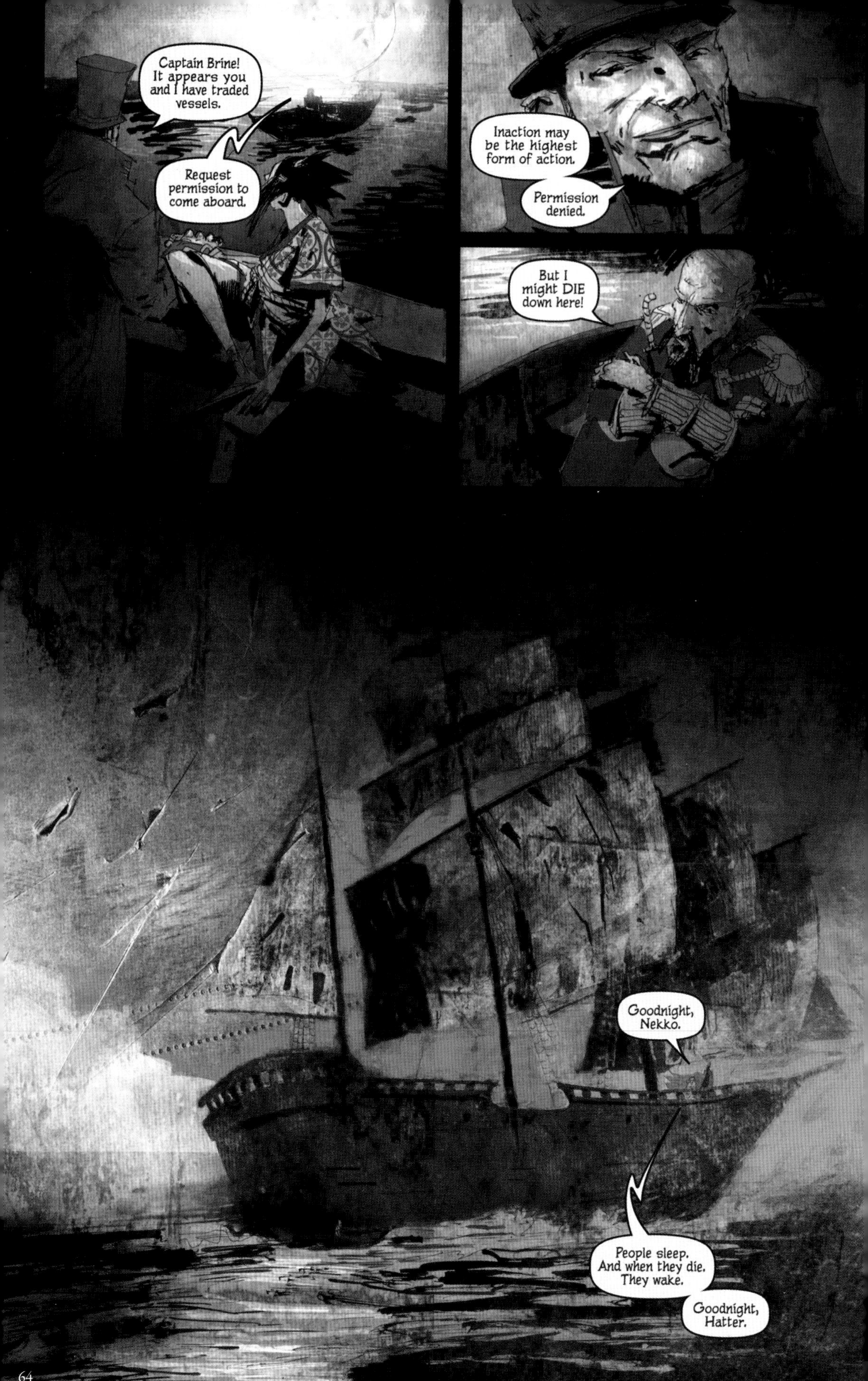
Captain Brine! It appears you and I have traded vessels.
Request permission to come aboard.
Inaction may be the highest form of action.
Permission denied.
But I might DIE down here!
Goodnight, Nekko.
People sleep. And when they die. They wake.
Goodnight, Hatter.

Why is it that little children are so intelligent and men so stupid?

Maybe we've had more practice at getting it wrong.

Or maybe we just forgot what life is meant to be.

GReeeeak

What do you think life is meant to be?

An adventure. Life should always be an adventure.

Goodnight, Captain.

If no snowflake falls in an inappropriate place...

SWOOOSH

... it appears my mourning was premature.

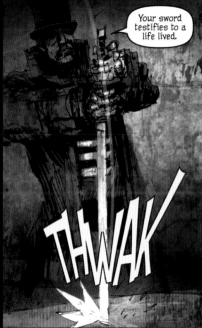

Your sword testifies to a life lived.

THWAK

Yet you chose to remain in this world.

Leaving only questions for those who lost you.

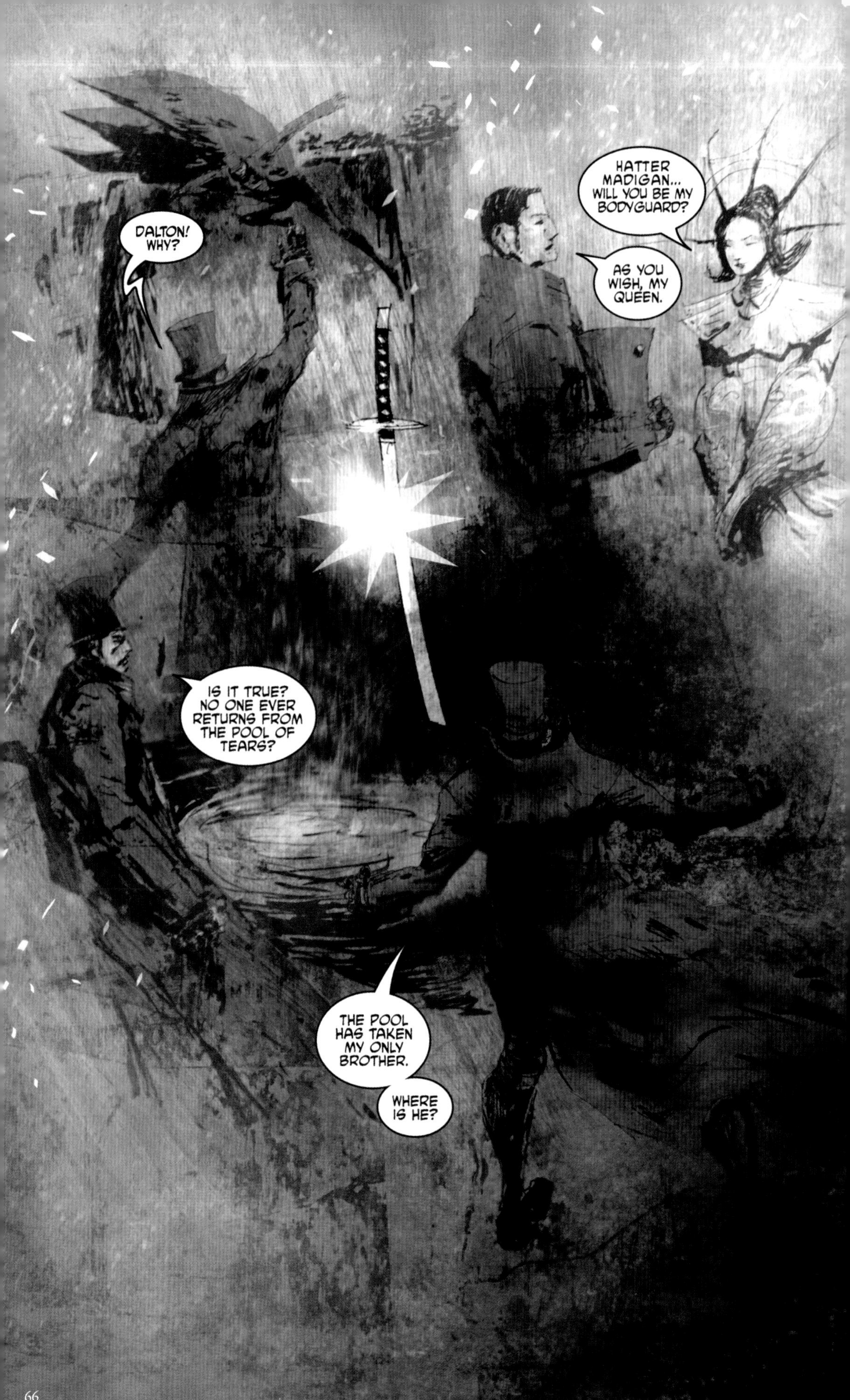
DALTON! WHY?
HATTER MADIGAN... WILL YOU BE MY BODYGUARD?
AS YOU WISH, MY QUEEN.
IS IT TRUE? NO ONE EVER RETURNS FROM THE POOL OF TEARS?
THE POOL HAS TAKEN MY ONLY BROTHER.
WHERE IS HE?

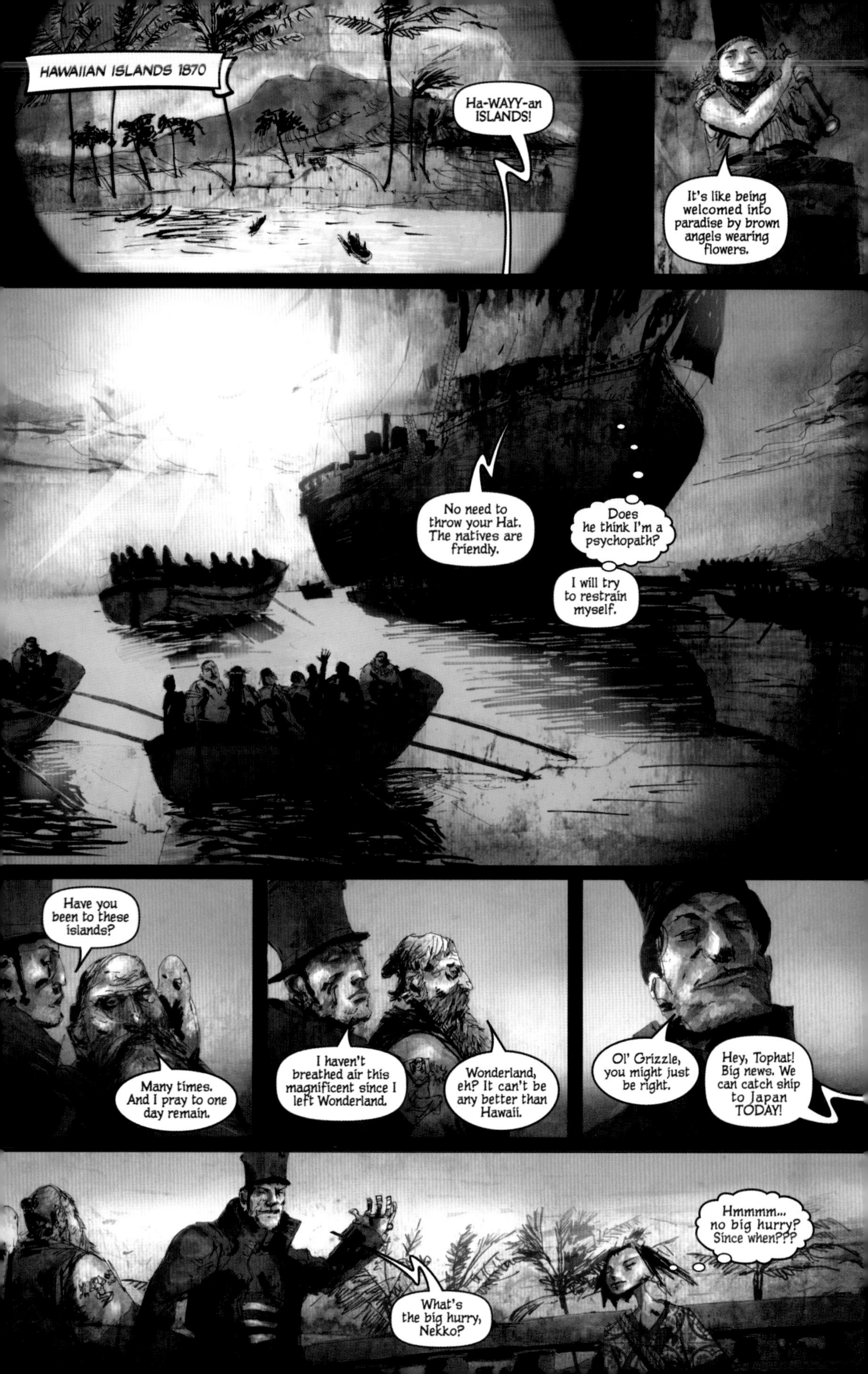
HAWAIIAN ISLANDS 1870
Ha-WAYY-an ISLANDS!
It's like being welcomed into paradise by brown angels wearing flowers.
No need to throw your Hat. The natives are friendly.
Does he think I'm a psychopath?
I will try to restrain myself.
Have you been to these islands?
Many times. And I pray to one day remain.
I haven't breathed air this magnificent since I left Wonderland.
Wonderland, eh? It can't be any better than Hawaii.
Ol' Grizzle, you might just be right.
Hey, Tophat! Big news. We can catch ship to Japan TODAY!
What's the big hurry, Nekko?
Hmmmm... no big hurry? Since when???

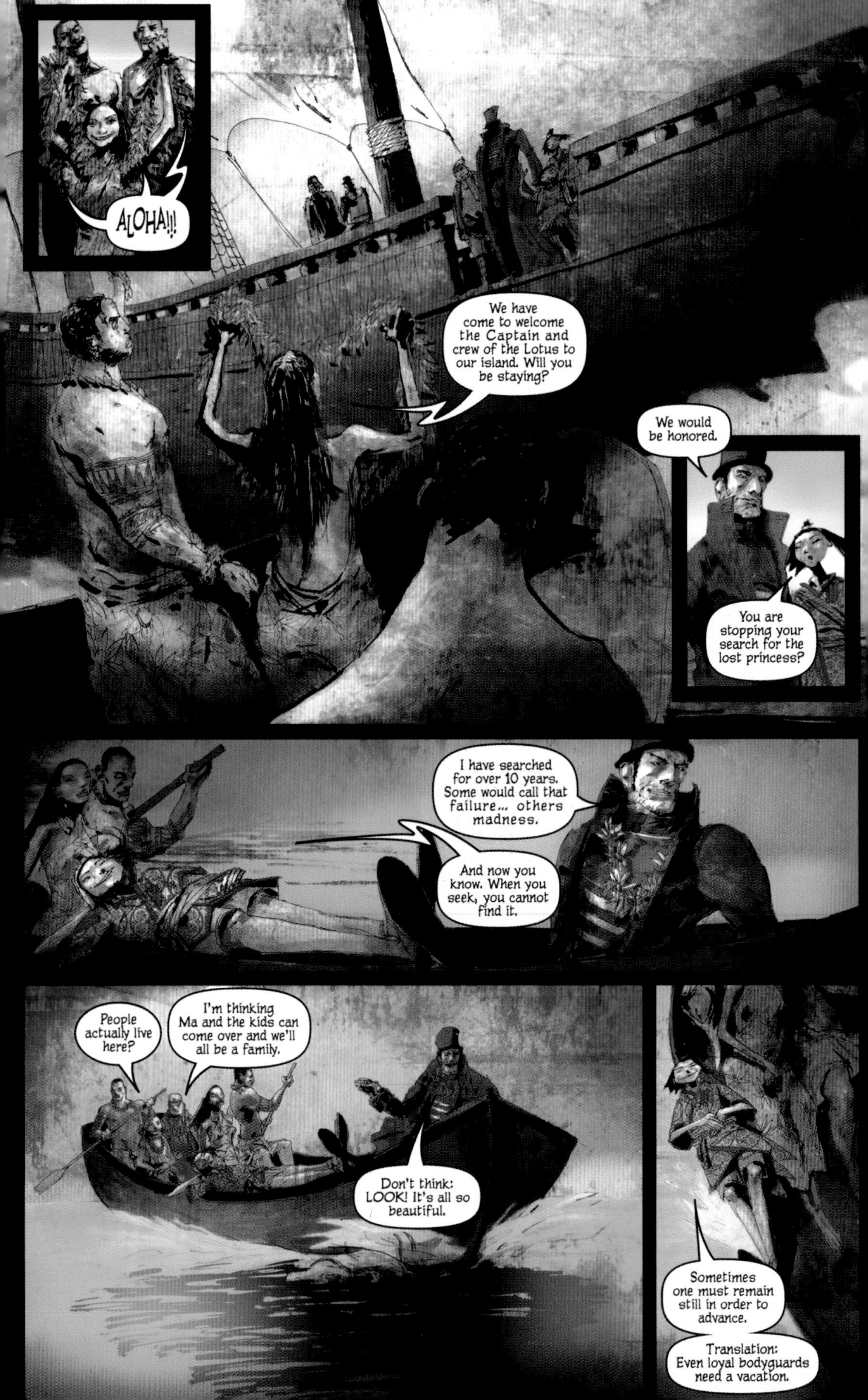

ALOHA!!!
We have come to welcome the Captain and crew of the Lotus to our island. Will you be staying?
We would be honored.
You are stopping your search for the lost princess?
I have searched for over 10 years. Some would call that failure... others madness.
And now you know. When you seek, you cannot find it.
People actually live here?
I'm thinking Ma and the kids can come over and we'll all be a family.
Don't think: LOOK! It's all so beautiful.
Sometimes one must remain still in order to advance.
Translation: Even loyal bodyguards need a vacation.

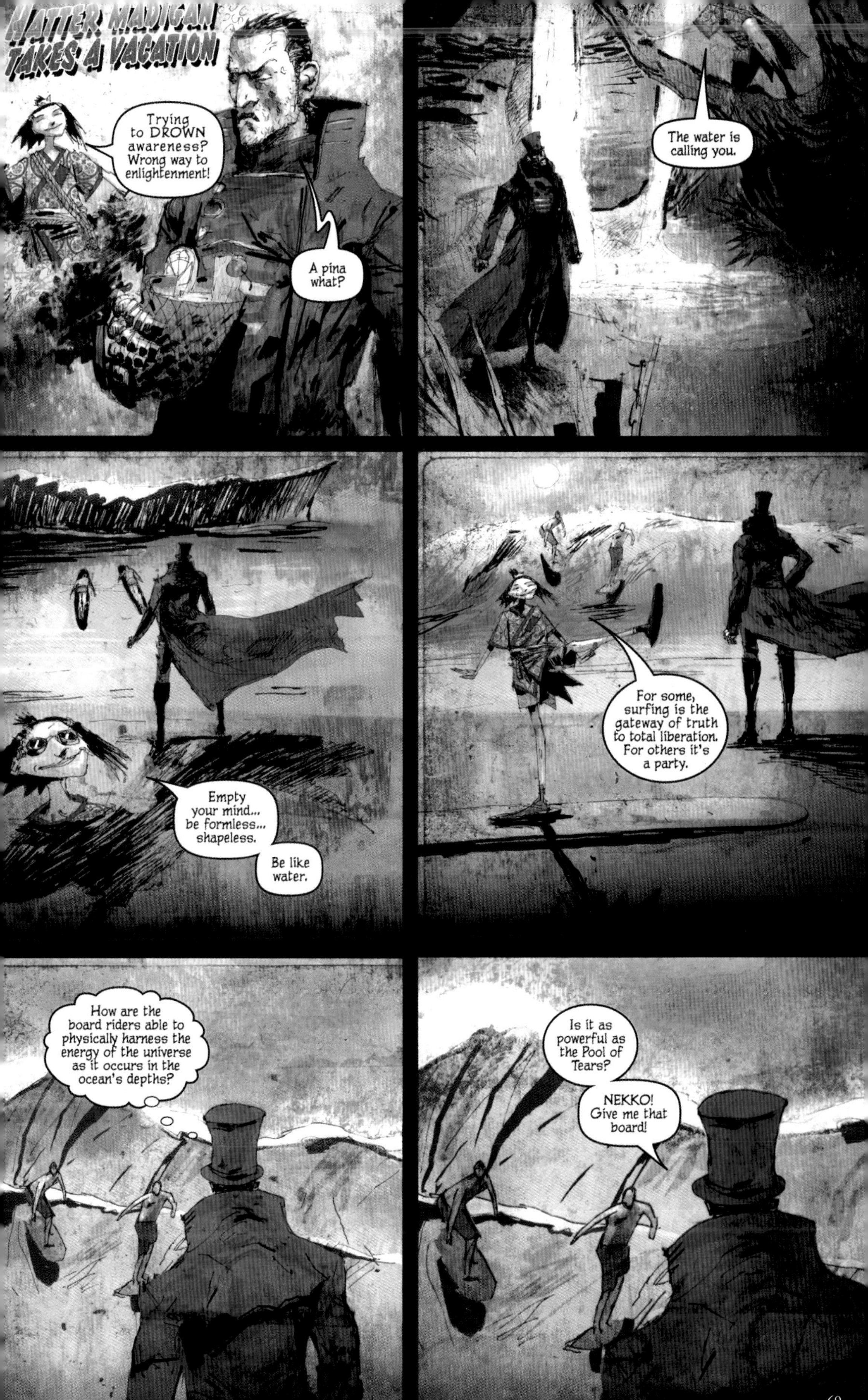
HATTER MADIGAN TAKES A VACATION
Trying to DROWN awareness? Wrong way to enlightenment!
A pina what?
The water is calling you.
Empty your mind... be formless... shapeless.
Be like water.
For some, surfing is the gateway of truth to total liberation. For others it's a party.
How are the board riders able to physically harness the energy of the universe as it occurs in the ocean's depths?
Is it as powerful as the Pool of Tears?
NEKKO! Give me that board!

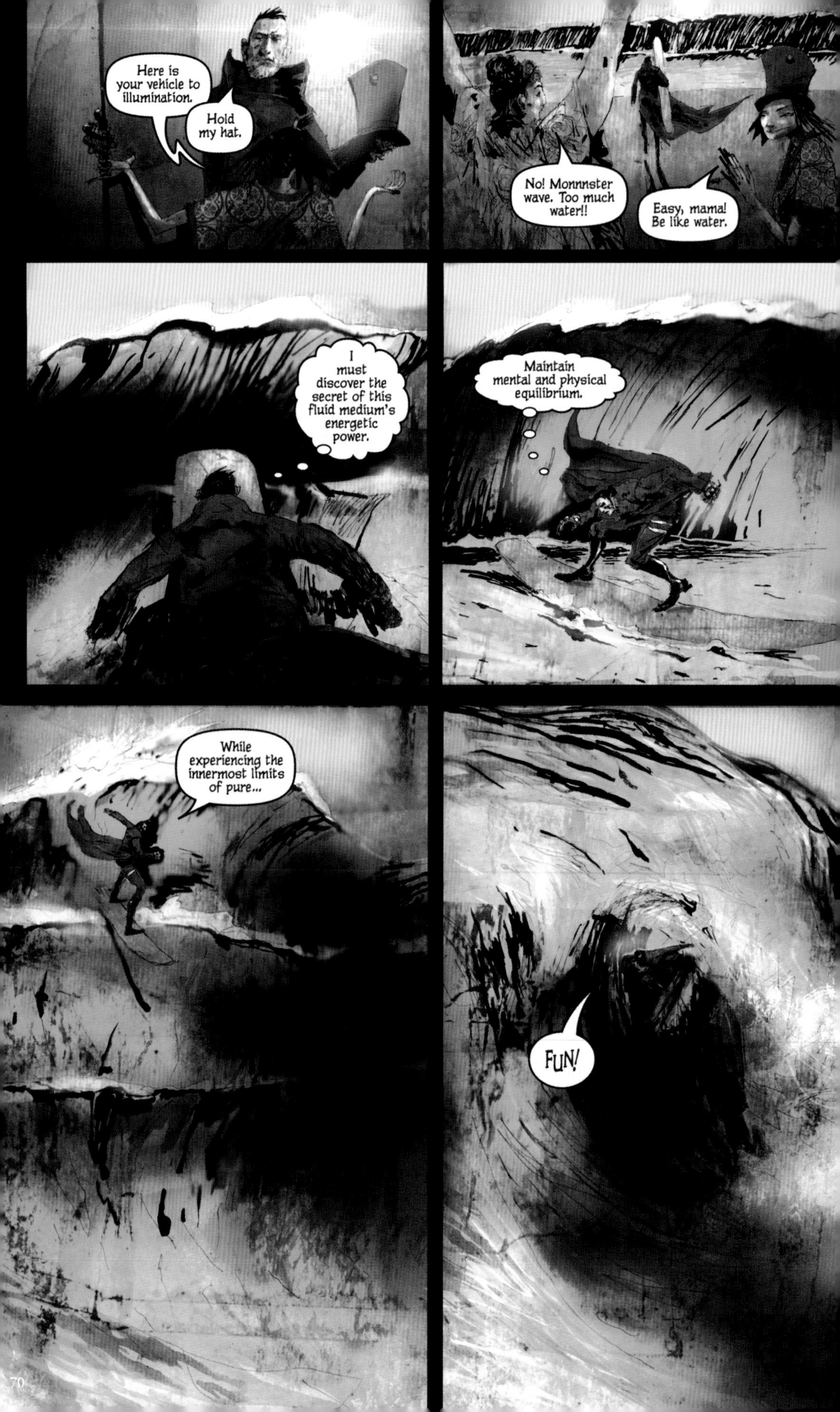
Here is your vehicle to illumination.
Hold my hat.
No! Monnnster wave. Too much water!!
Easy, mama! Be like water.
I must discover the secret of this fluid medium's energetic power.
Maintain mental and physical equilibrium.
While experiencing the innermost limits of pure...
FUN!

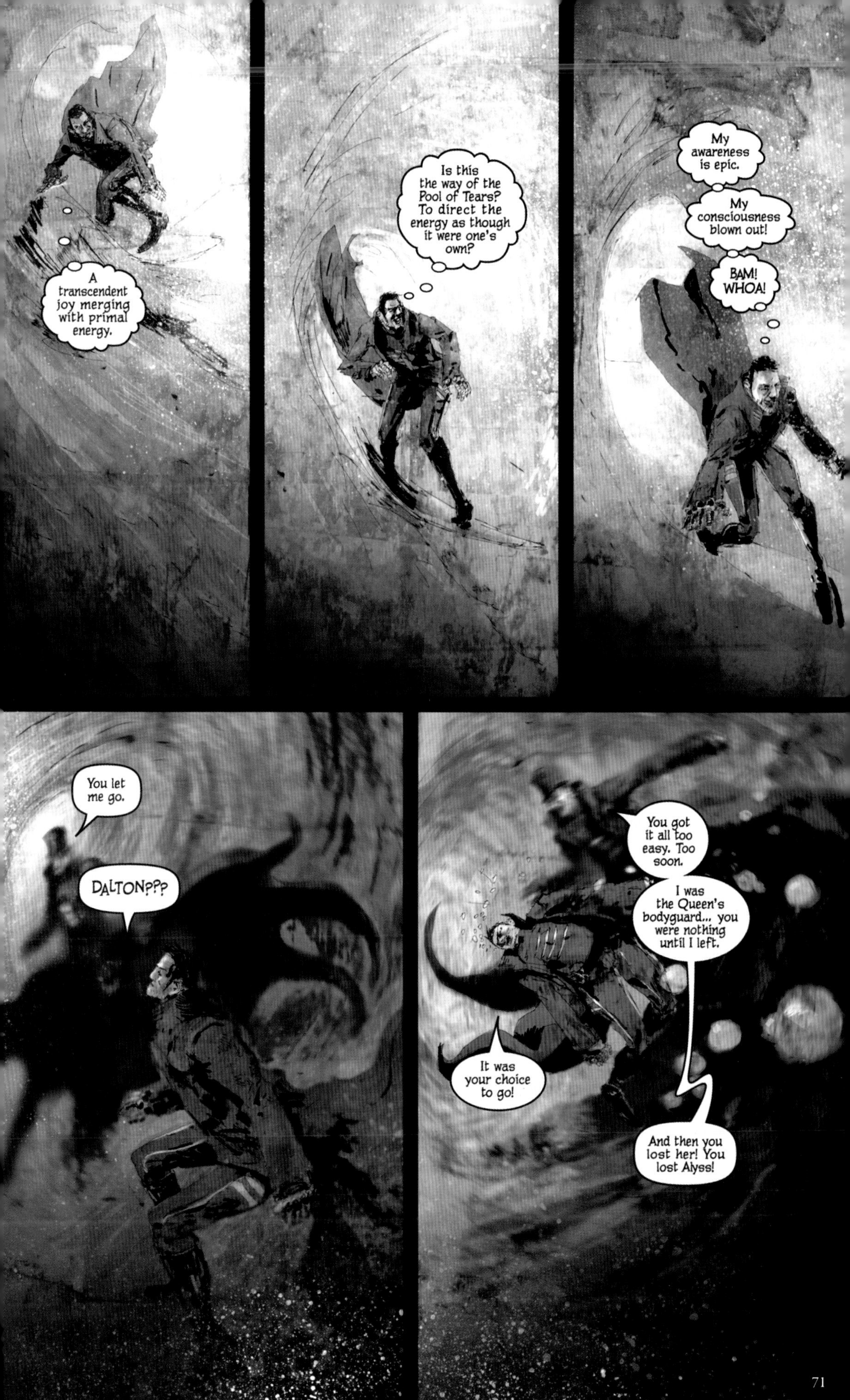
A transcendent joy merging with primal energy.
Is this the way of the Pool of Tears? To direct the energy as though it were one's own?
My awareness is epic.
My consciousness blown out!
BAM! WHOA!
You let me go.
DALTON???
You got it all too easy. Too soon.
I was the Queen's bodyguard... you were nothing until I left.
It was your choice to go!
And then you lost her! You lost Alyss!

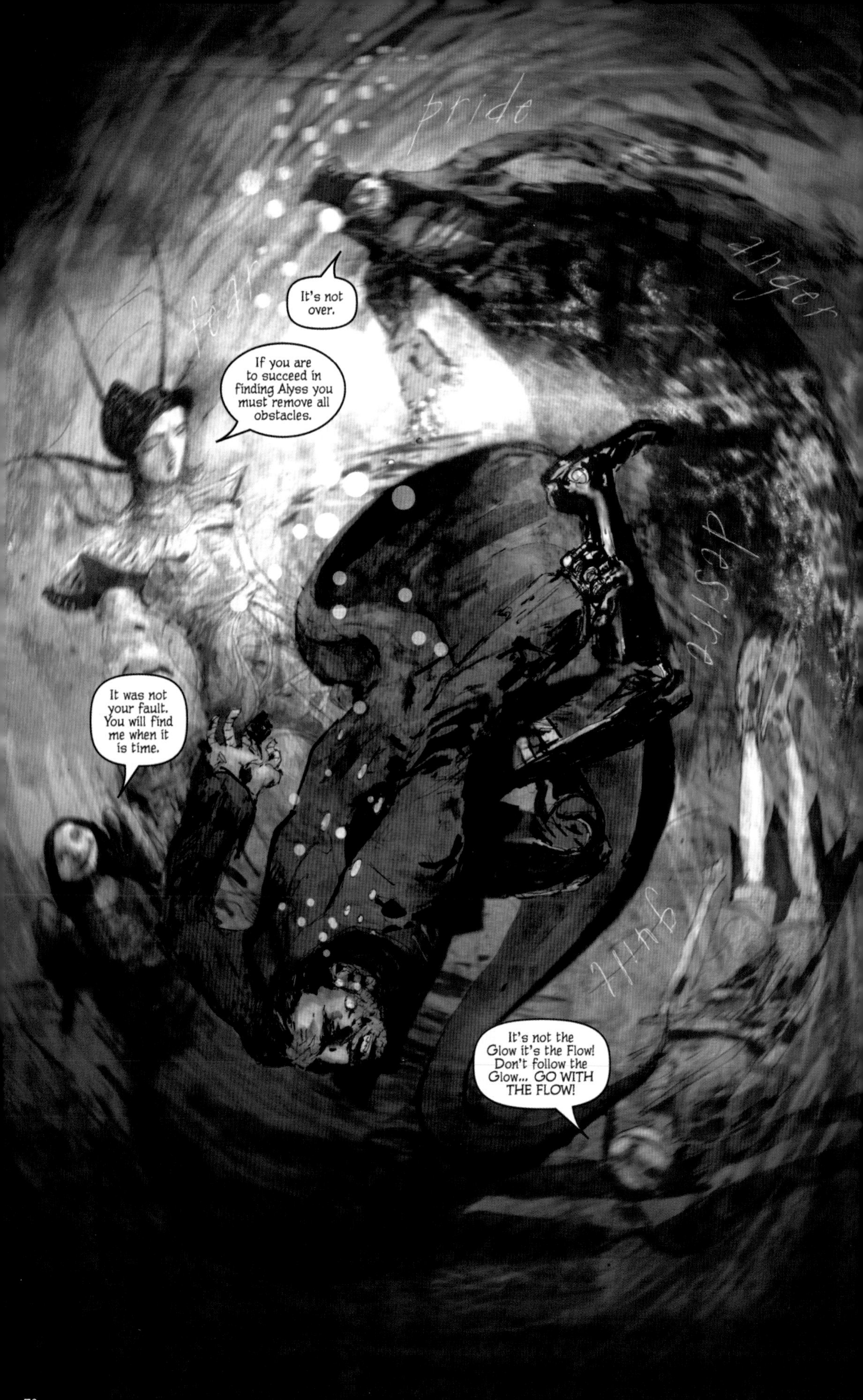
pride
anger
fear
It's not over.
If you are to succeed in finding Alyss you must remove all obstacles.
desire
It was not your fault. You will find me when it is time.
guilt
It's not the Glow it's the Flow! Don't follow the Glow... GO WITH THE FLOW!

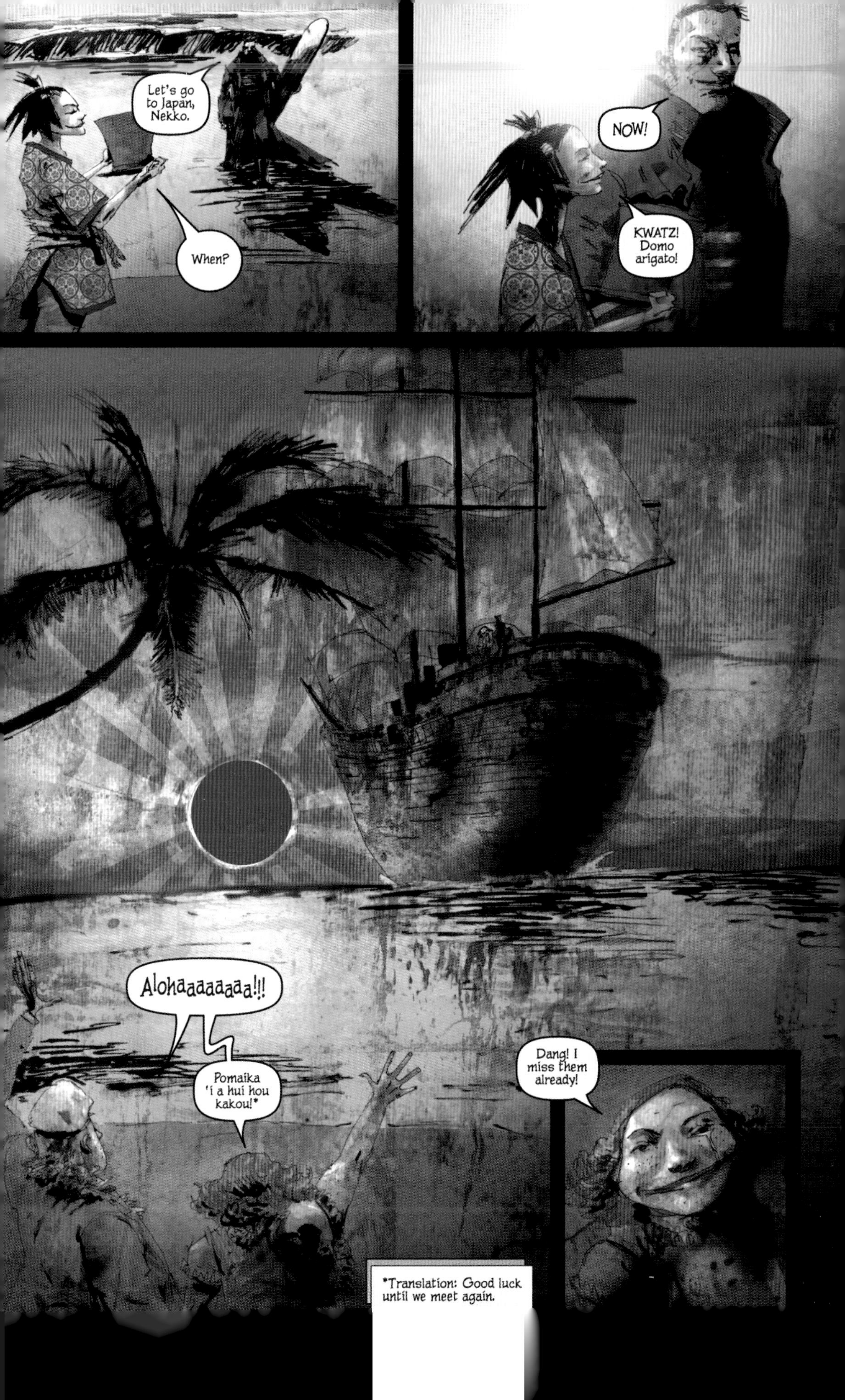
Let's go to Japan, Nekko.
When?
NOW!
KWATZ! Domo arigato!
Alohaaaaaaaa!!!
Pomaika 'i a hui hou kakou!*
Dang! I miss them already!
*Translation: Good luck until we meet again.

Zen is to have the heart and
soul of a little child.
                    -Takuan

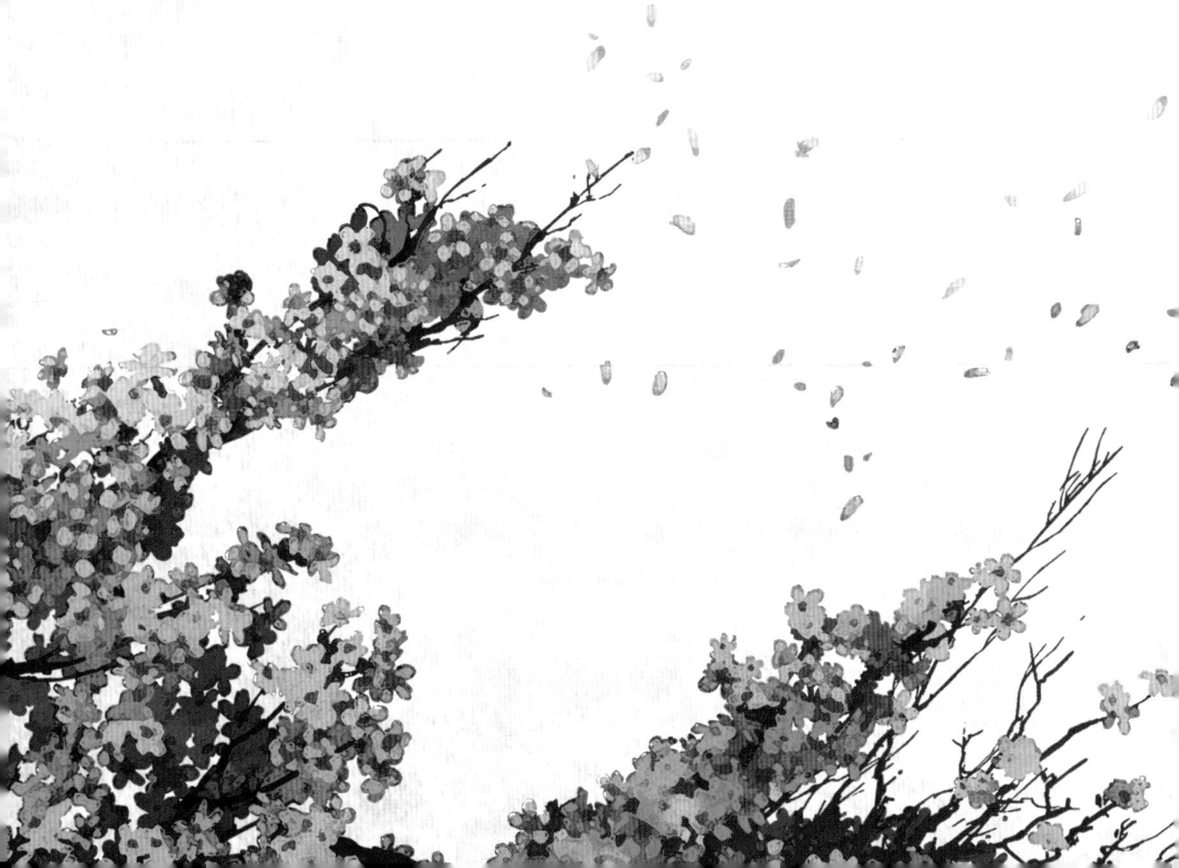

nature has no fear
of loss or demons or death
only the wind moves

恐怖と笑

CHAPTER 3
FEAR AND LAUGHTER

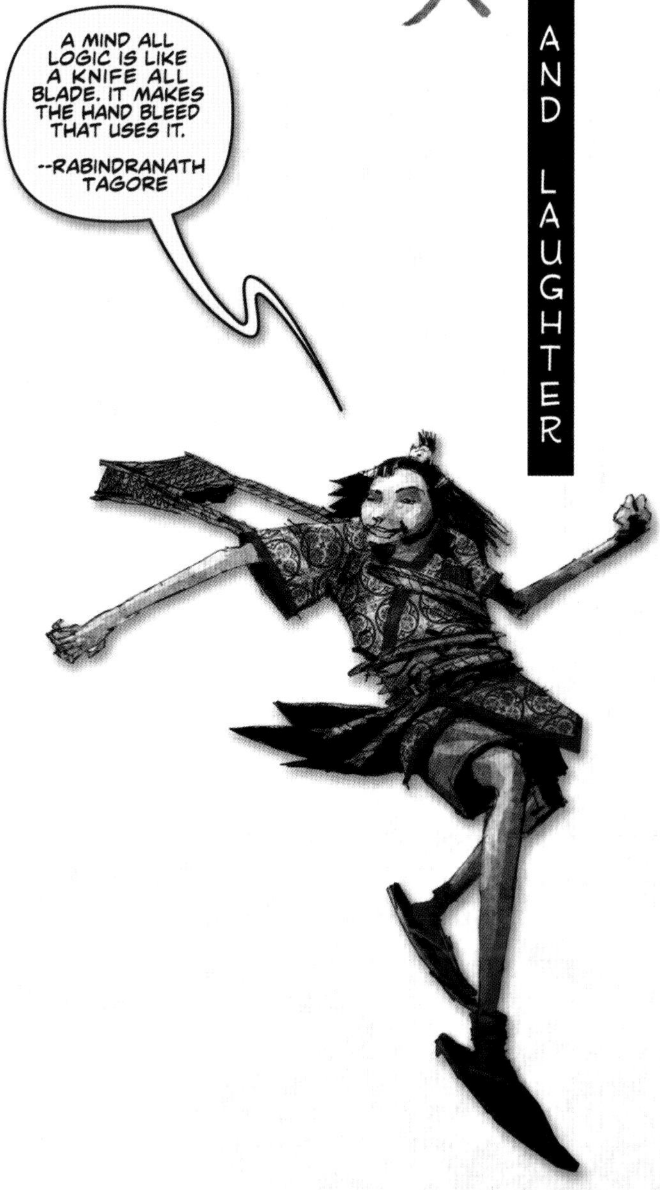
A MIND ALL LOGIC IS LIKE A KNIFE ALL BLADE. IT MAKES THE HAND BLEED THAT USES IT.
--RABINDRANATH TAGORE

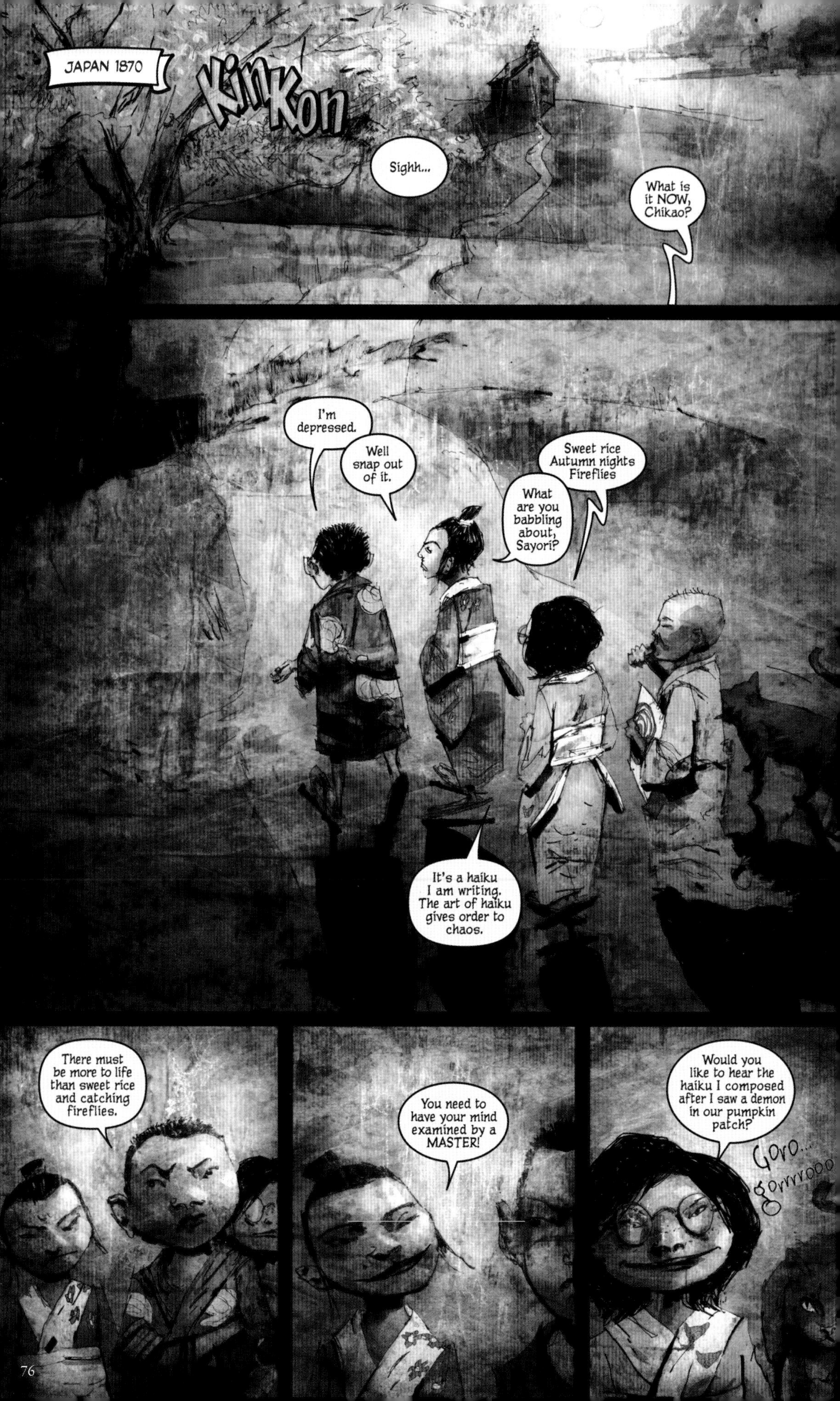
JAPAN 1870
KinKon
Sighh...
What is it NOW, Chikao?
I'm depressed.
Well snap out of it.
Sweet rice Autumn nights Fireflies
What are you babbling about, Sayori?
It's a haiku I am writing. The art of haiku gives order to chaos.
There must be more to life than sweet rice and catching fireflies.
You need to have your mind examined by a MASTER!
Would you like to hear the haiku I composed after I saw a demon in our pumpkin patch?
Goro... gorrrooo

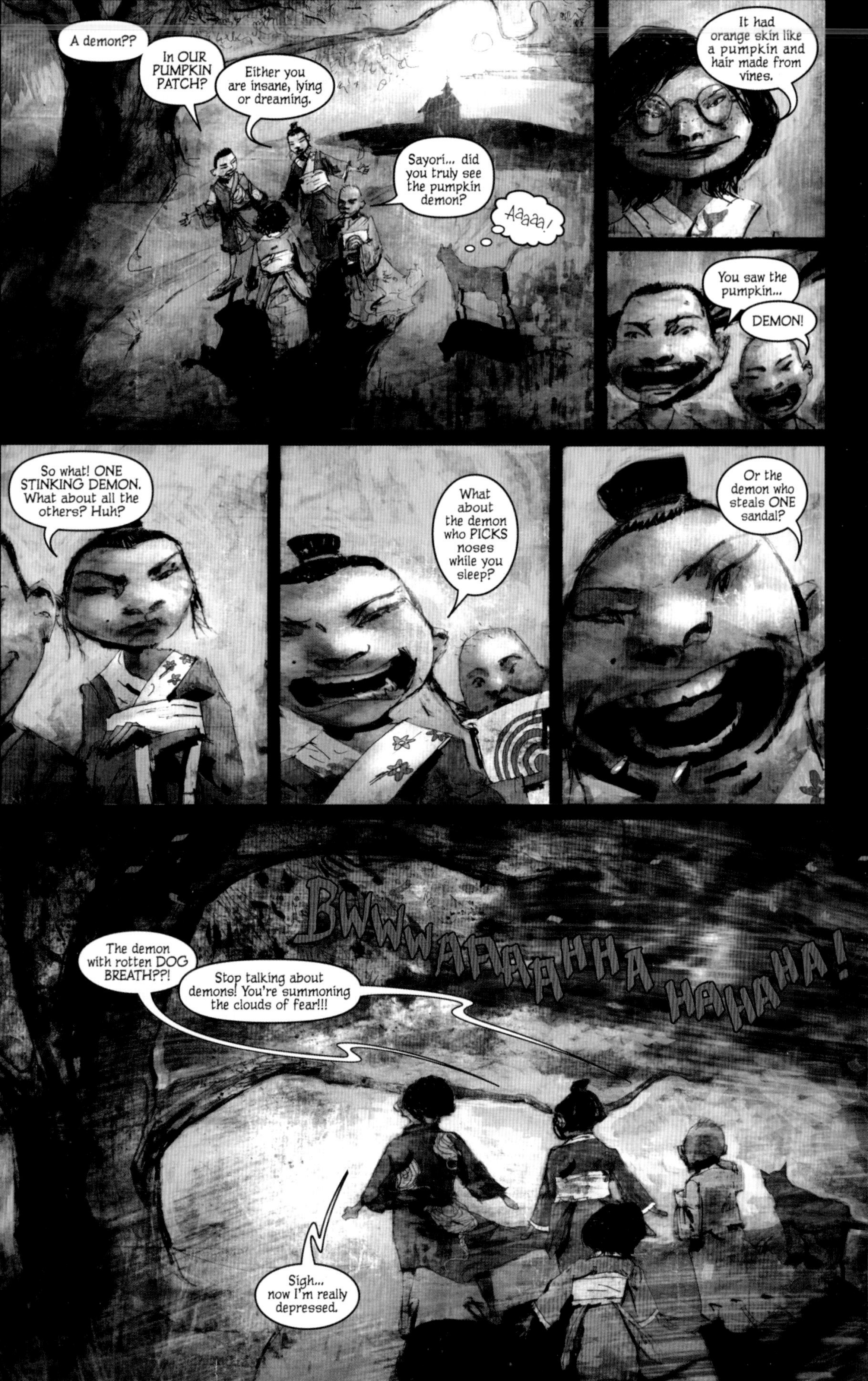
A demon??
In OUR PUMPKIN PATCH?
Either you are insane, lying or dreaming.
Sayori... did you truly see the pumpkin demon?
Aaaaa!
It had orange skin like a pumpkin and hair made from vines.
You saw the pumpkin...
DEMON!
So what! ONE STINKING DEMON. What about all the others? Huh?
What about the demon who PICKS noses while you sleep?
Or the demon who steals ONE sandal?
BWWWAHAHAHHHA HAHAHA!
The demon with rotten DOG BREATH??!
Stop talking about demons! You're summoning the clouds of fear!!!
Sigh... now I'm really depressed.

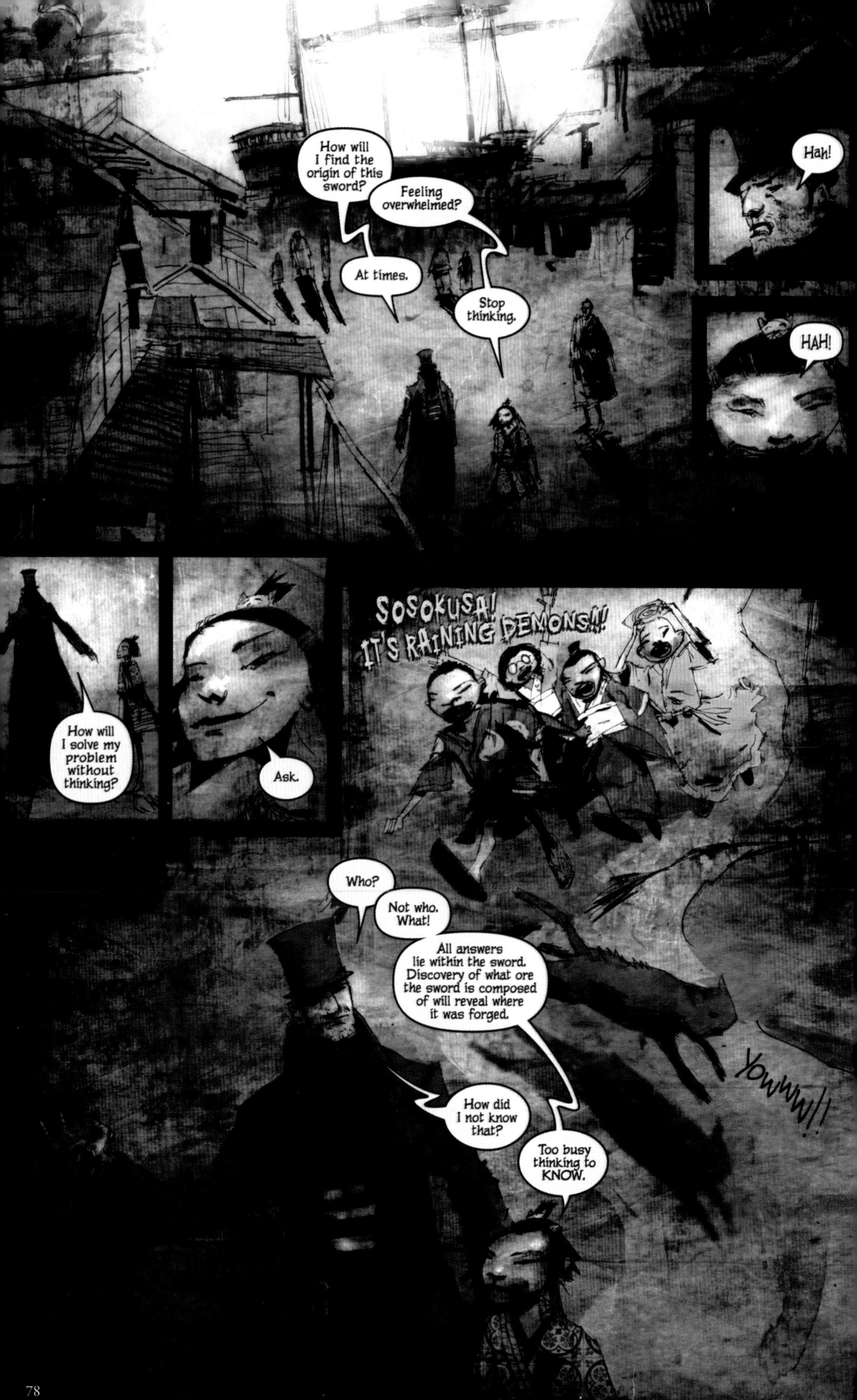

How will I find the origin of this sword?
Feeling overwhelmed?
At times.
Stop thinking.
Hah!
HAH!
How will I solve my problem without thinking?
Ask.
SOSOKUSA! IT'S RAINING DEMONS!!!
Who?
Not who. What!
All answers lie within the sword. Discovery of what ore the sword is composed of will reveal where it was forged.
How did I not know that?
Too busy thinking to KNOW.
YOWWWL!

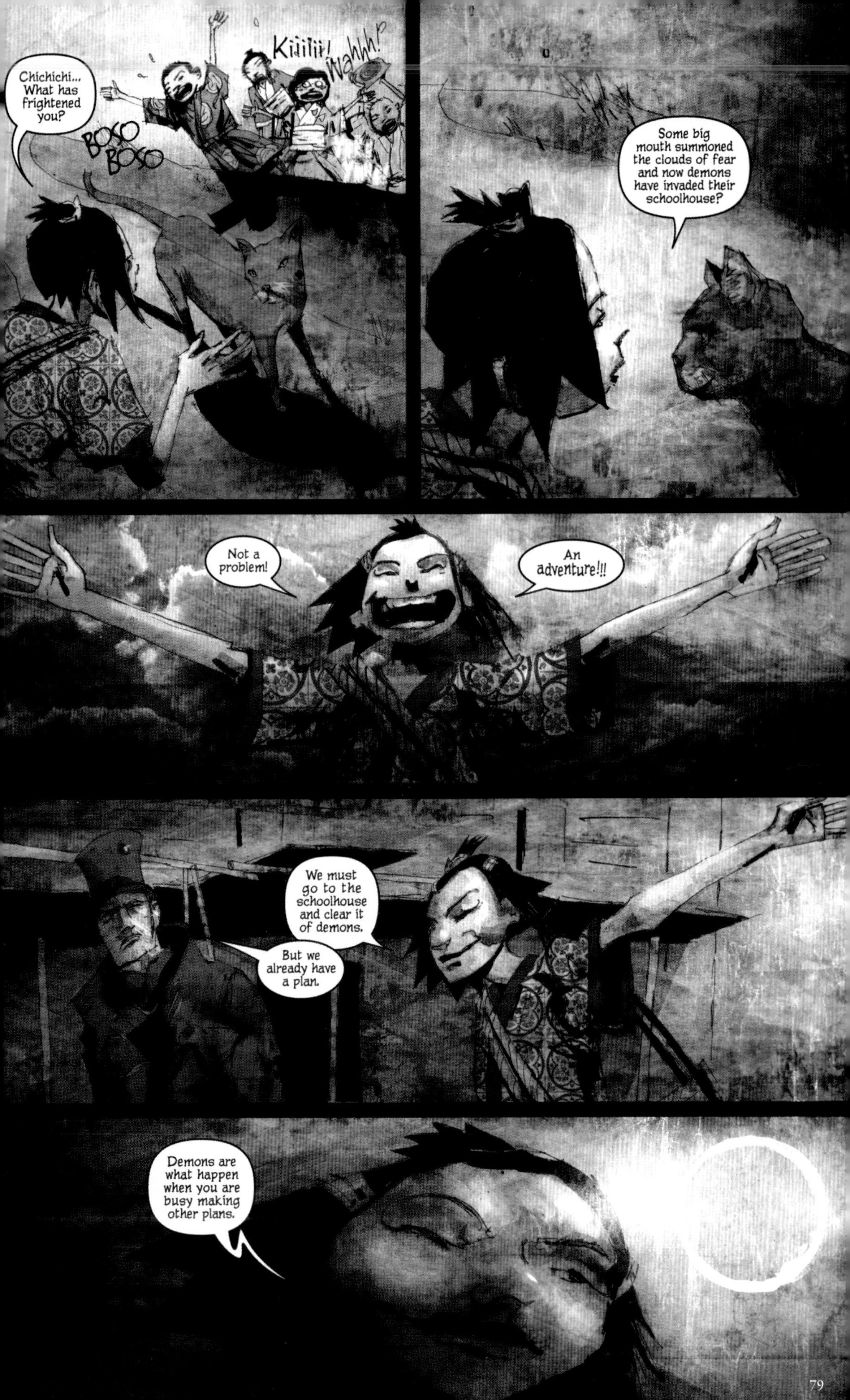

Chichichi... What has frightened you?
Kiiiiii!
Wahhh!
BOSO BOSO
Some big mouth summoned the clouds of fear and now demons have invaded their schoolhouse?
Not a problem!
An adventure!!!
We must go to the schoolhouse and clear it of demons.
But we already have a plan.
Demons are what happen when you are busy making other plans.

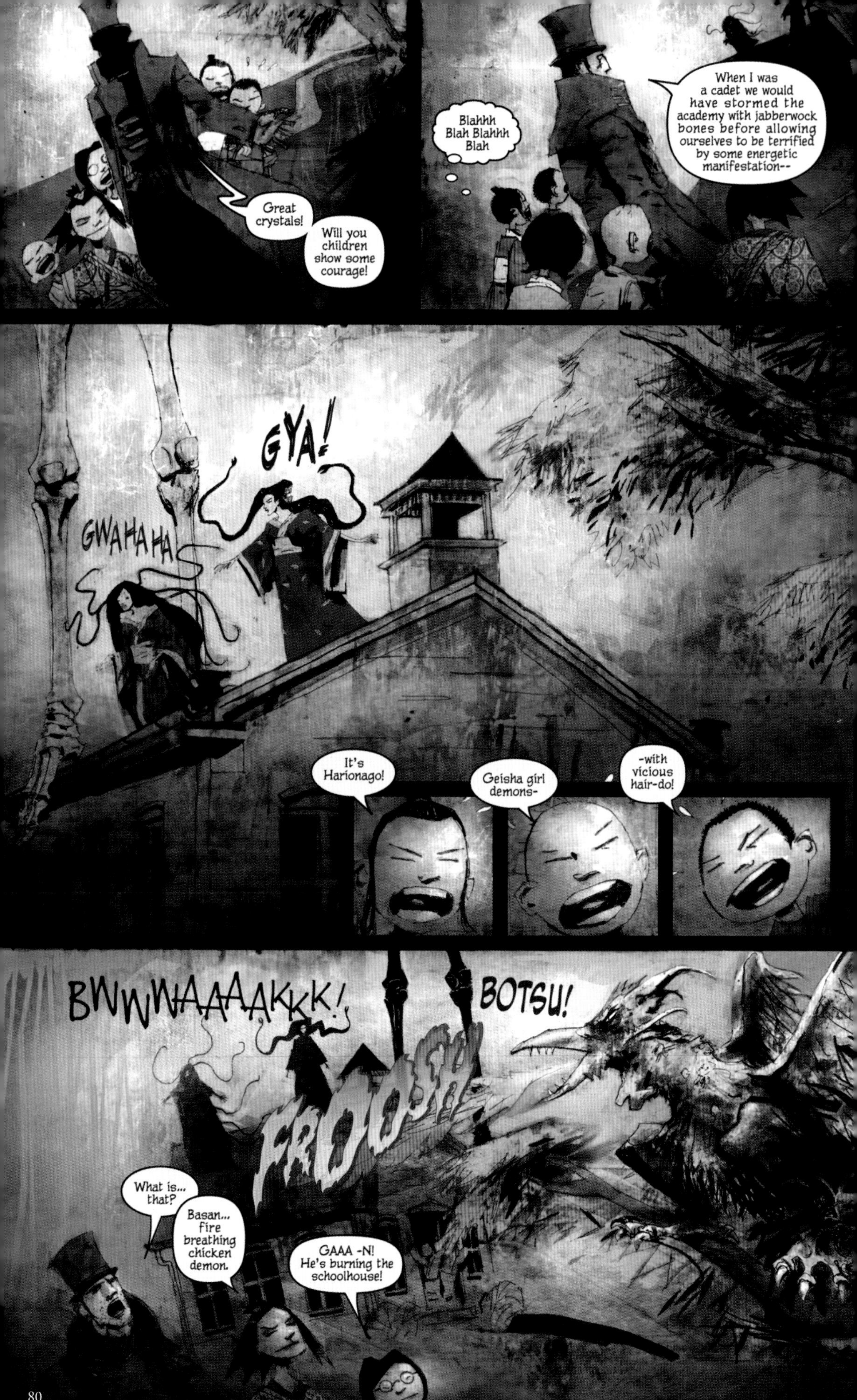
Great crystals!
Will you children show some courage!
Blahhh Blah Blahhh Blah
When I was a cadet we would have stormed the academy with jabberwock bones before allowing ourselves to be terrified by some energetic manifestation--
GYA!
GWAHAHA
It's Harionago!
Geisha girl demons-
-with vicious hair-do!
BWWWAAAAKKK!
BOTSU!
FROOSH!
What is... that?
Basan... fire breathing chicken demon.
GAAA -N! He's burning the schoolhouse!

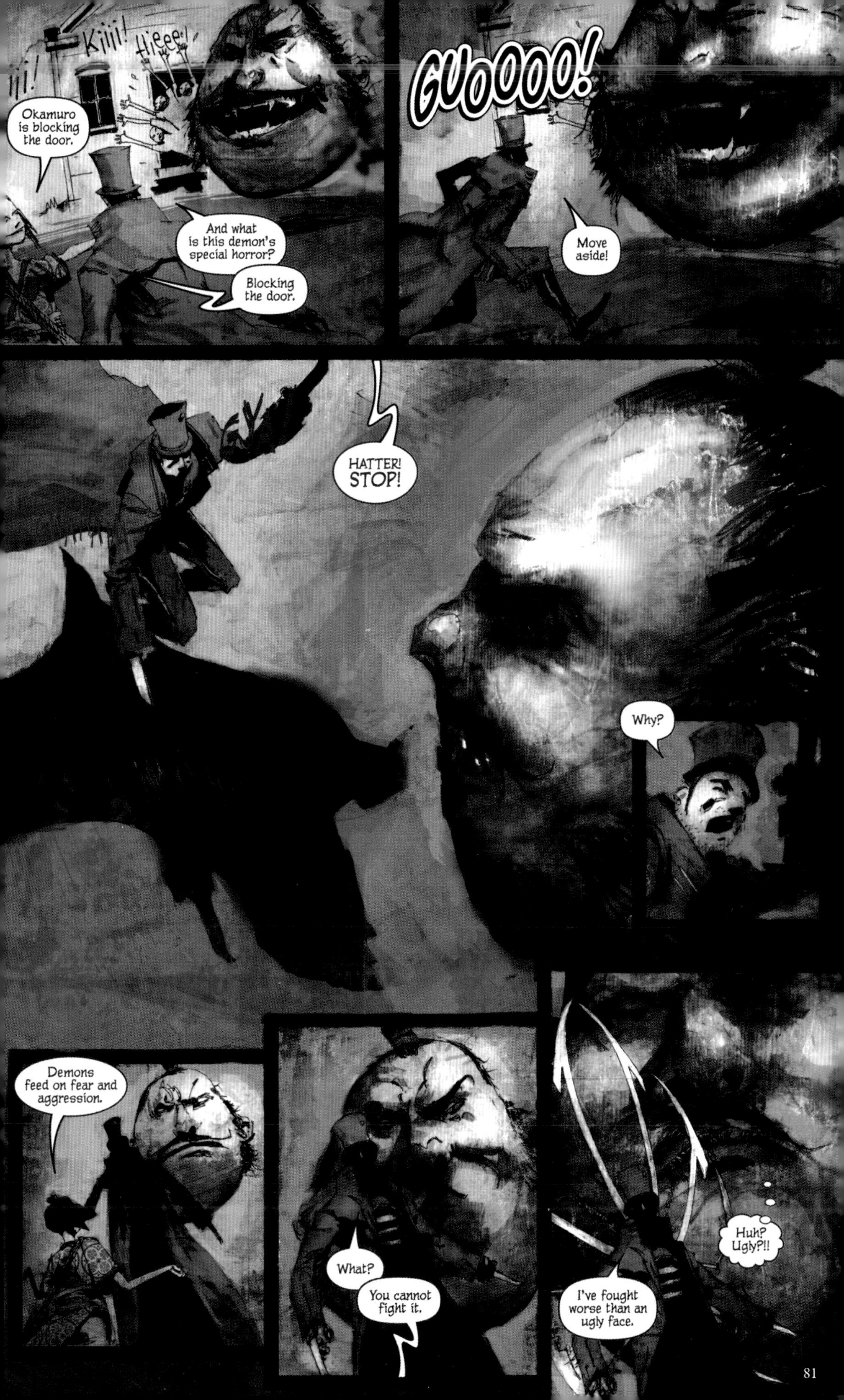
Kiiii! Hieee!
Okamuro is blocking the door.
And what is this demon's special horror?
Blocking the door.
GUOOOO!
Move aside!
HATTER! STOP!
Why?
Demons feed on fear and aggression.
What?
You cannot fight it.
I've fought worse than an ugly face.
Huh? Ugly?!!

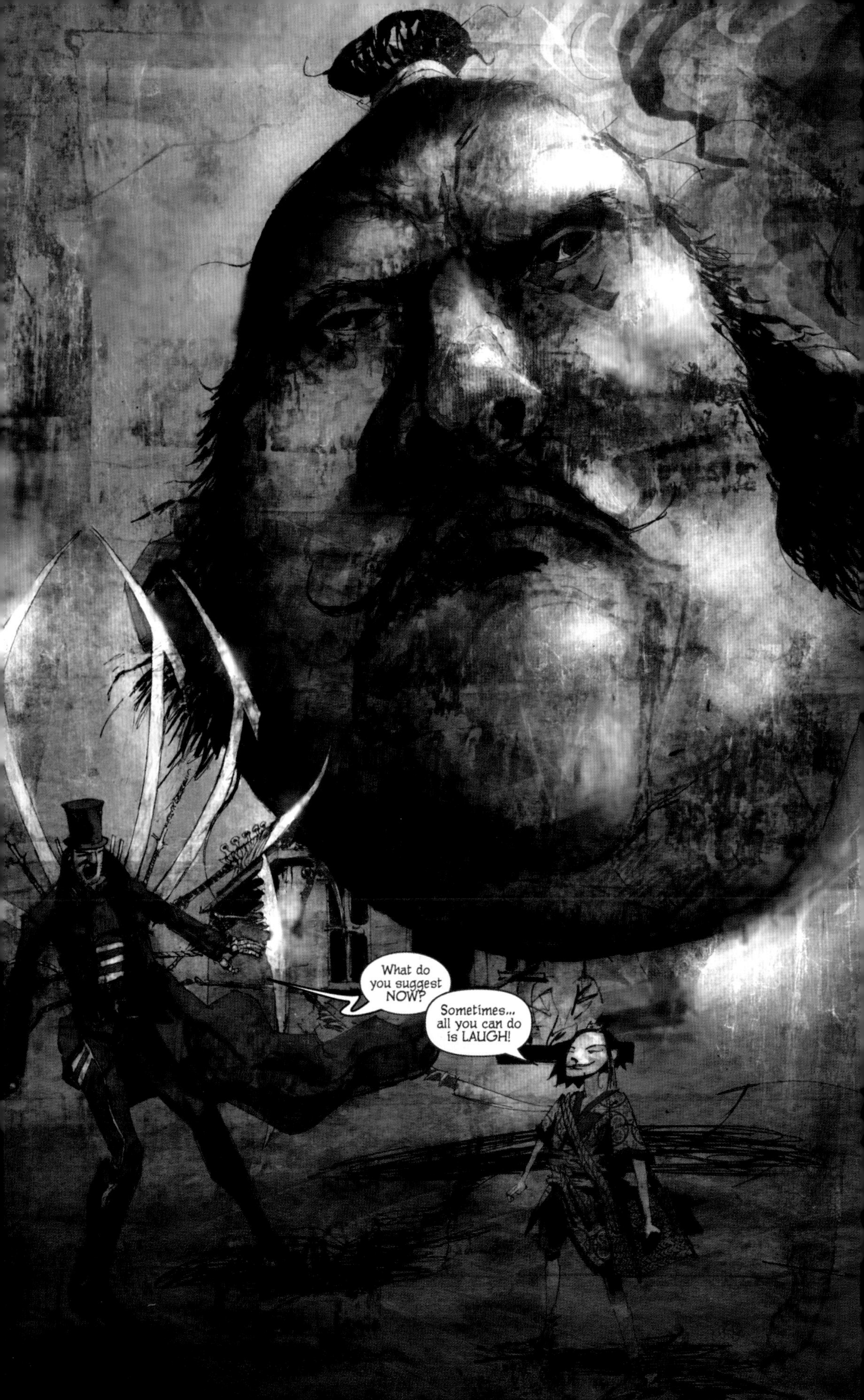
What do you suggest NOW?
Sometimes... all you can do is LAUGH!

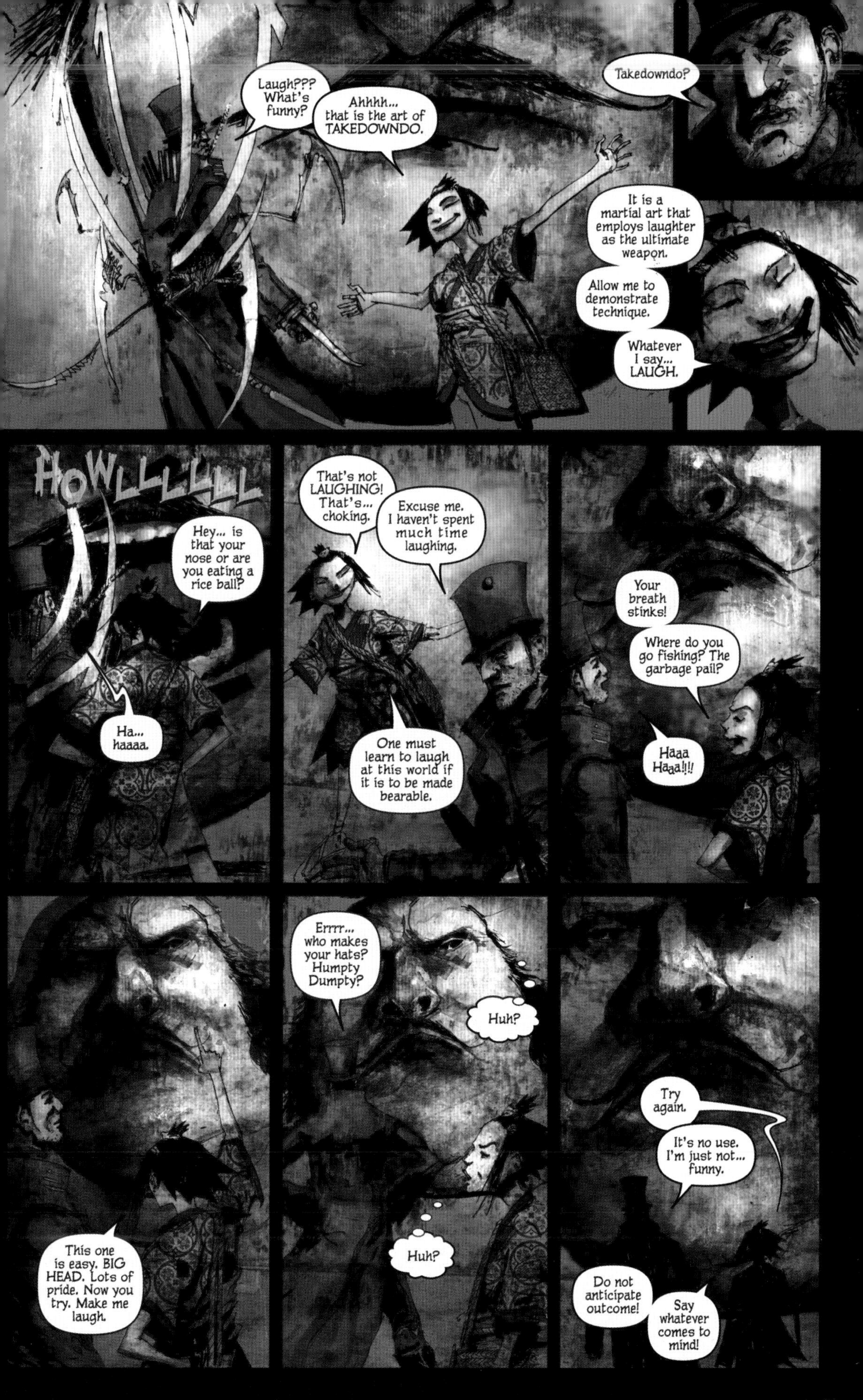
Laugh??? What's funny?
Ahhhh... that is the art of TAKEDOWNDO.
Takedowndo?
It is a martial art that employs laughter as the ultimate weapon.
Allow me to demonstrate technique.
Whatever I say... LAUGH.
HOWLLLLLL
Hey... is that your nose or are you eating a rice ball?
Ha... haaaa.
That's not LAUGHING! That's... choking.
Excuse me. I haven't spent much time laughing.
One must learn to laugh at this world if it is to be made bearable.
Your breath stinks!
Where do you go fishing? The garbage pail?
Haaa Haaa!!!!
This one is easy. BIG HEAD. Lots of pride. Now you try. Make me laugh.
Errrr... who makes your hats? Humpty Dumpty?
Huh?
Huh?
Try again.
It's no use. I'm just not... funny.
Do not anticipate outcome!
Say whatever comes to mind!

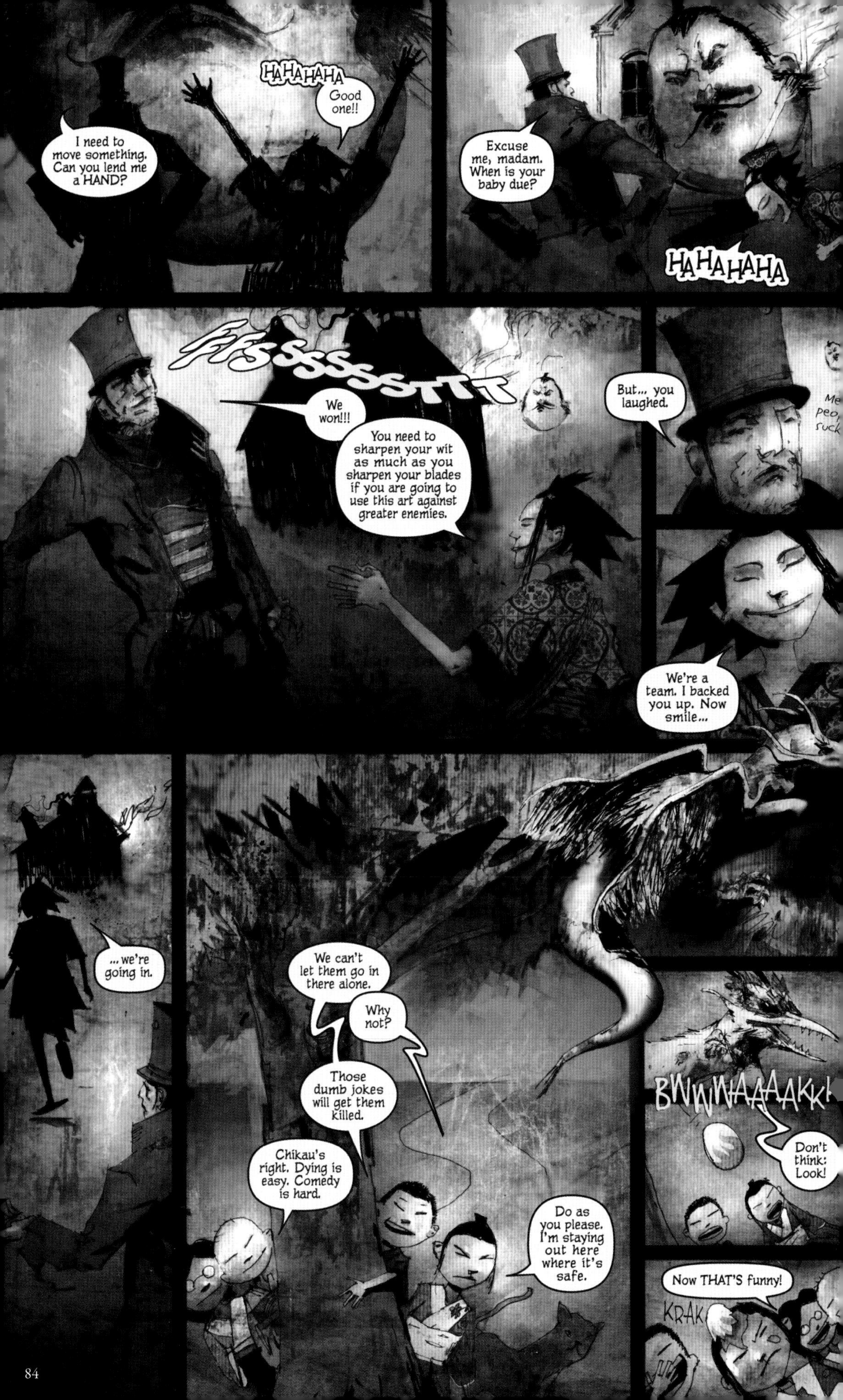
I need to move something. Can you lend me a HAND?
HAHAHAHA
Good one!!
Excuse me, madam. When is your baby due?
HAHAHAHA
FFSSSSSSTTT
We won!!!
You need to sharpen your wit as much as you sharpen your blades if you are going to use this art against greater enemies.
But... you laughed.
We're a team. I backed you up. Now smile...
...we're going in.
We can't let them go in there alone.
Why not?
Those dumb jokes will get them killed.
Chikau's right. Dying is easy. Comedy is hard.
Do as you please. I'm staying out here where it's safe.
BWWWAAAAKK
Don't think: Look!
Now THAT'S funny!
KRAK

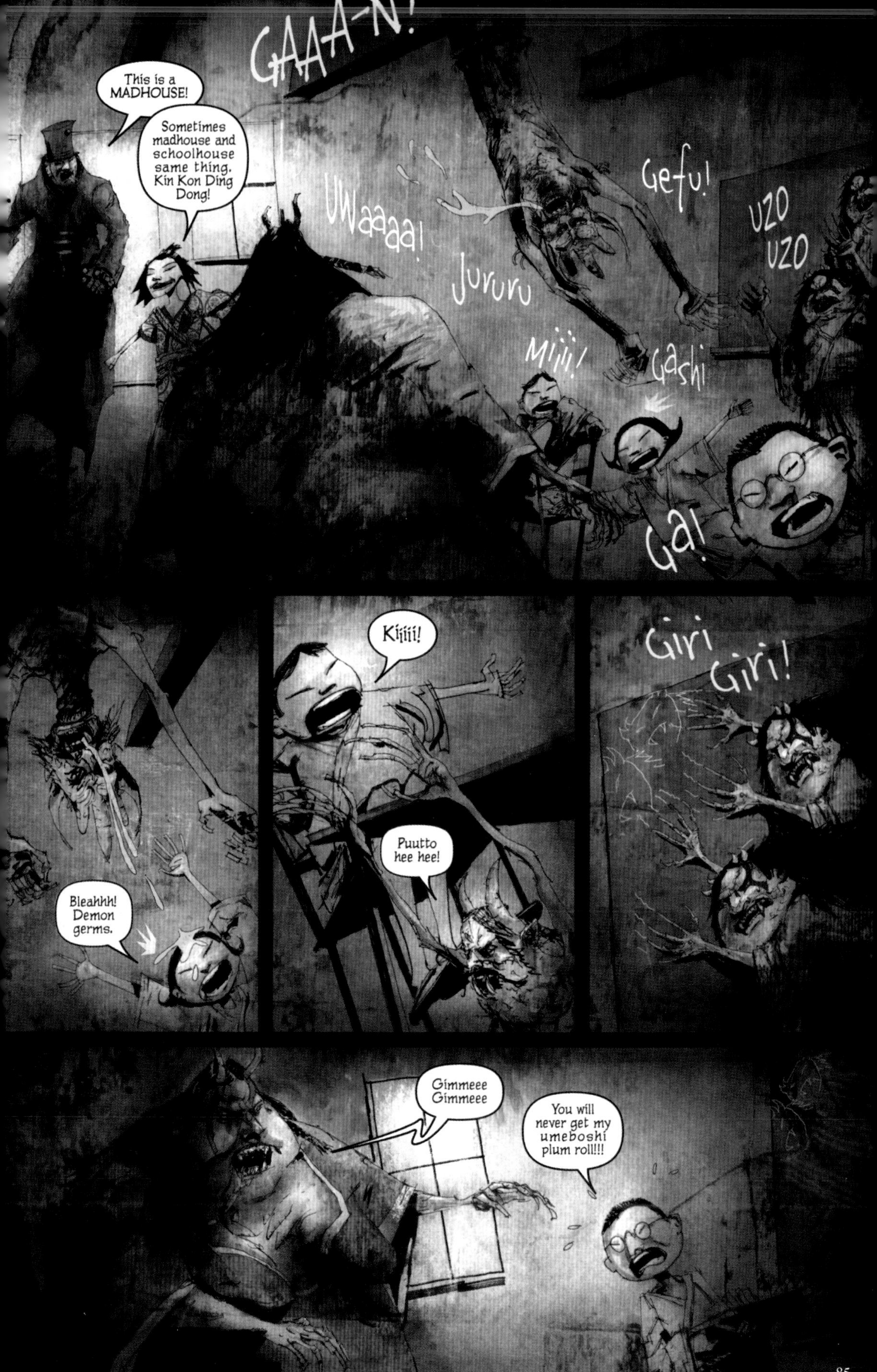
GAAA-N!
This is a MADHOUSE!
Sometimes madhouse and schoolhouse same thing. Kin Kon Ding Dong!
Uwaaaaa!
Jururu
Gefu!
UZO UZO
Miiii!
Gashi
Ga!
Bleahhh! Demon germs.
Kiiiii!
Puutto hee hee!
Giri Giri!
Gimmeee Gimmeee
You will never get my umeboshi plum roll!!!

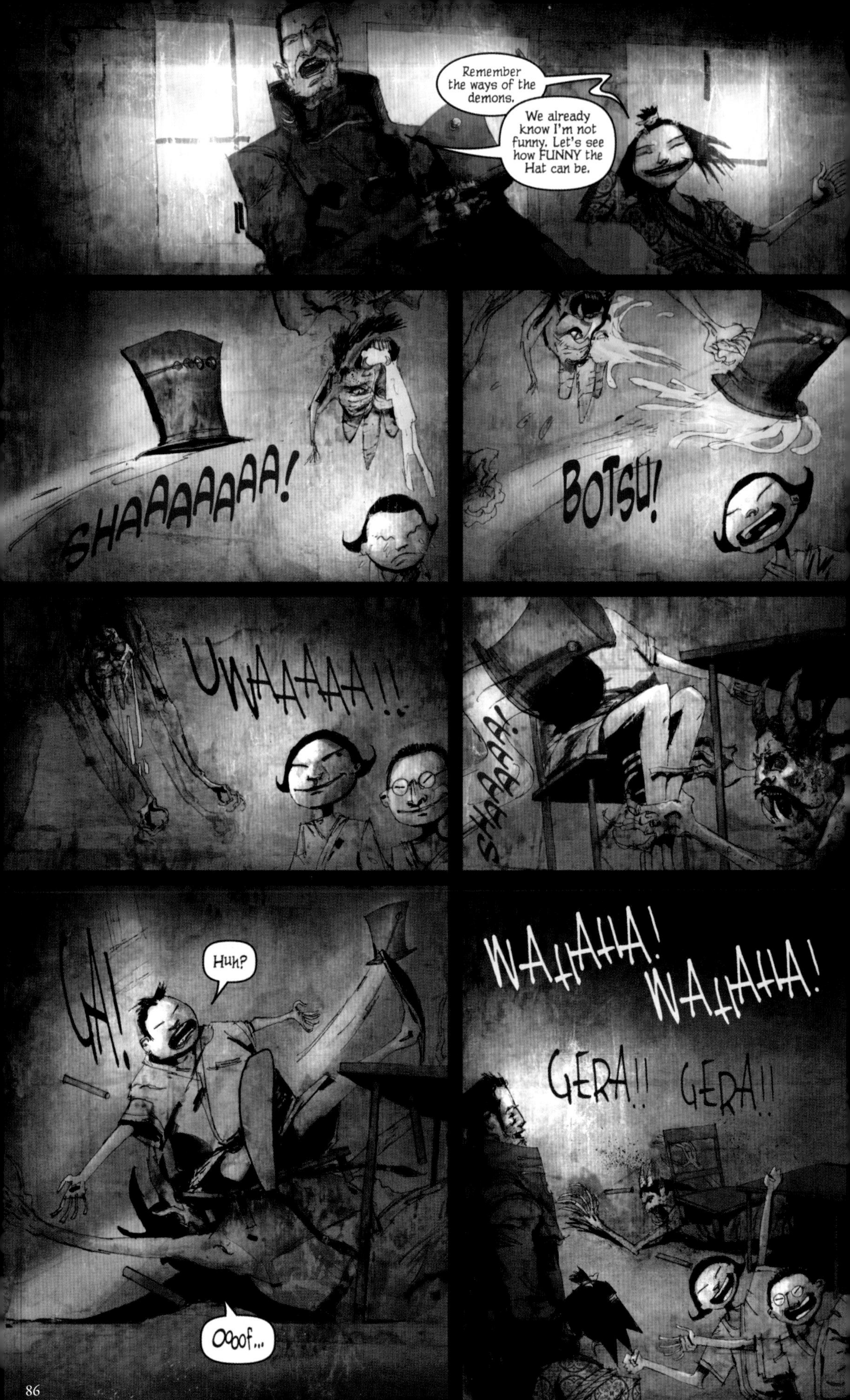
Remember the ways of the demons.
We already know I'm not funny. Let's see how FUNNY the Hat can be.
SHAAAAAAA!
BOTSU!
UWAAAAAA!!
SHAAAA!
GA!
Huh?
Ooof...
WAHAHA! WAHAHA!
GERA!! GERA!!

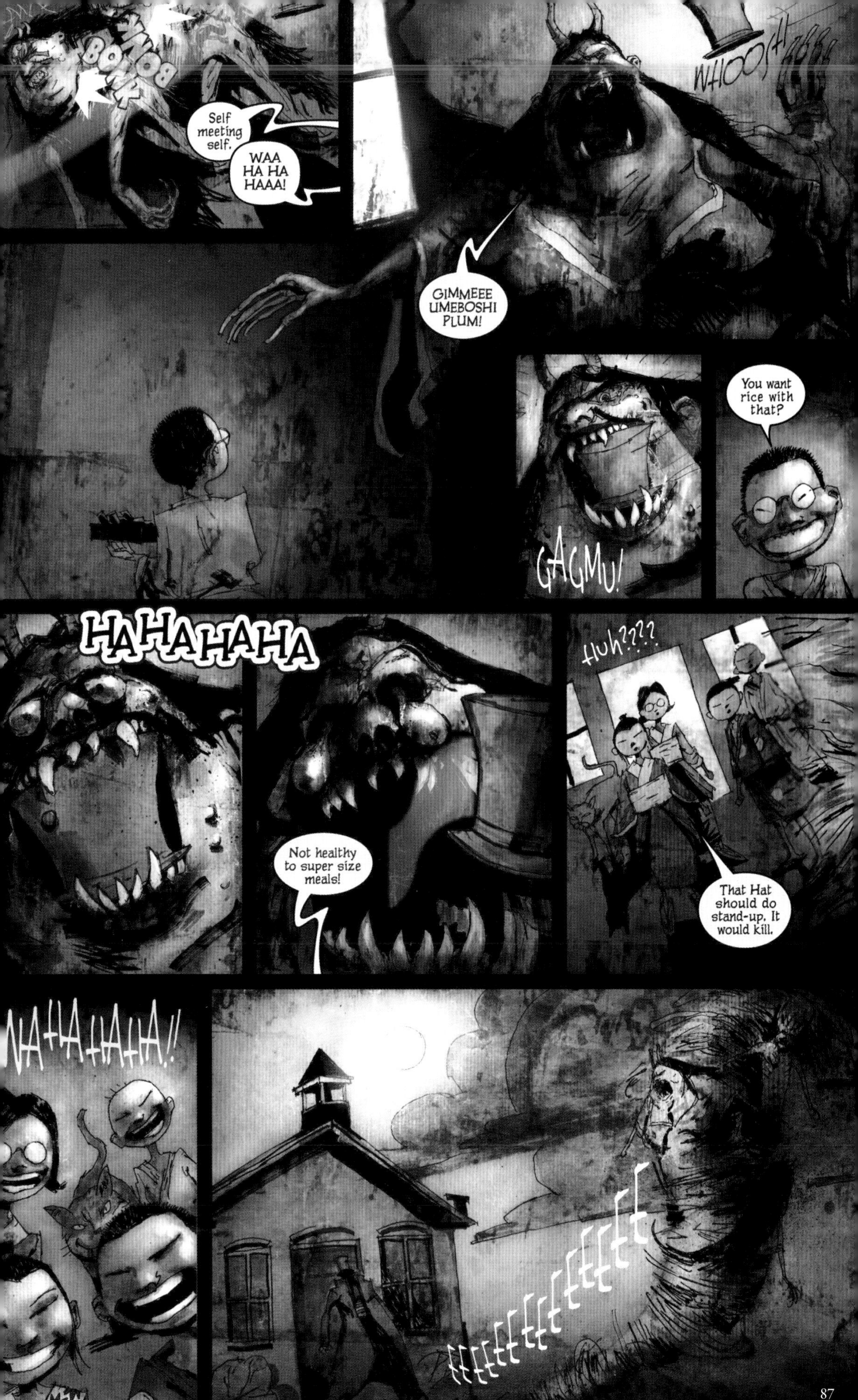
BONK
Self meeting self.
WAA HA HA HAAA!
WHOOSH
GIMMEEE UMEBOSHI PLUM!
GAGMU!
You want rice with that?
HAHAHAHA
Not healthy to super size meals!
Huh????
That Hat should do stand-up. It would kill.
NAHAHAHA!!
EEEEEEEEEEEEEEEEE

Let's go someplace depressing. See you in your nightmares!

Hena... Hena...

Help me... please...

It's Mr. Murakami!

He's being held captive in the outhouse by Toire-no-hanakosan!

Which demon is this?

THE DEMON WHO LURKS IN GRADE SCHOOL OUTHOUSES!

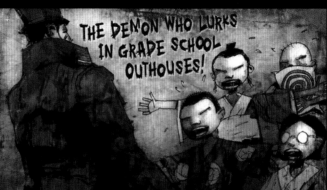

In the crapper?

HAHAHAHA So that's the HOME of Toire-no-hanakosan?

What's so funny? HAHAHAHA YOU!!!!

Arig... ariga... ARIGATO!

When a monk asked, "What is the Buddha?"

*Ummon replied, "A shit wiping stick."

HA!

*Ummon Bun'en Zenji (Japanese) was a Zen Master during the golden age of Zen in T'ang Dynasty China (864-949 AD)

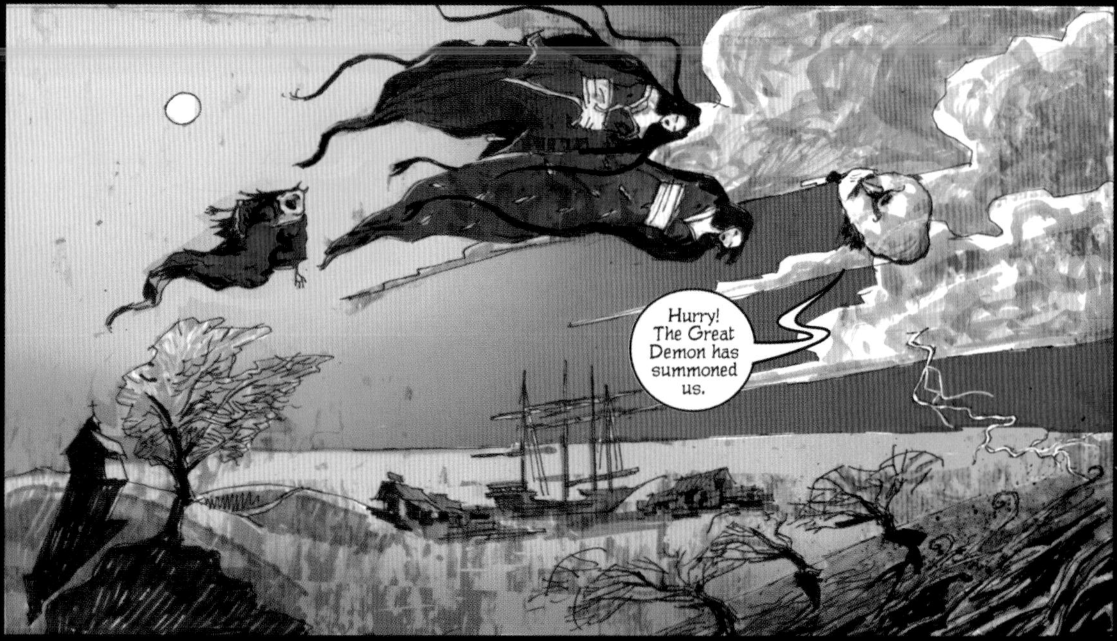
Hurry! The Great Demon has summoned us.

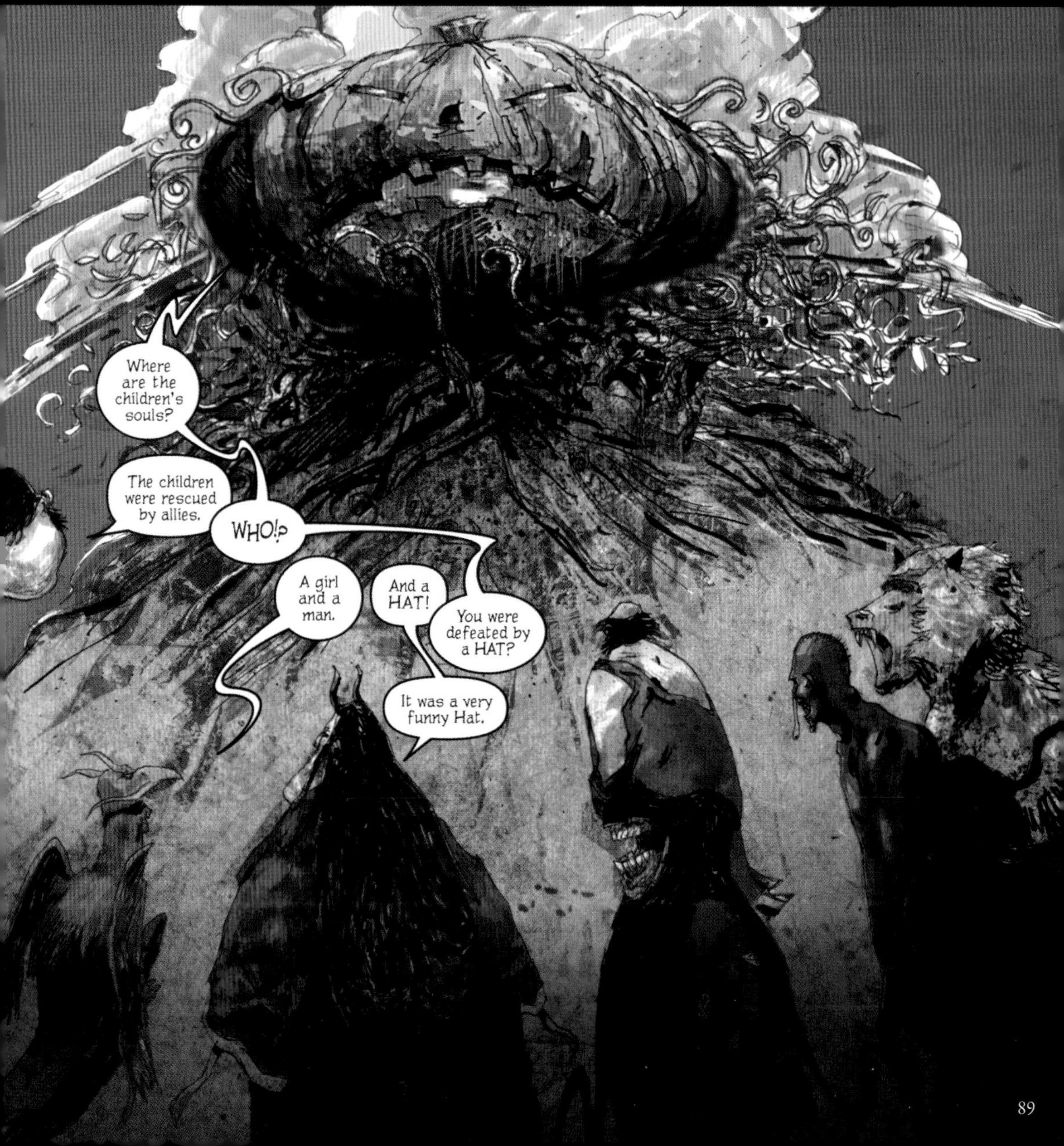
Where are the children's souls?
The children were rescued by allies.
WHO!?
A girl and a man.
And a HAT!
You were defeated by a HAT?
It was a very funny Hat.

We all feel we are going to crash.
But the satori is – we bounce.
-Anonymous

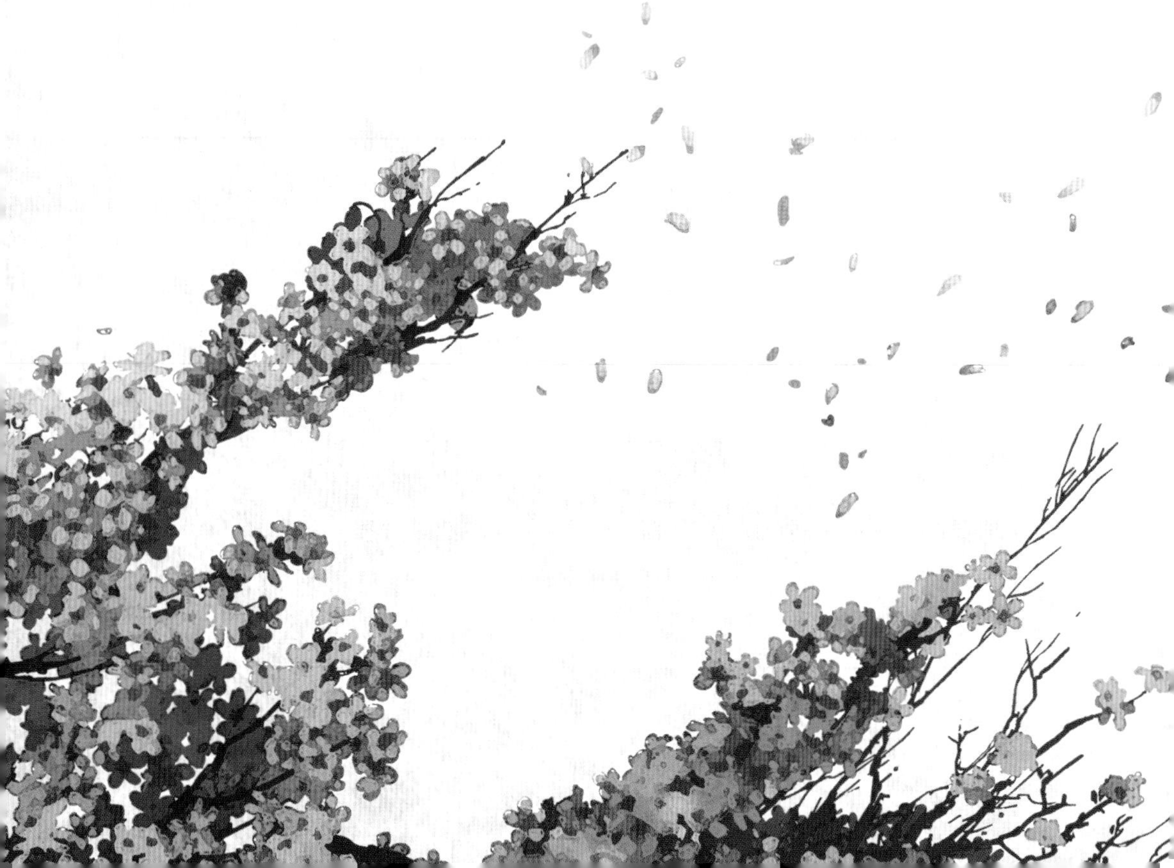

crushed by gravity
swept by invisible landslides
laughing, the seeker escapes

悟り
CHAPTER 4
SATORI

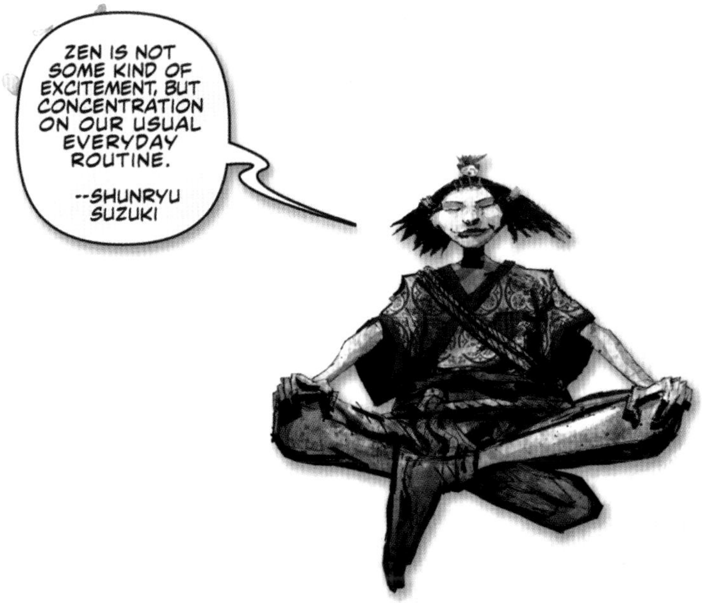
ZEN IS NOT SOME KIND OF EXCITEMENT, BUT CONCENTRATION ON OUR USUAL EVERYDAY ROUTINE.
--SHUNRYU SUZUKI

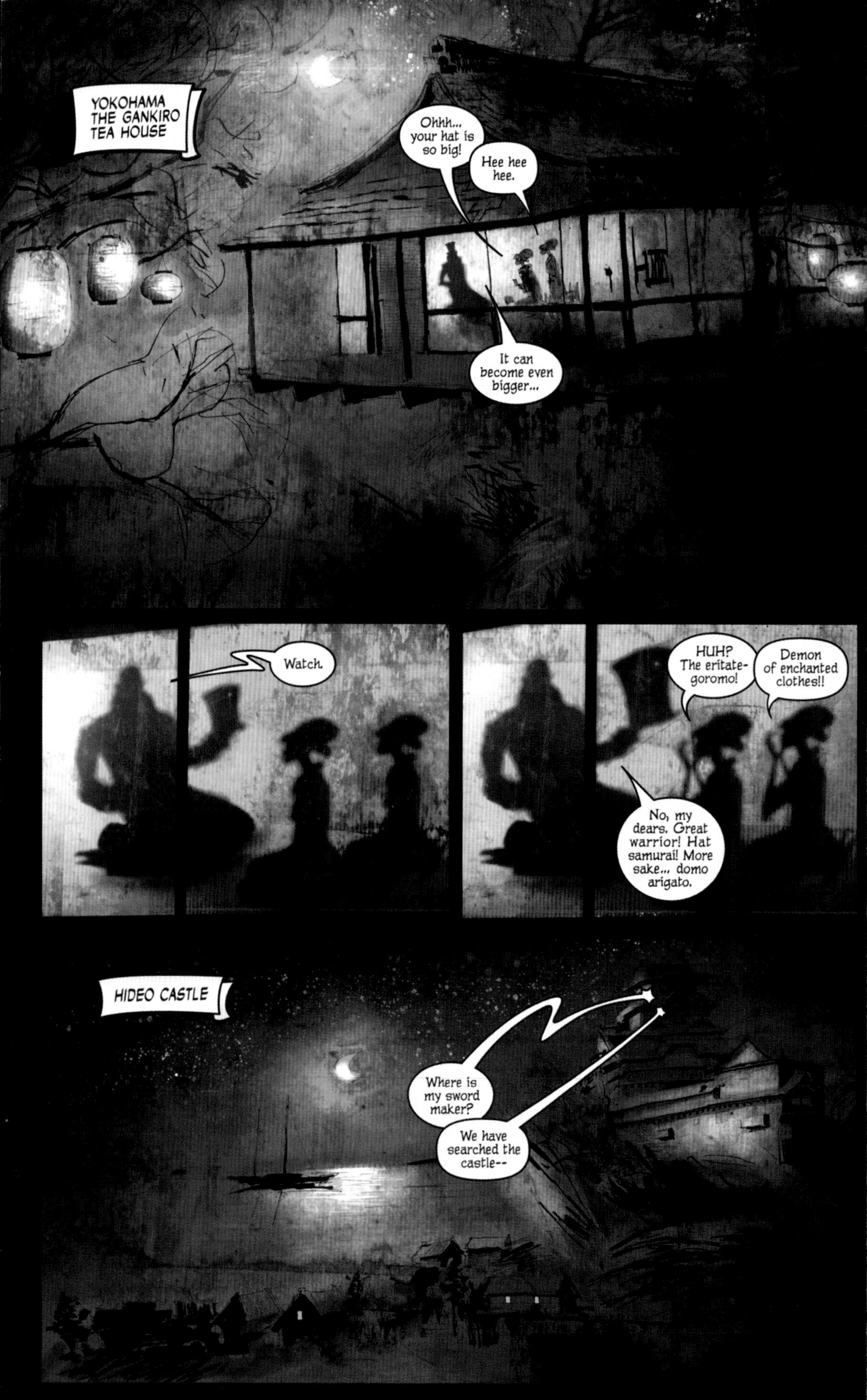

YOKOHAMA THE GANKIRO TEA HOUSE
Ohhh... your hat is so big!
Hee hee hee.
It can become even bigger...
Watch.
HUH? The eritate-goromo!
Demon of enchanted clothes!!
No, my dears. Great warrior! Hat samurai! More sake... domo arigato.
HIDEO CASTLE
Where is my sword maker?
We have searched the castle--

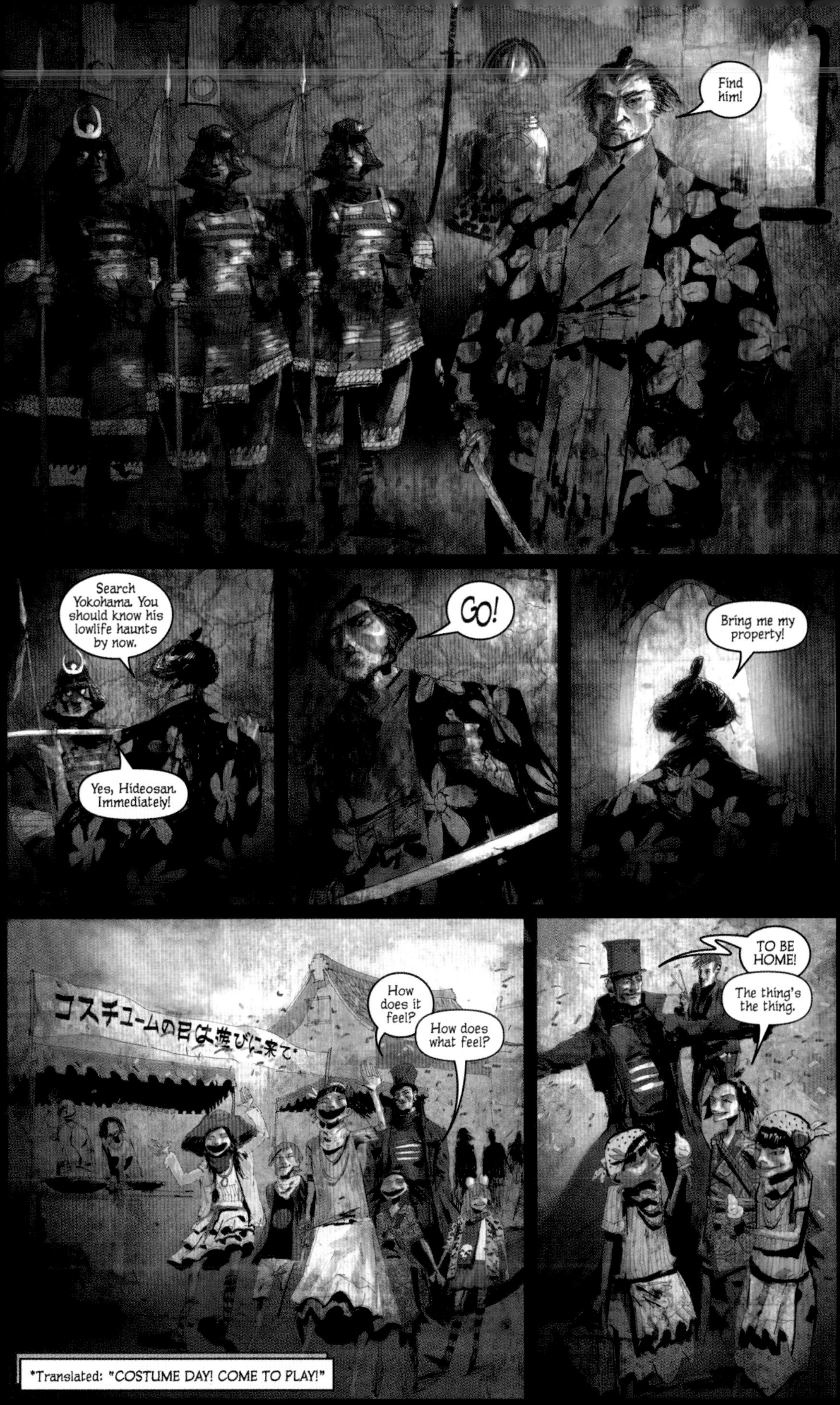

Find him!
Search Yokohama. You should know his lowlife haunts by now.
Yes, Hideosan. Immediately!
GO!
Bring me my property!
コスチュームの日は遊びに来て*
How does it feel?
How does what feel?
TO BE HOME!
The thing's the thing.
*Translated: "COSTUME DAY! COME TO PLAY!"

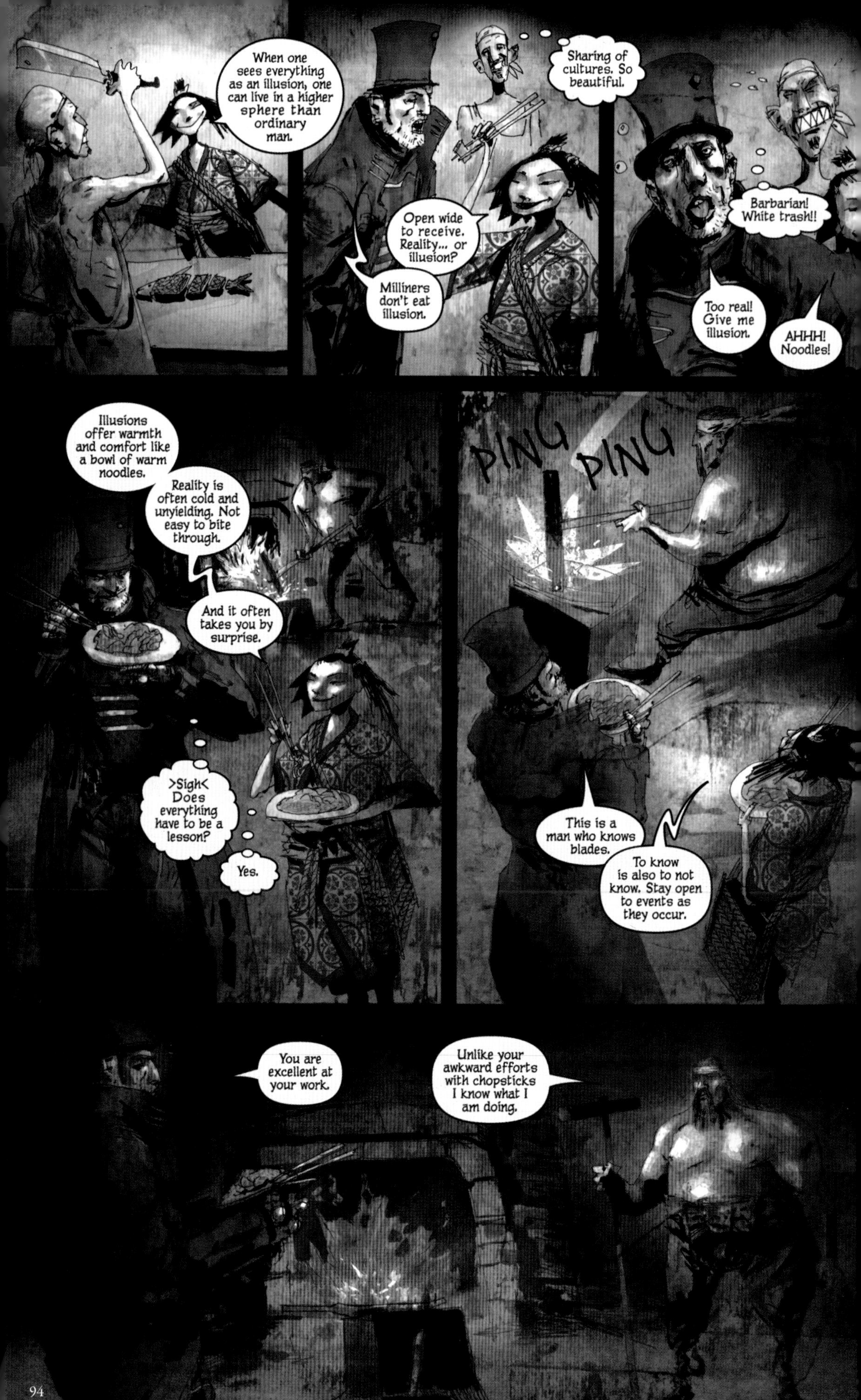
When one sees everything as an illusion, one can live in a higher sphere than ordinary man.
Sharing of cultures. So beautiful.
Open wide to receive. Reality... or illusion?
Milliners don't eat illusion.
Barbarian! White trash!!
Too real! Give me illusion.
AHHH! Noodles!
Illusions offer warmth and comfort like a bowl of warm noodles.
Reality is often cold and unyielding. Not easy to bite through.
And it often takes you by surprise.
>Sigh< Does everything have to be a lesson?
Yes.
PING PING
This is a man who knows blades.
To know is also to not know. Stay open to events as they occur.
You are excellent at your work.
Unlike your awkward efforts with chopsticks I know what I am doing.

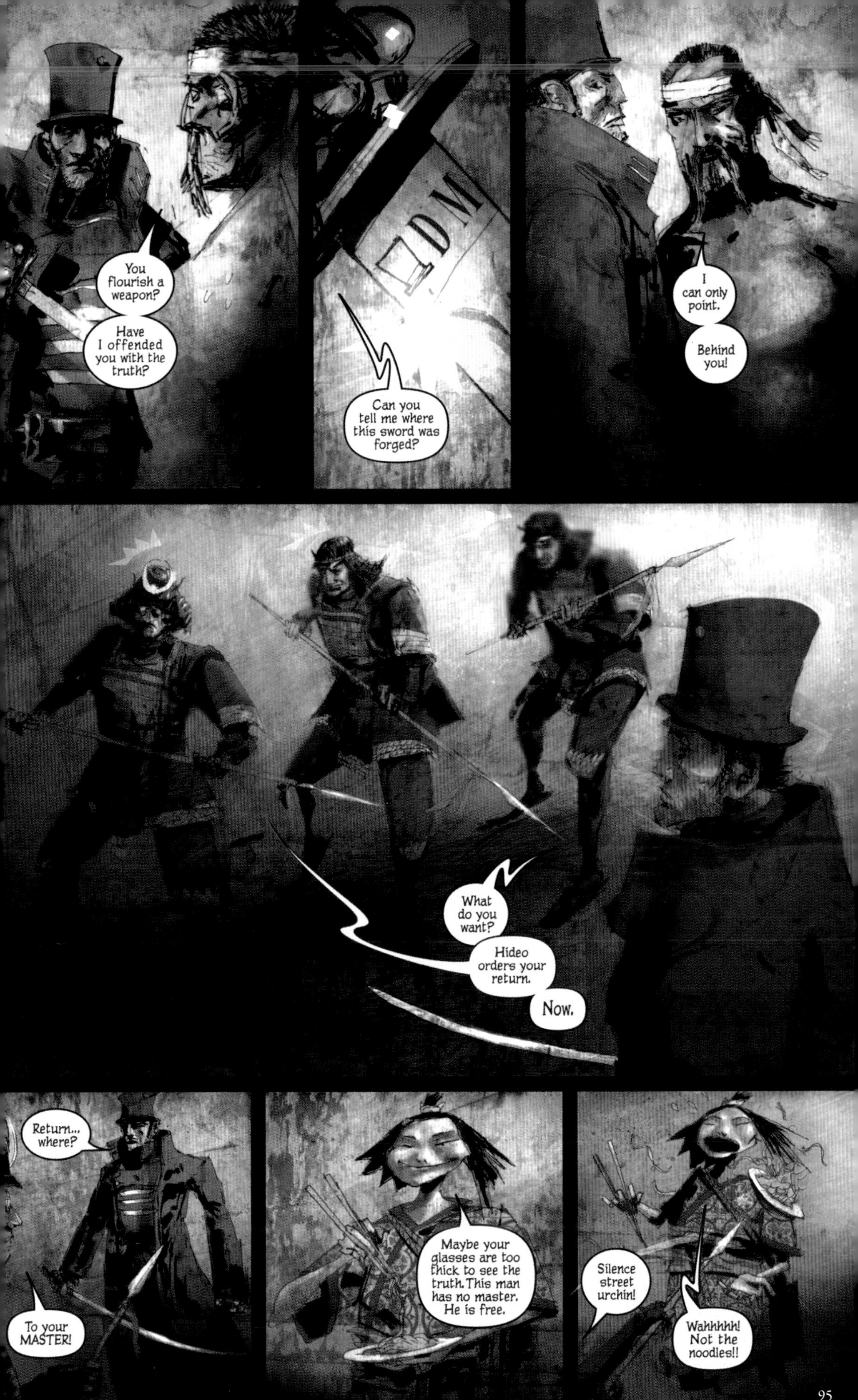
You flourish a weapon?
Have I offended you with the truth?
Can you tell me where this sword was forged?
I can only point.
Behind you!
What do you want?
Hideo orders your return.
Now.
Return... where?
To your MASTER!
Maybe your glasses are too thick to see the truth. This man has no master. He is free.
Silence street urchin!
Wahhhhh! Not the noodles!!

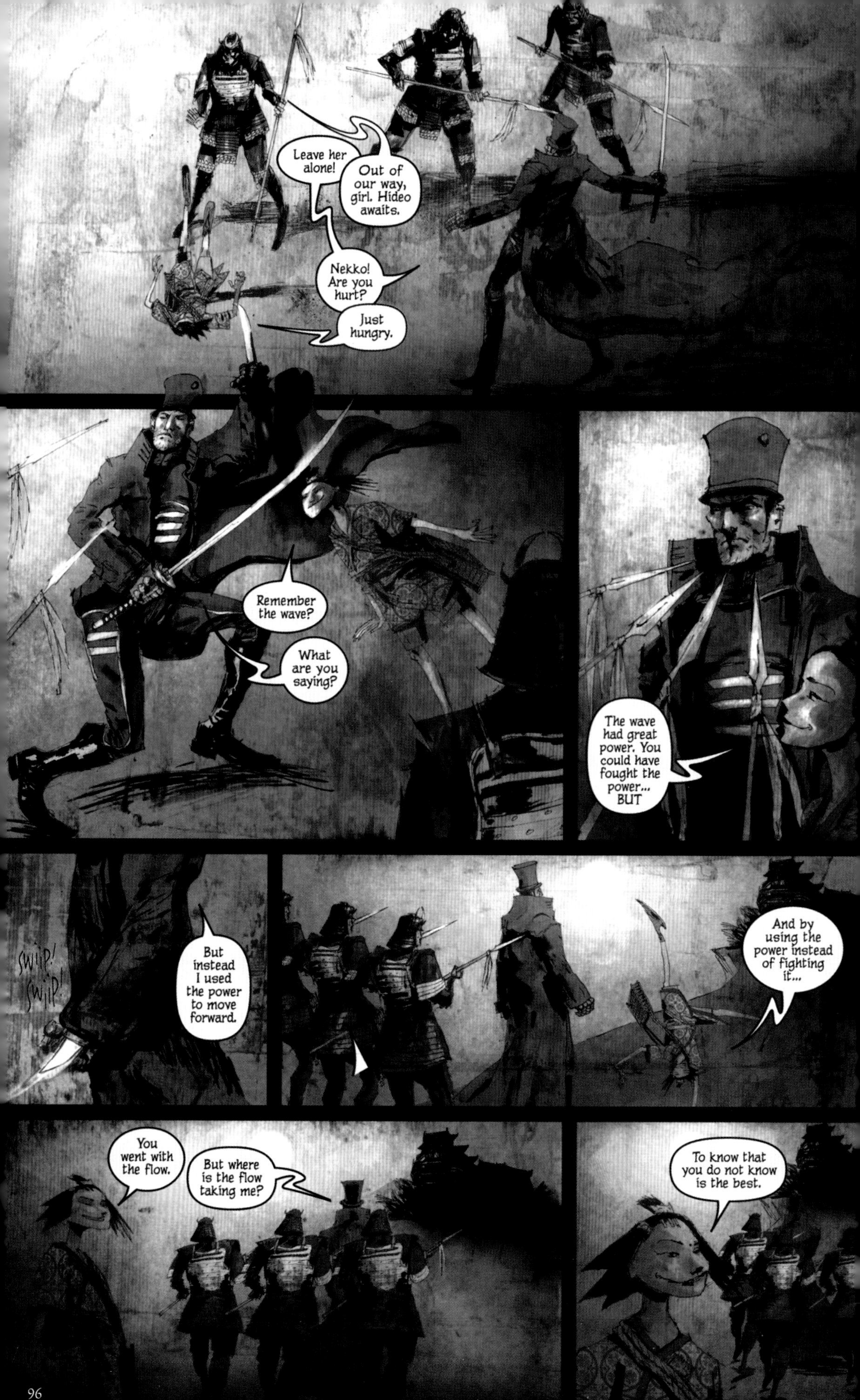
Leave her alone!
Out of our way, girl. Hideo awaits.
Nekko! Are you hurt?
Just hungry.
Remember the wave?
What are you saying?
The wave had great power. You could have fought the power... BUT
SWIIP! SWIIP!
But instead I used the power to move forward.
And by using the power instead of fighting it...
You went with the flow.
But where is the flow taking me?
To know that you do not know is the best.

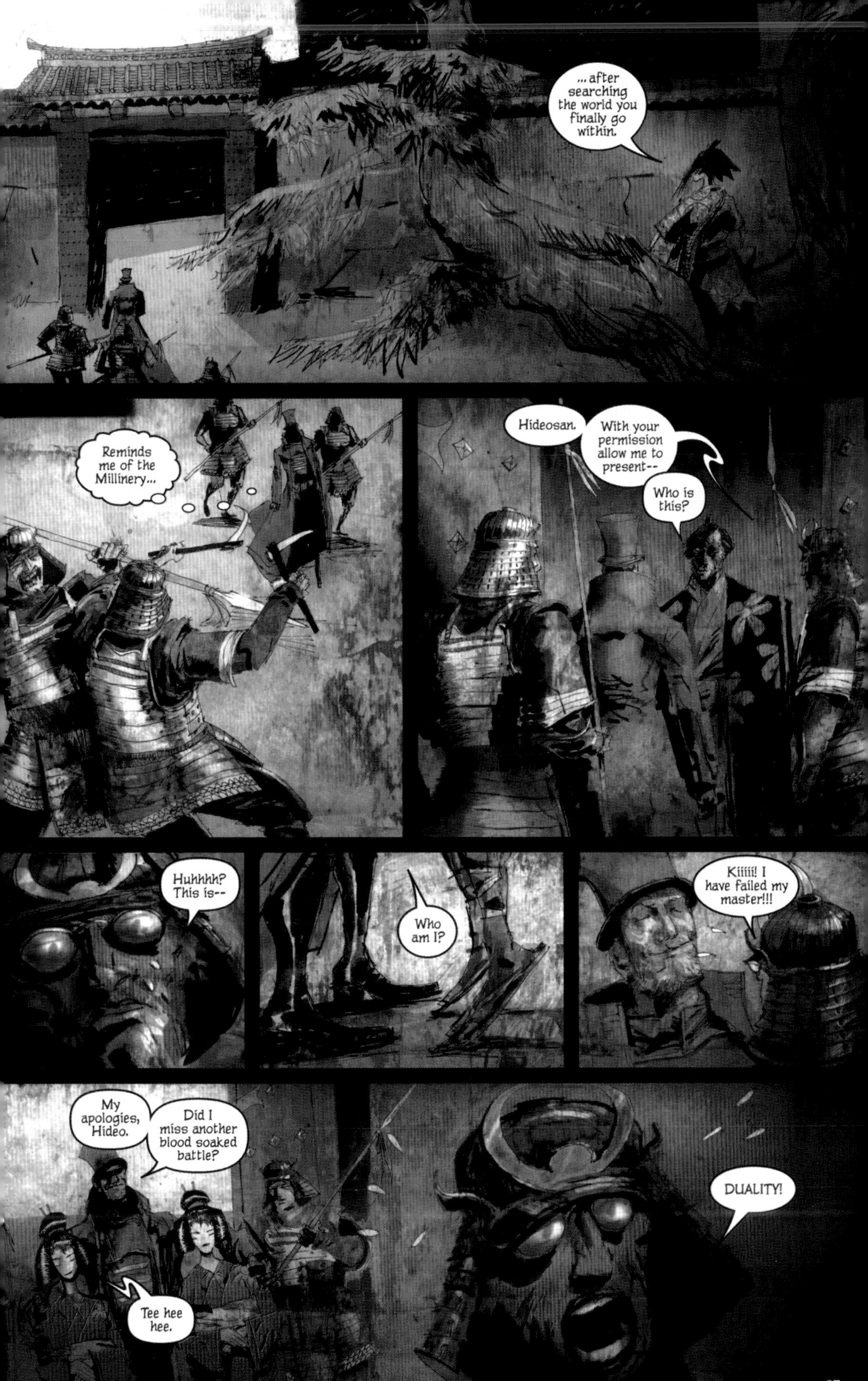
...after searching the world you finally go within.
Reminds me of the Millinery...
Hideosan.
With your permission allow me to present--
Who is this?
Huhhhh? This is--
Who am I?
Kiiiii! I have failed my master!!!
My apologies, Hideo.
Did I miss another blood soaked battle?
Tee hee hee.
DUALITY!

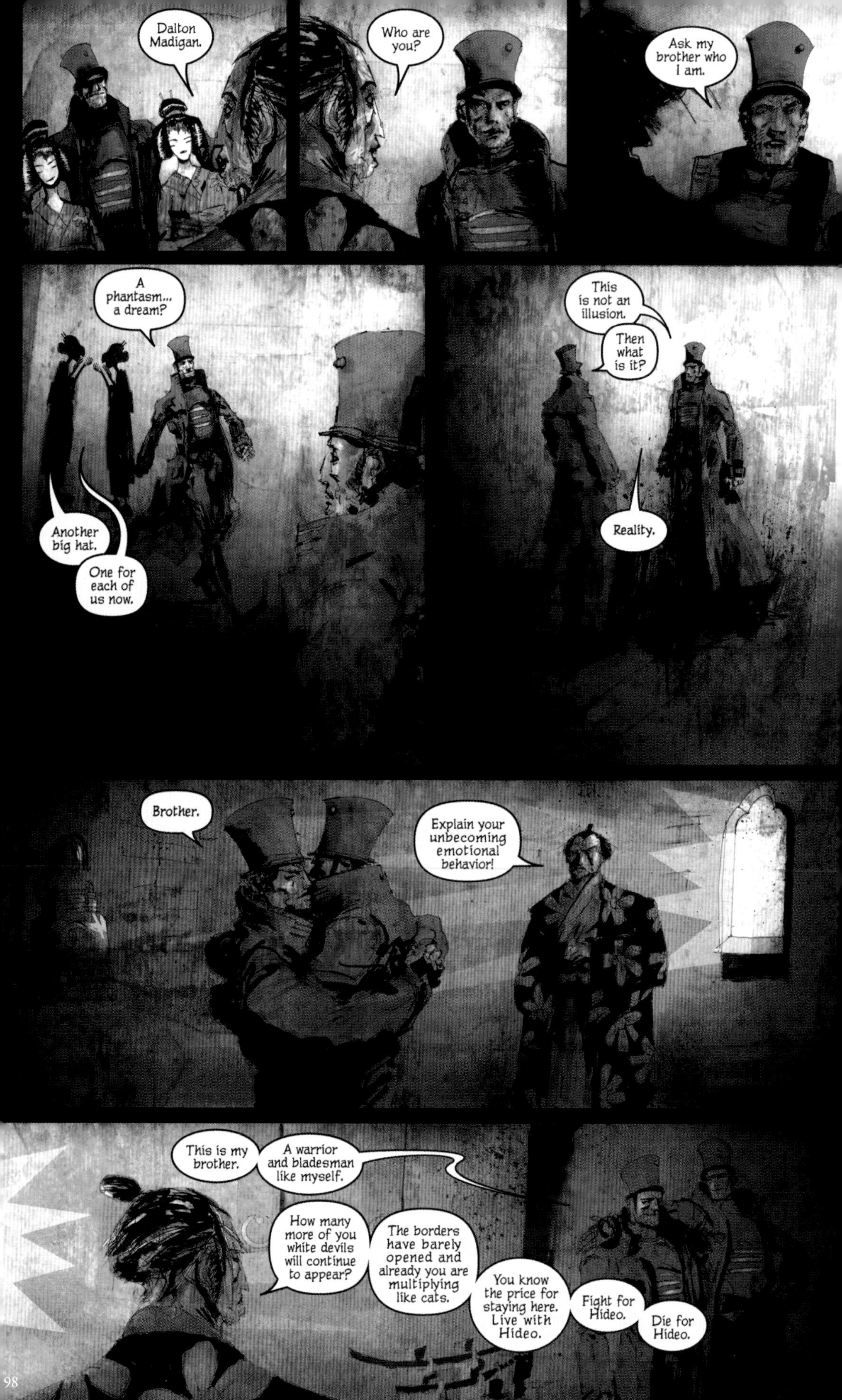
Dalton Madigan.
Who are you?
Ask my brother who I am.
A phantasm... a dream?
Another big hat.
One for each of us now.
This is not an illusion.
Then what is it?
Reality.
Brother.
Explain your unbecoming emotional behavior!
This is my brother.
A warrior and bladesman like myself.
How many more of you white devils will continue to appear?
The borders have barely opened and already you are multiplying like cats.
You know the price for staying here. Live with Hideo.
Fight for Hideo.
Die for Hideo.

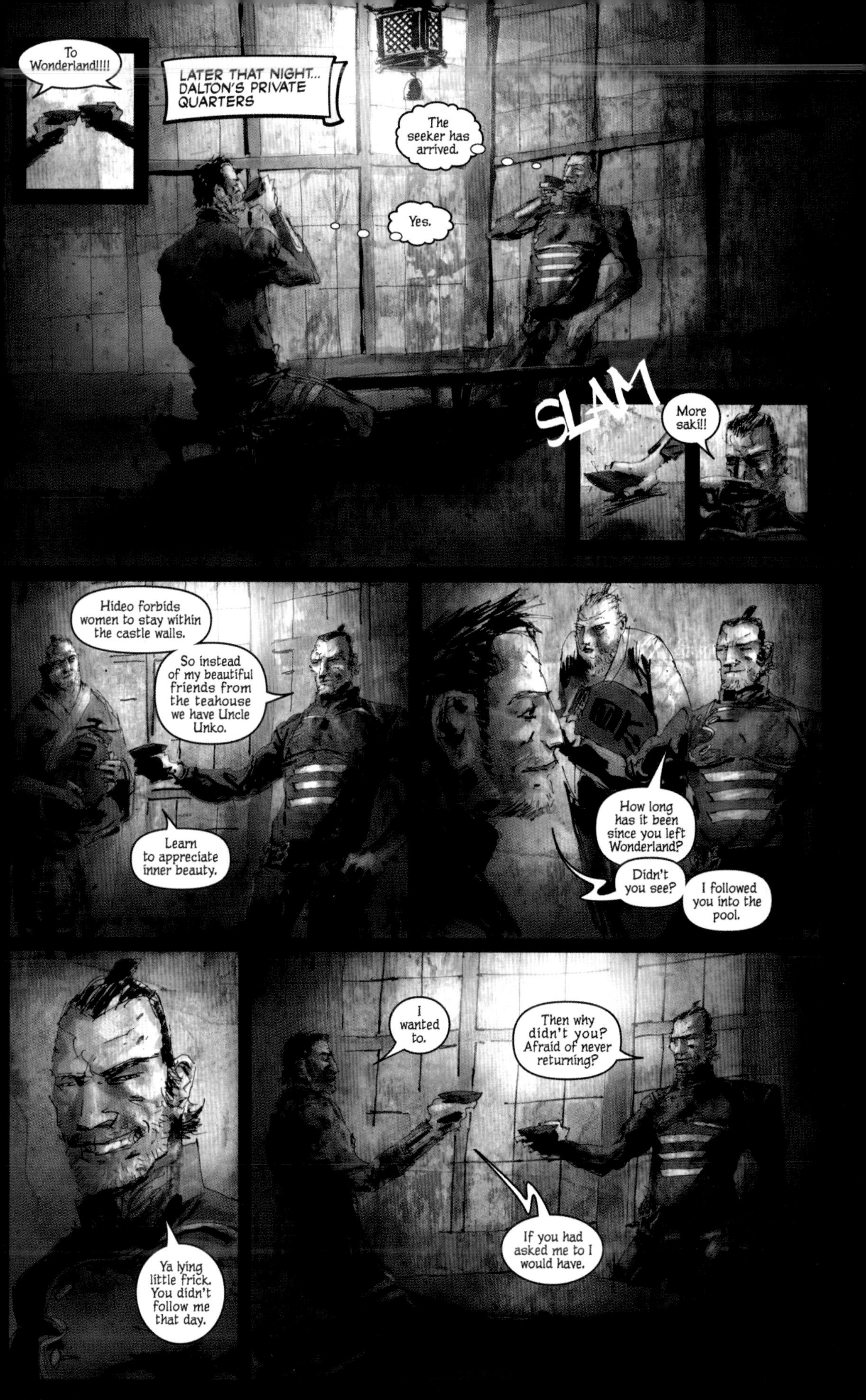
To Wonderland!!!!
LATER THAT NIGHT... DALTON'S PRIVATE QUARTERS
The seeker has arrived.
Yes.
SLAM
More saki!!
Hideo forbids women to stay within the castle walls.
So instead of my beautiful friends from the teahouse we have Uncle Unko.
Learn to appreciate inner beauty.
How long has it been since you left Wonderland?
Didn't you see?
I followed you into the pool.
Ya lying little frick. You didn't follow me that day.
I wanted to.
Then why didn't you? Afraid of never returning?
If you had asked me to I would have.

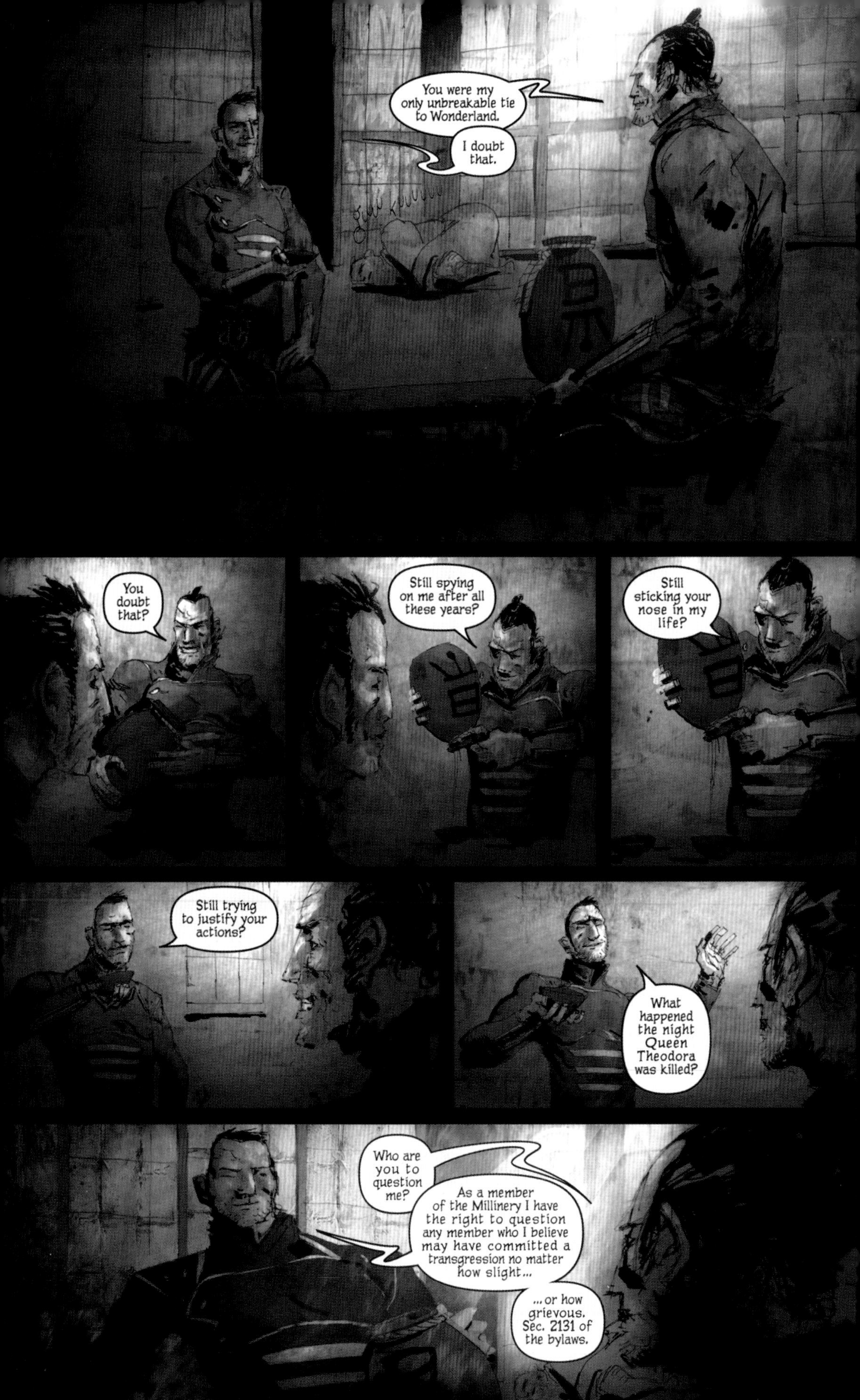
You were my only unbreakable tie to Wonderland.
I doubt that.
You doubt that?
Still spying on me after all these years?
Still sticking your nose in my life?
Still trying to justify your actions?
What happened the night Queen Theodora was killed?
Who are you to question me?
As a member of the Millinery I have the right to question any member who I believe may have committed a transgression no matter how slight...
...or how grievous. Sec. 2131 of the bylaws.

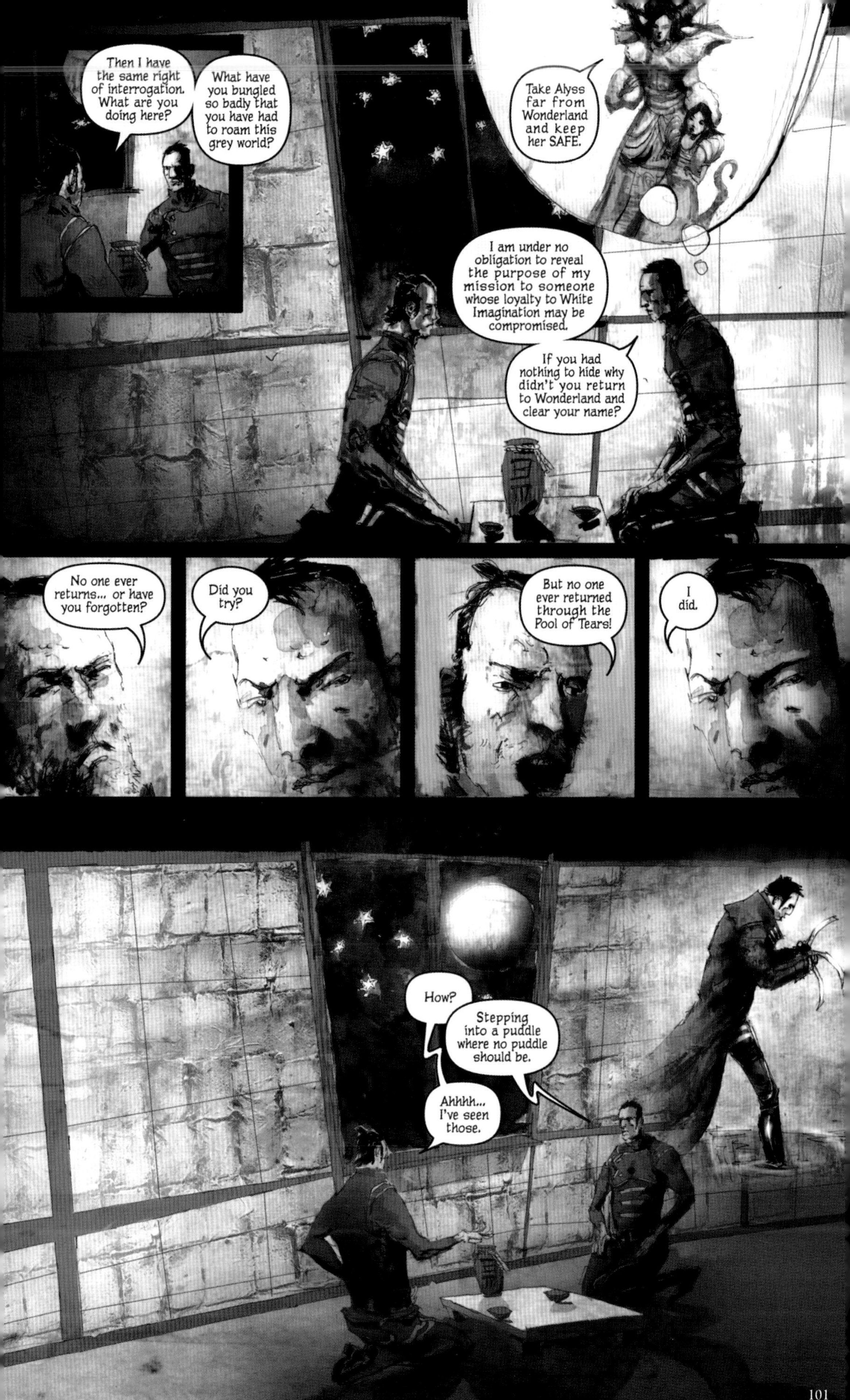
Then I have the same right of interrogation. What are you doing here?
What have you bungled so badly that you have had to roam this grey world?
Take Alyss far from Wonderland and keep her SAFE.
I am under no obligation to reveal the purpose of my mission to someone whose loyalty to White Imagination may be compromised.
If you had nothing to hide why didn't you return to Wonderland and clear your name?
No one ever returns... or have you forgotten?
Did you try?
But no one ever returned through the Pool of Tears!
I did.
How?
Stepping into a puddle where no puddle should be.
Ahhhh... I've seen those.

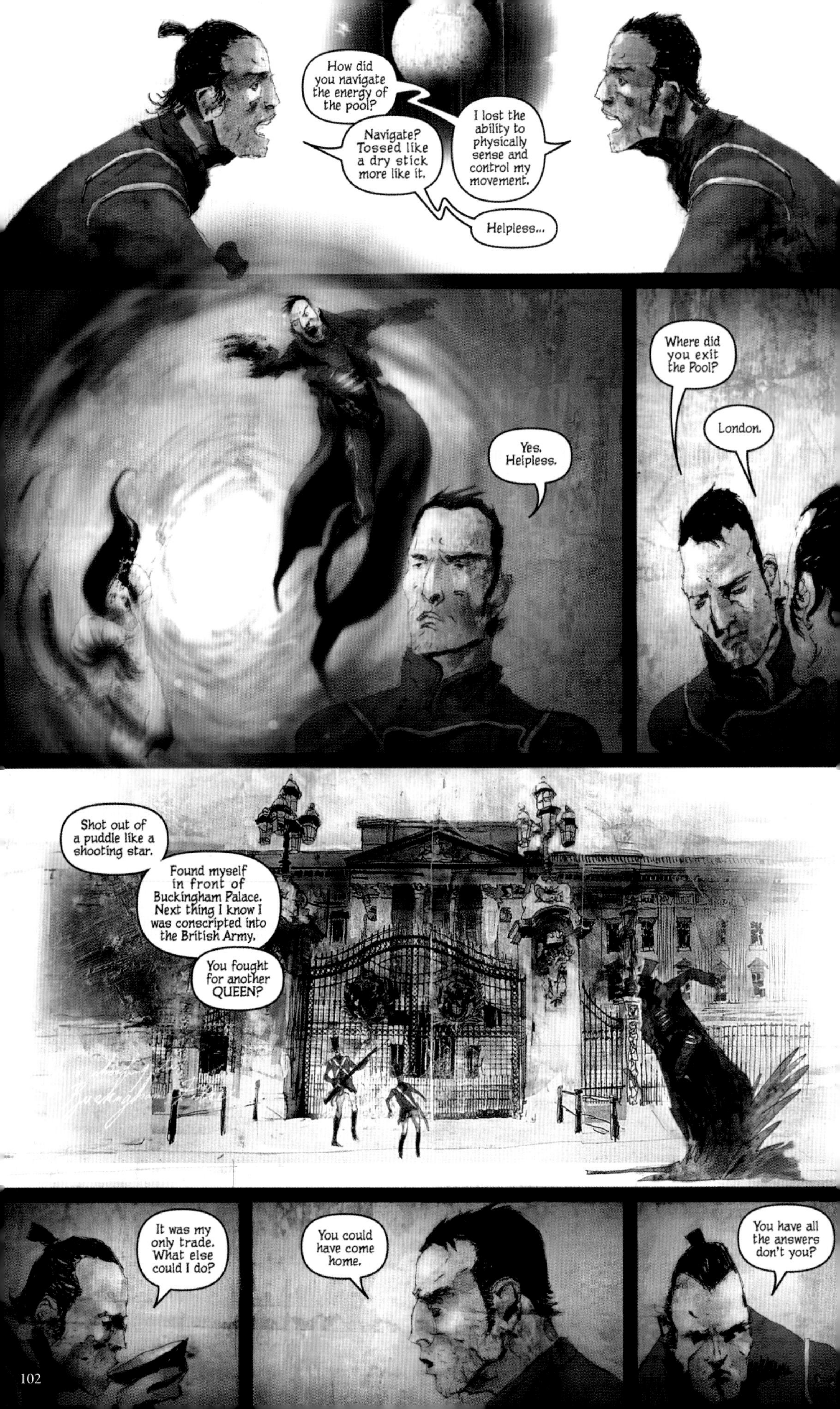
How did you navigate the energy of the pool?
I lost the ability to physically sense and control my movement.
Navigate? Tossed like a dry stick more like it.
Helpless...
Yes. Helpless.
Where did you exit the Pool?
London.
Shot out of a puddle like a shooting star.
Found myself in front of Buckingham Palace. Next thing I know I was conscripted into the British Army.
You fought for another QUEEN?
It was my only trade. What else could I do?
You could have come home.
You have all the answers don't you?

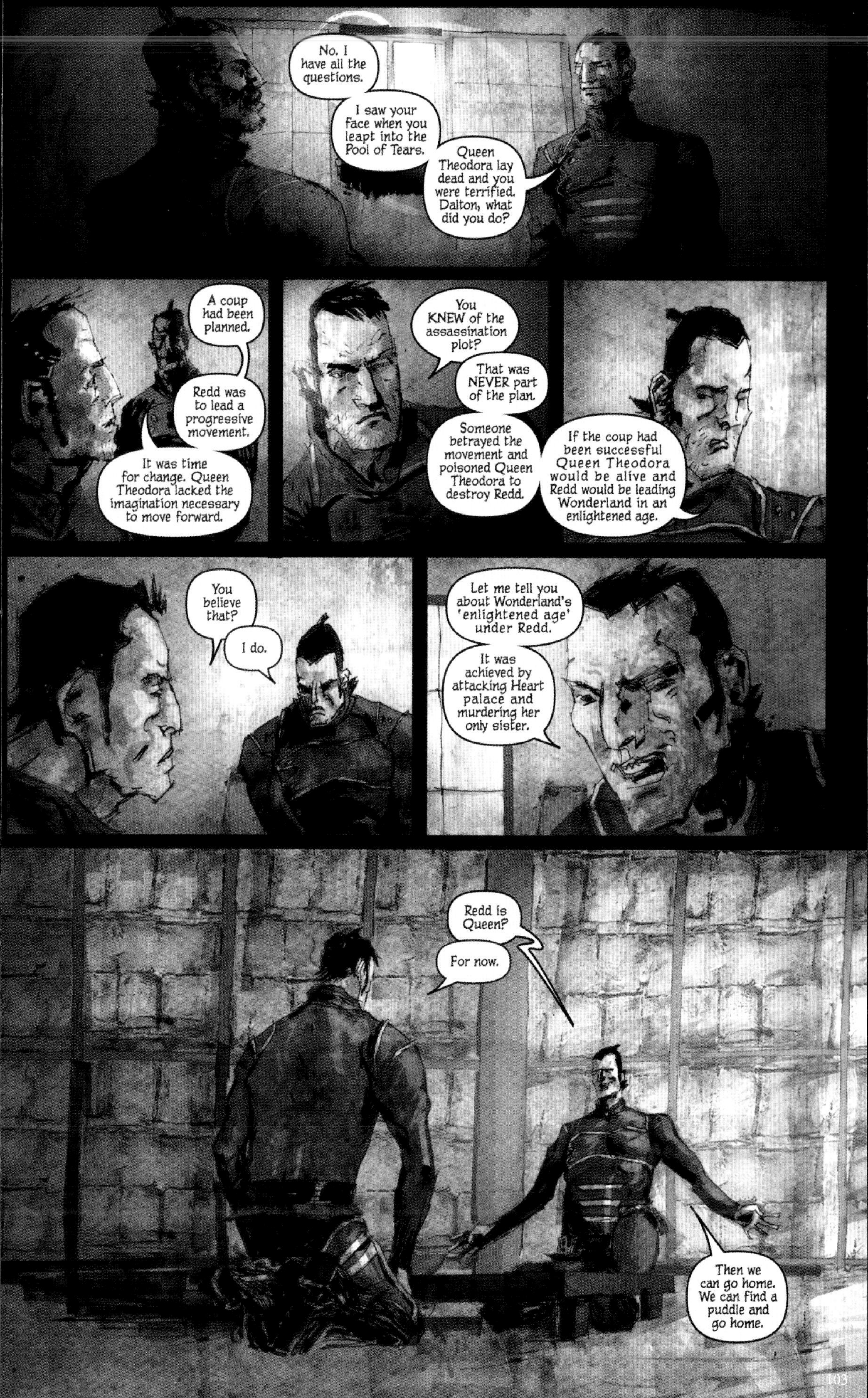
No. I have all the questions.
I saw your face when you leapt into the Pool of Tears.
Queen Theodora lay dead and you were terrified. Dalton, what did you do?
A coup had been planned.
Redd was to lead a progressive movement.
It was time for change. Queen Theodora lacked the imagination necessary to move forward.
You KNEW of the assassination plot?
That was NEVER part of the plan.
Someone betrayed the movement and poisoned Queen Theodora to destroy Redd.
If the coup had been successful Queen Theodora would be alive and Redd would be leading Wonderland in an enlightened age.
You believe that?
I do.
Let me tell you about Wonderland's 'enlightened age' under Redd.
It was achieved by attacking Heart palace and murdering her only sister.
Redd is Queen?
For now.
Then we can go home. We can find a puddle and go home.

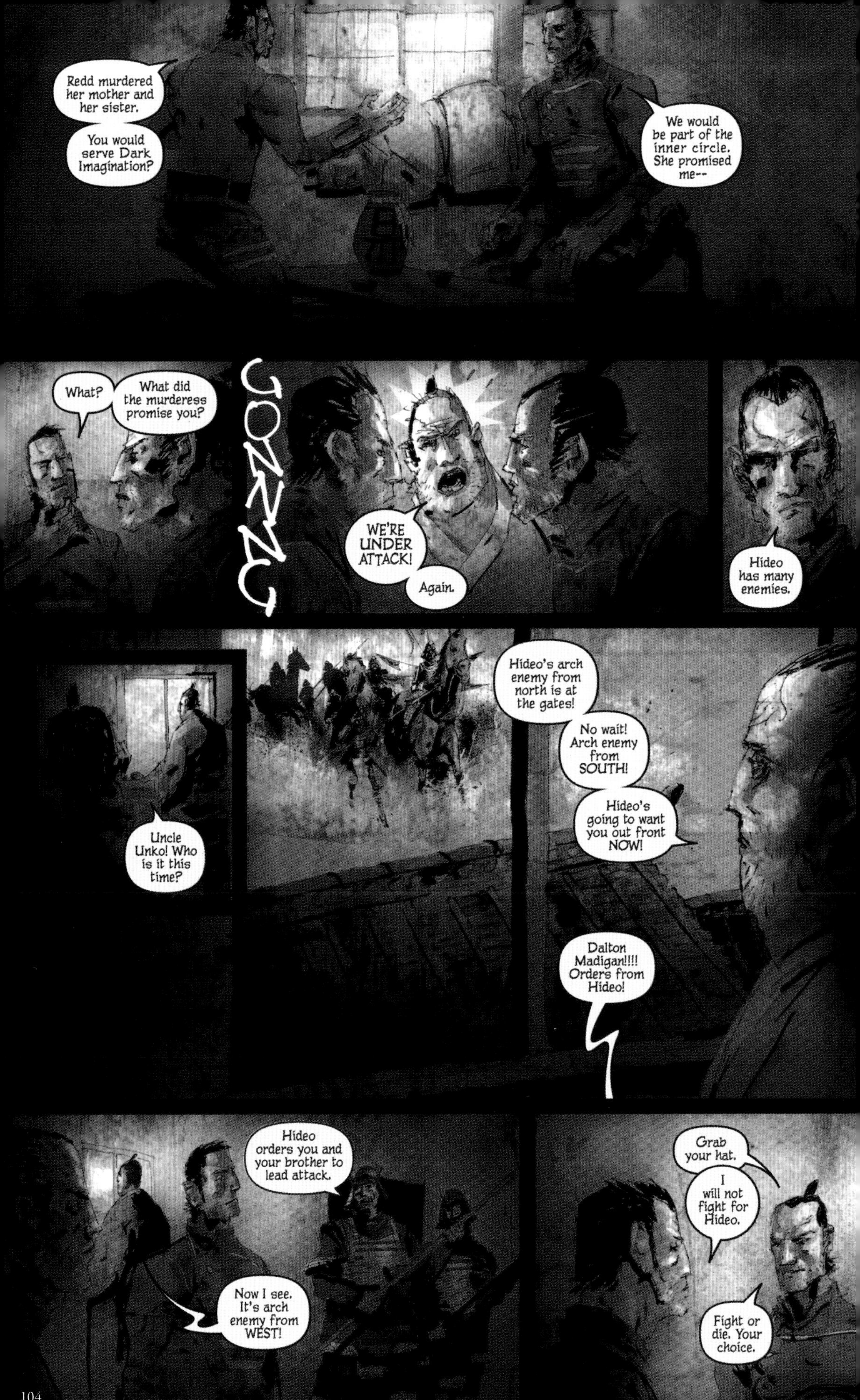

Redd murdered her mother and her sister.
You would serve Dark Imagination?
We would be part of the inner circle. She promised me--
What?
What did the murderess promise you?
WE'RE UNDER ATTACK!
Again.
Hideo has many enemies.
Uncle Unko! Who is it this time?
Hideo's arch enemy from north is at the gates!
No wait! Arch enemy from SOUTH!
Hideo's going to want you out front NOW!
Dalton Madigan!!!! Orders from Hideo!
Hideo orders you and your brother to lead attack.
Now I see. It's arch enemy from WEST!
Grab your hat.
I will not fight for Hideo.
Fight or die. Your choice.

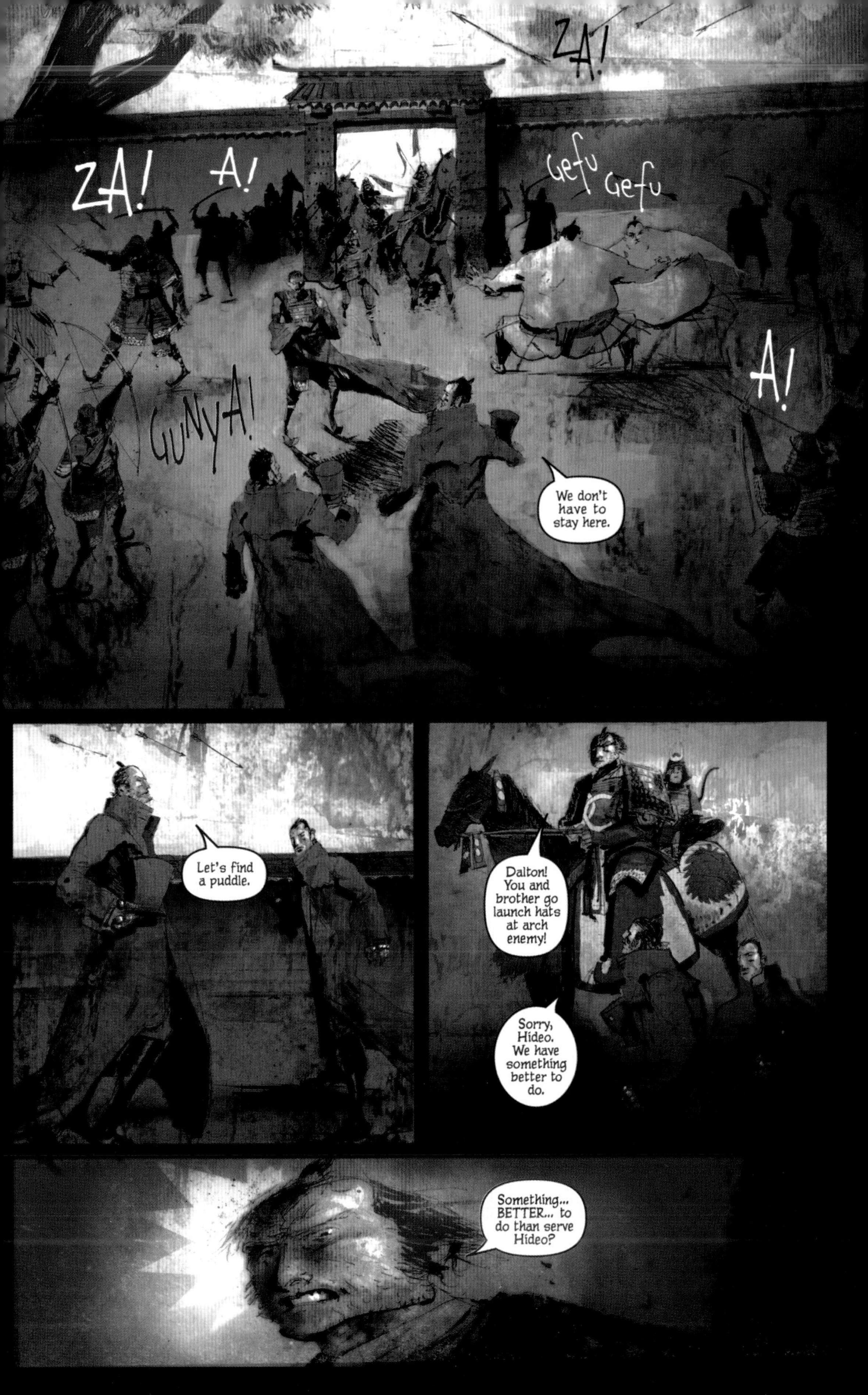

ZA!
ZA!
A!
Gefu Gefu
A!
GUNYA!
We don't have to stay here.
Let's find a puddle.
Dalton! You and brother go launch hats at arch enemy!
Sorry, Hideo. We have something better to do.
Something... BETTER... to do than serve Hideo?

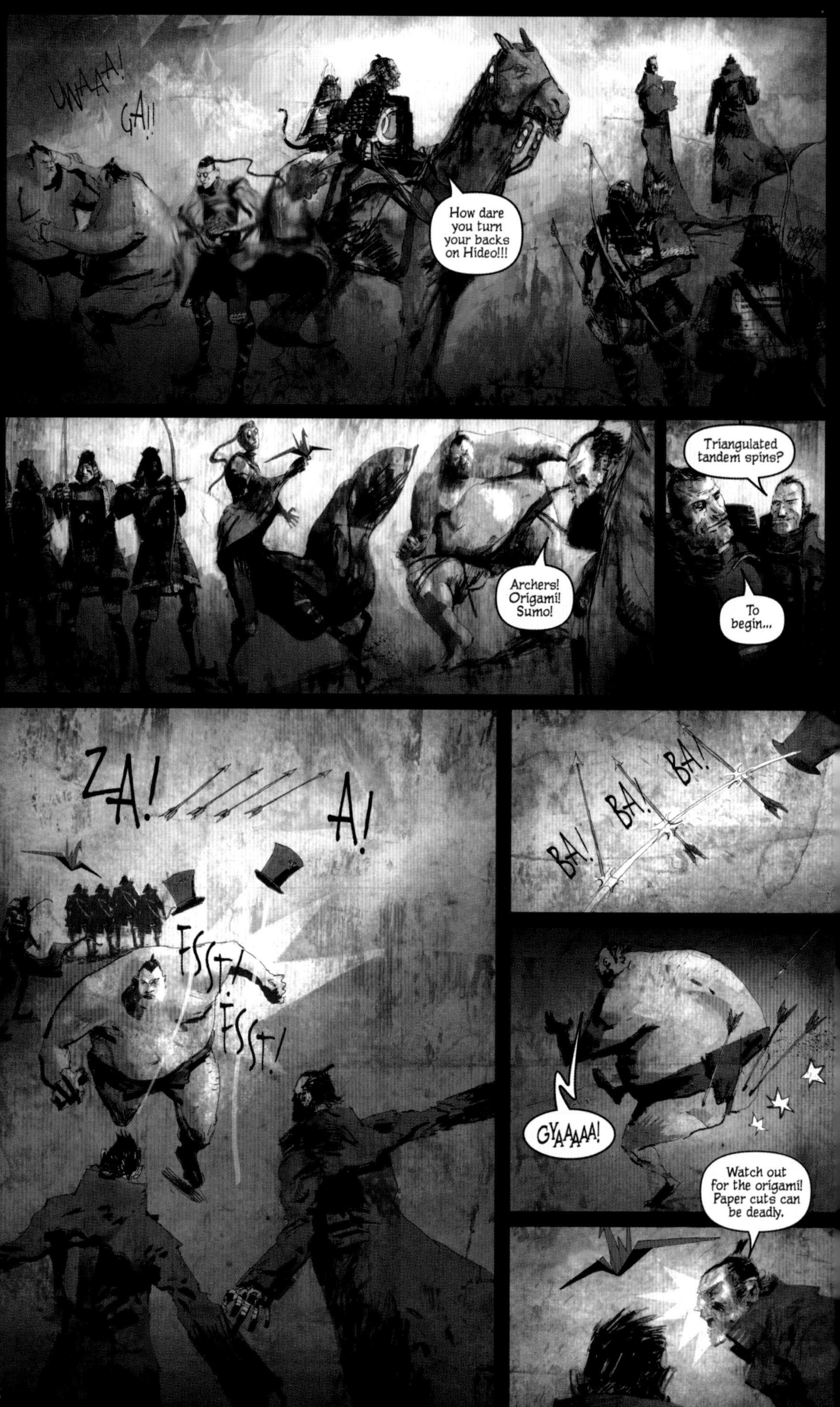
UNAAA!
GA!!
How dare you turn your backs on Hideo!!!
Archers! Origami! Sumo!
Triangulated tandem spins?
To begin...
ZA!
A!
FSST!
FSST!
BA!
BA!
BA!
GYAAAAA!
Watch out for the origami! Paper cuts can be deadly.

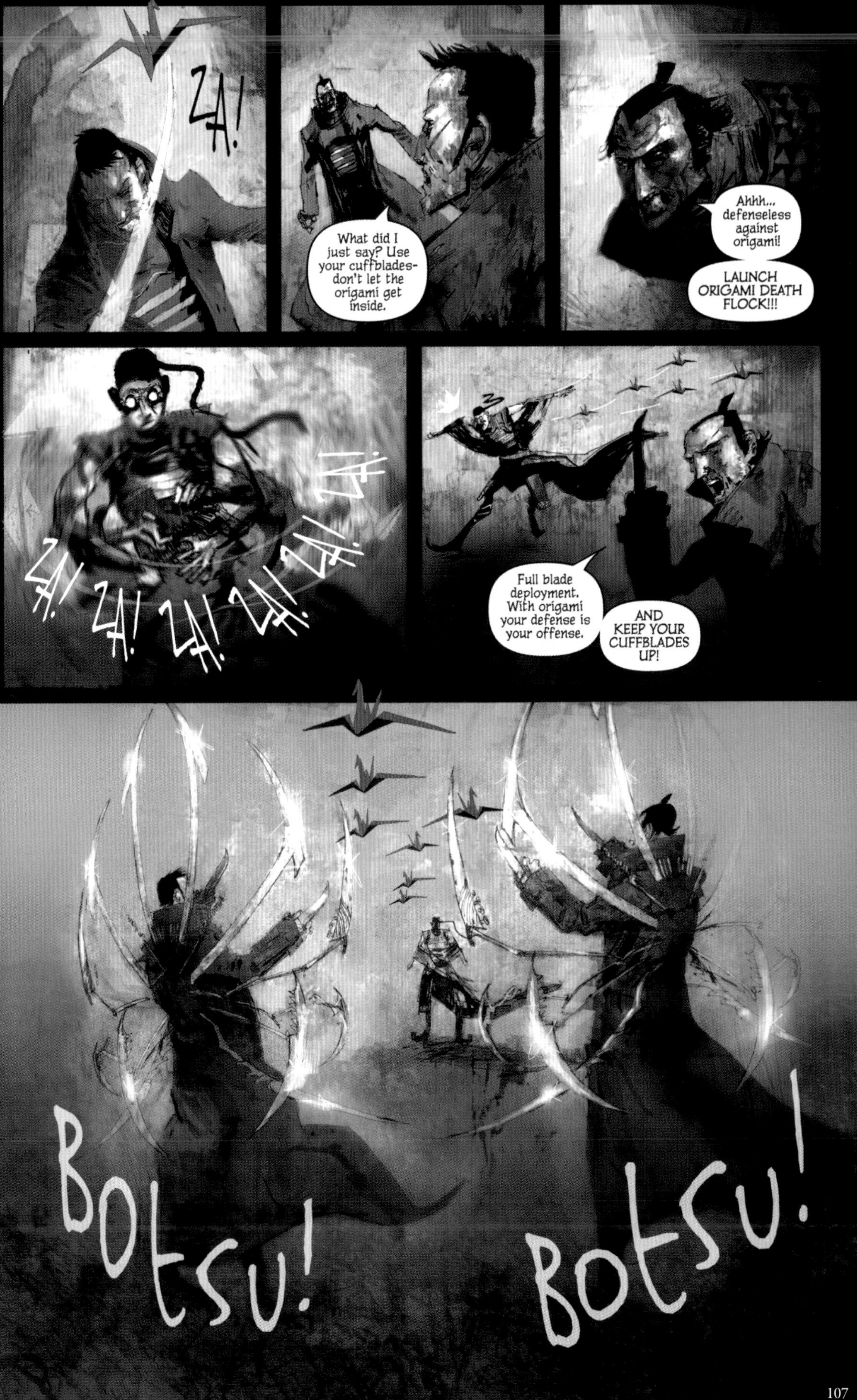
ZA!
What did I just say? Use your cuffblades- don't let the origami get inside.
Ahhh... defenseless against origami!
LAUNCH ORIGAMI DEATH FLOCK!!!
ZA! ZA! ZA! ZA! ZA! ZA!
Full blade deployment. With origami your defense is your offense.
AND KEEP YOUR CUFFBLADES UP!
Botsu!
Botsu!

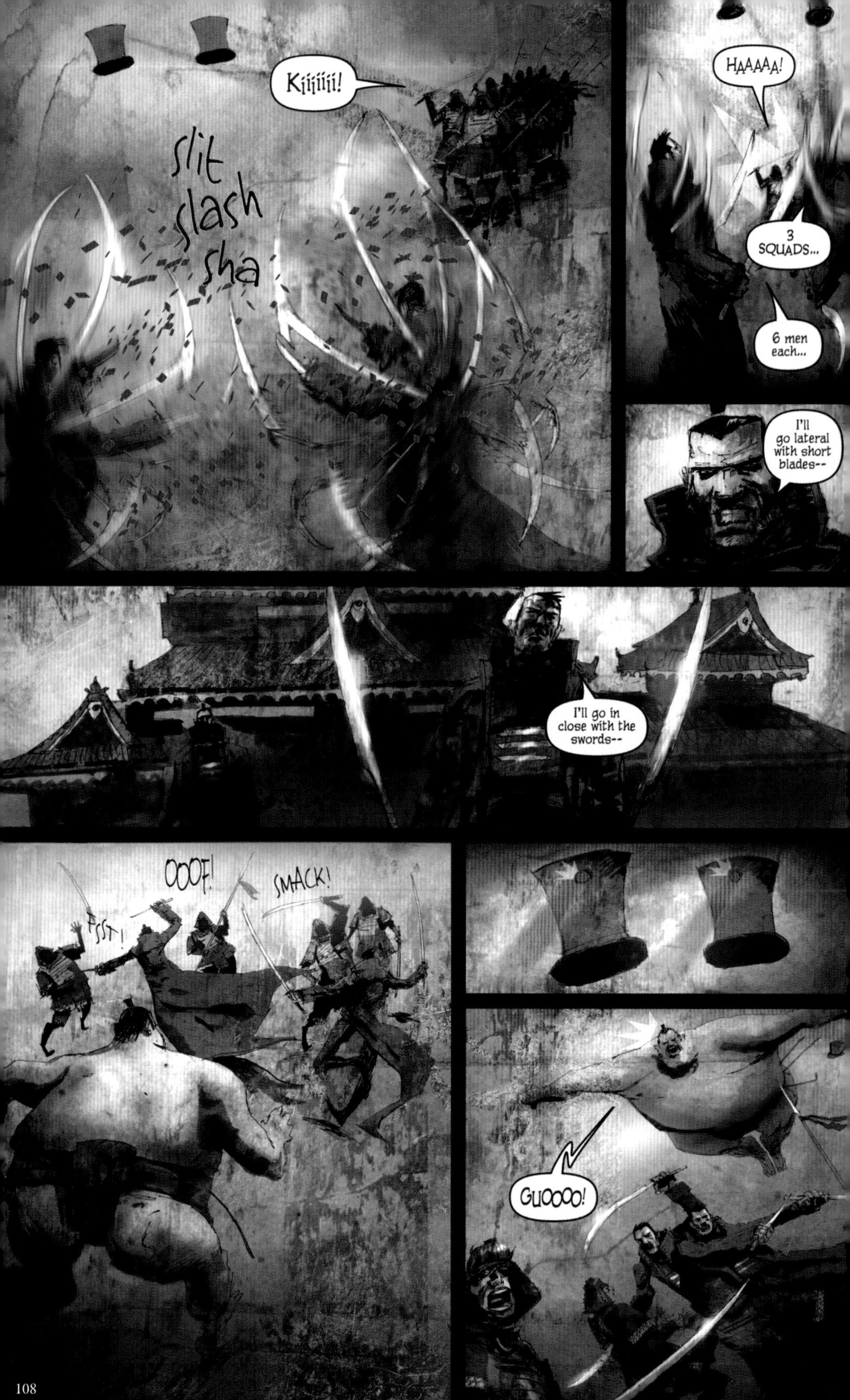
Kiiiiii!
slit
slash
sha
HAAAAA!
3 SQUADS...
6 men each...
I'll go lateral with short blades--
I'll go in close with the swords--
OOOF!
SMACK!
FSST!
GUOOOO!

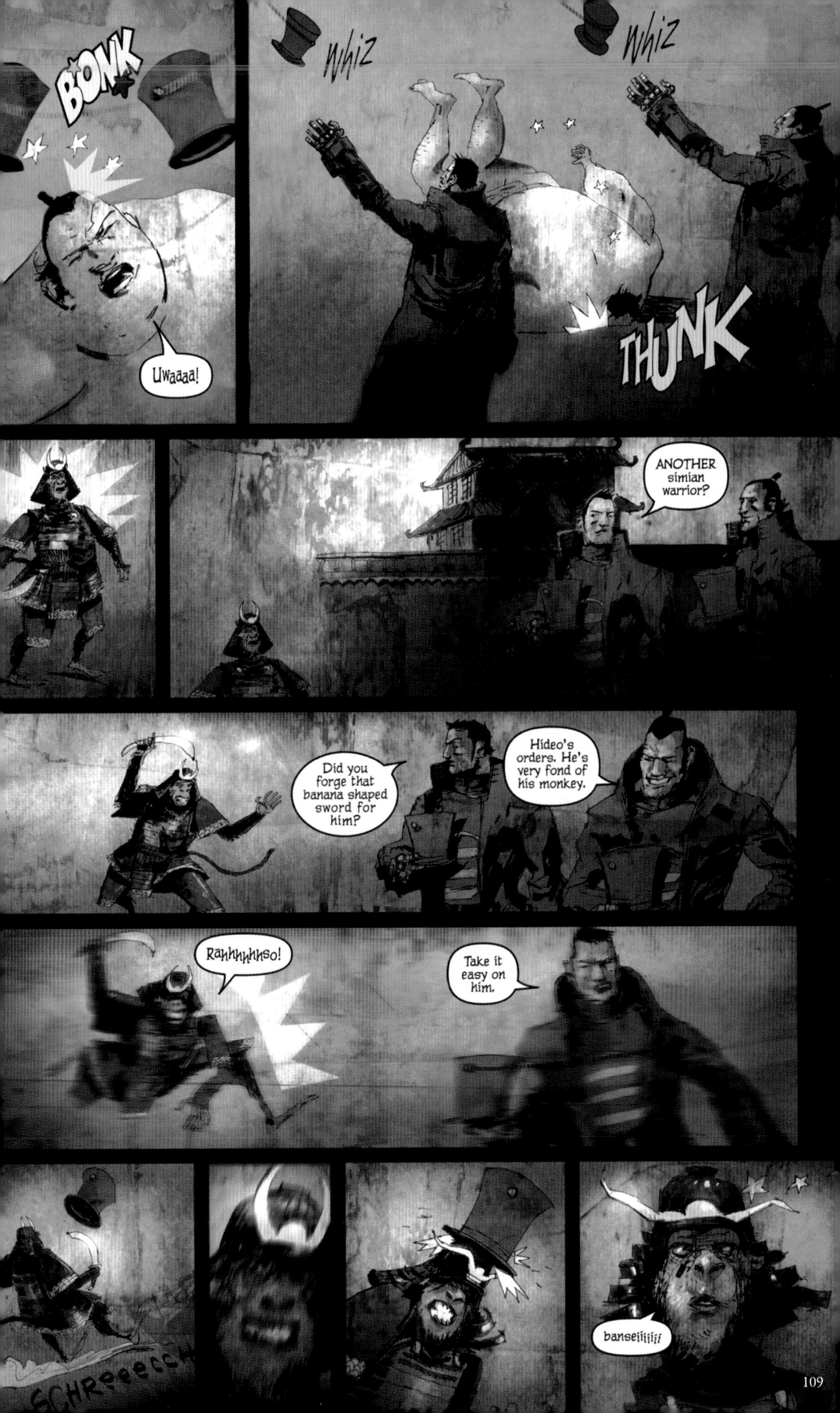
BONK
Uwaaaa!
Whiz
Whiz
THUNK
ANOTHER simian warrior?
Did you forge that banana shaped sword for him?
Hideo's orders. He's very fond of his monkey.
Ranhhhhhso!
Take it easy on him.
SCHReeeech
banseiiiiiii

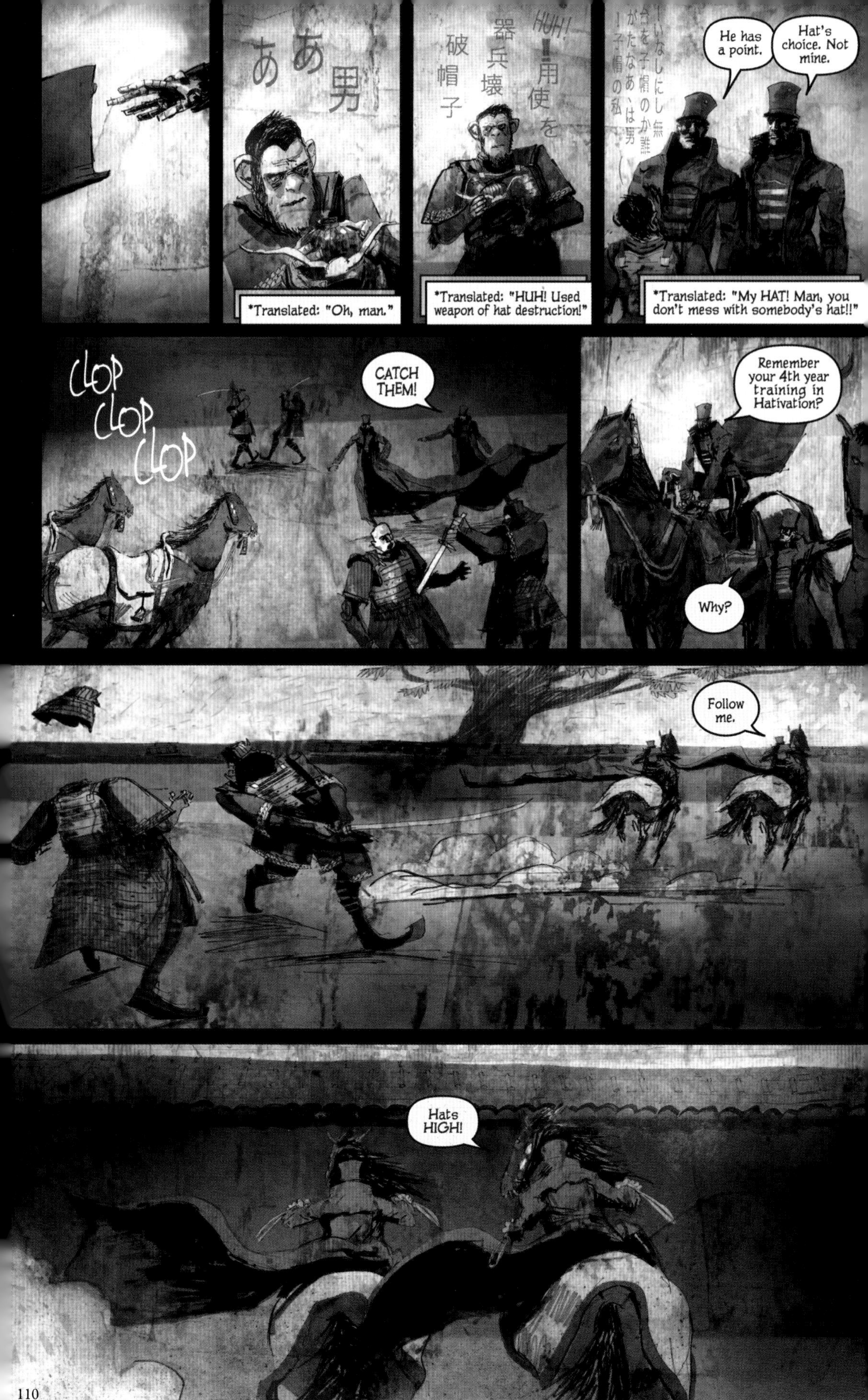

男ああ
*Translated: "Oh, man."
HUH!
用使を
器兵壊
破帽子
*Translated: "HUH! Used weapon of hat destruction!"
He has a point.
Hat's choice. Not mine.
*Translated: "My HAT! Man, you don't mess with somebody's hat!!"
CLOP CLOP CLOP
CATCH THEM!
Remember your 4th year training in Hativation?
Why?
Follow me.
Hats HIGH!

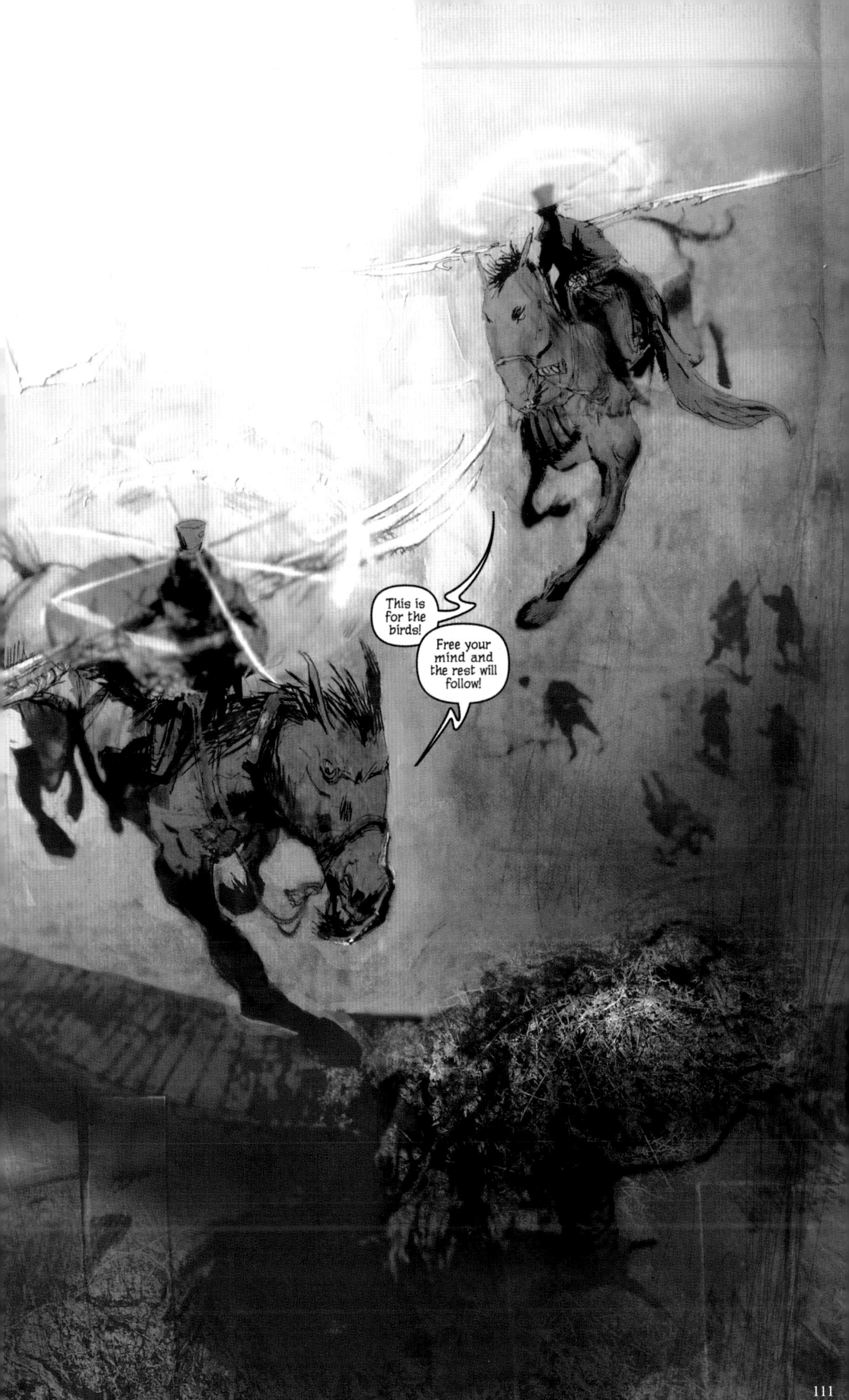
This is for the birds!
Free your mind and the rest will follow!

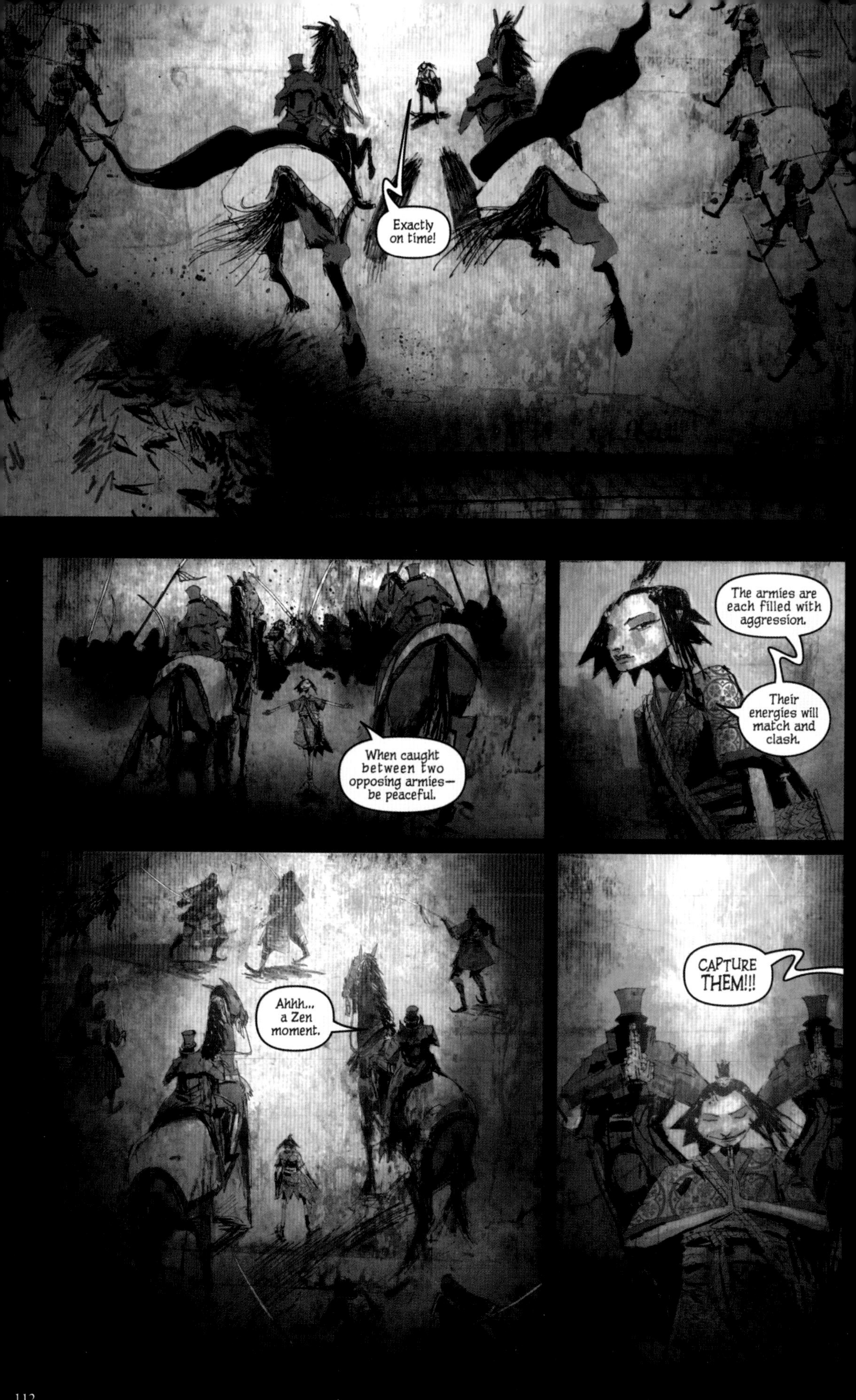
Exactly on time!
When caught between two opposing armies— be peaceful.
The armies are each filled with aggression.
Their energies will match and clash.
Ahhh... a Zen moment.
CAPTURE THEM!!!

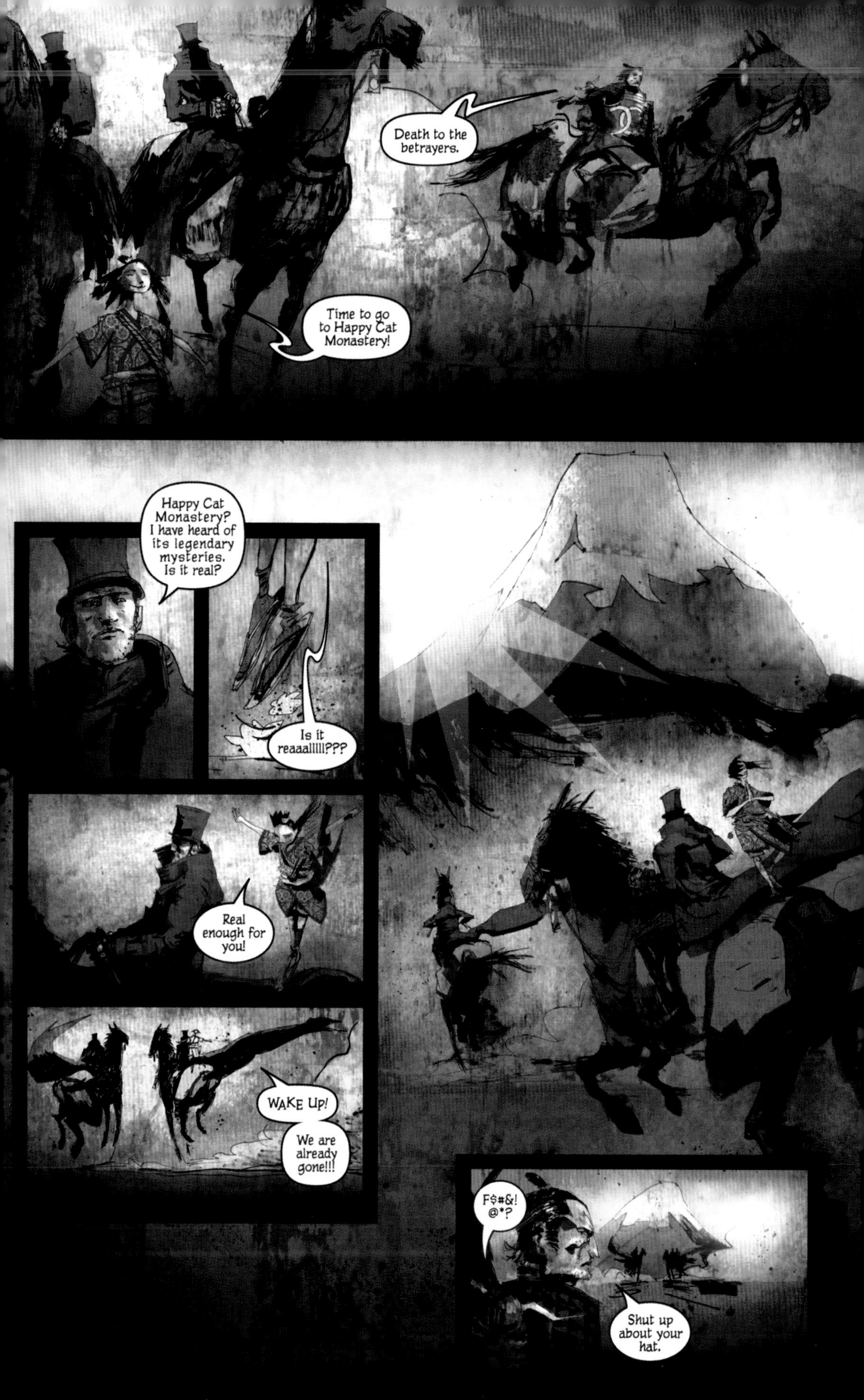
Death to the betrayers.
Time to go to Happy Cat Monastery!
Happy Cat Monastery? I have heard of its legendary mysteries. Is it real?
Is it reaaallllll???
Real enough for you!
WAKE UP!
We are already gone!!!
F$#&! @*?
Shut up about your hat.

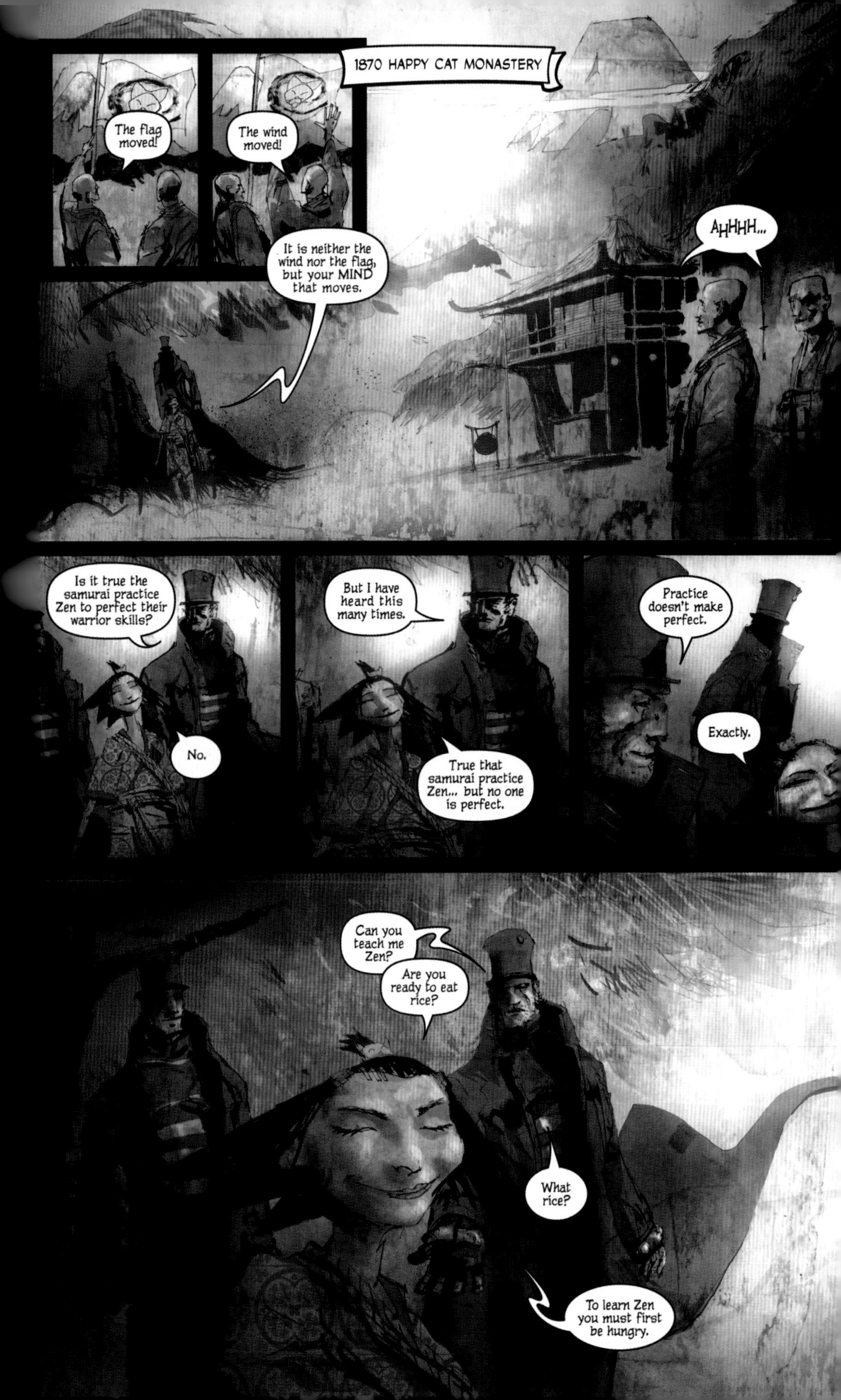

1870 HAPPY CAT MONASTERY
The flag moved!
The wind moved!
It is neither the wind nor the flag, but your MIND that moves.
AHHHH...
Is it true the samurai practice Zen to perfect their warrior skills?
No.
But I have heard this many times.
True that samurai practice Zen... but no one is perfect.
Practice doesn't make perfect.
Exactly.
Can you teach me Zen?
Are you ready to eat rice?
What rice?
To learn Zen you must first be hungry.

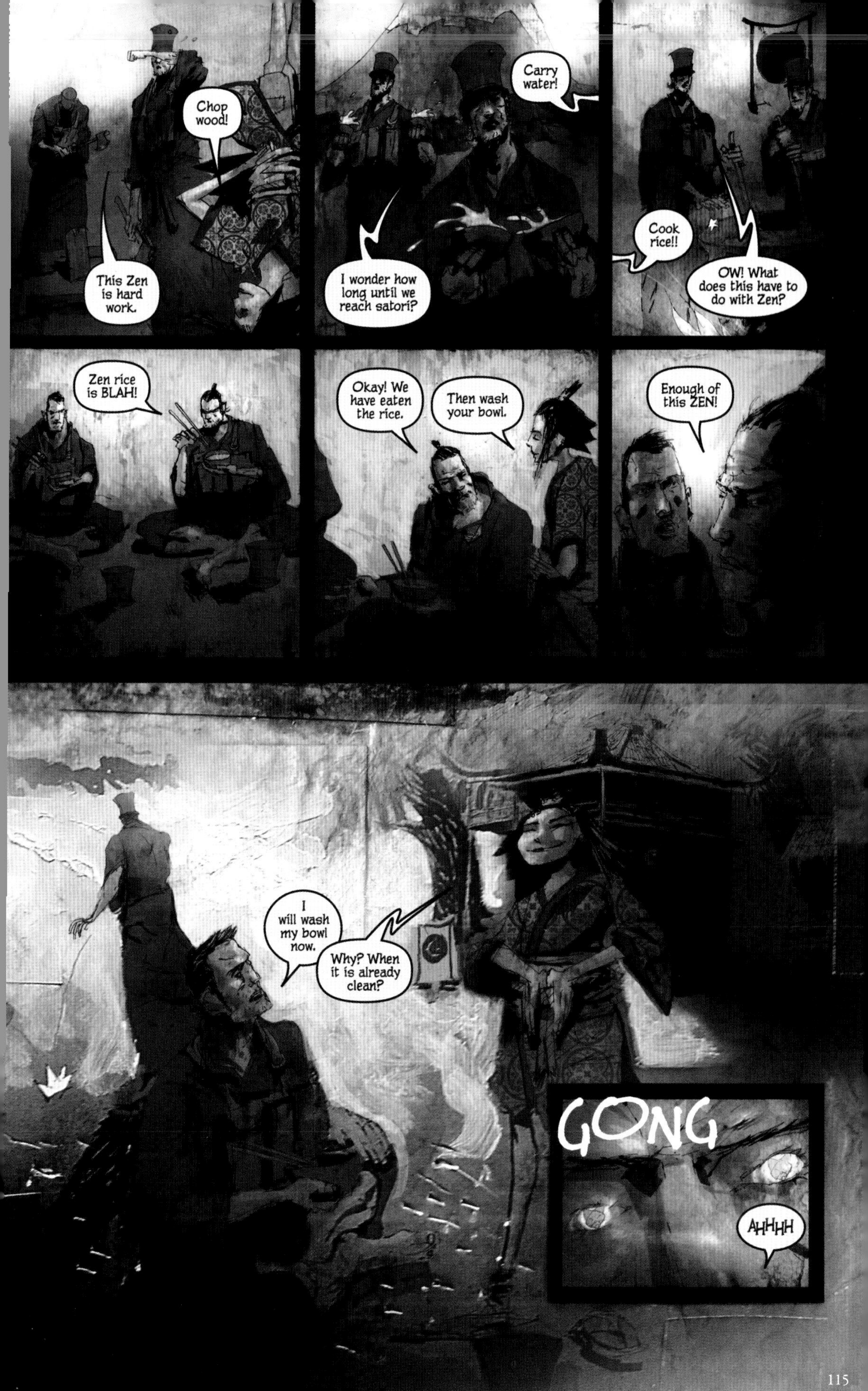
Chop wood!
This Zen is hard work.
Carry water!
I wonder how long until we reach satori?
Cook rice!!
OW! What does this have to do with Zen?
Zen rice is BLAH!
Okay! We have eaten the rice.
Then wash your bowl.
Enough of this ZEN!
I will wash my bowl now.
Why? When it is already clean?
GONG
AHHHH

YOUR TRAVELS ON THE INNER PATH HAVE BEGUN...

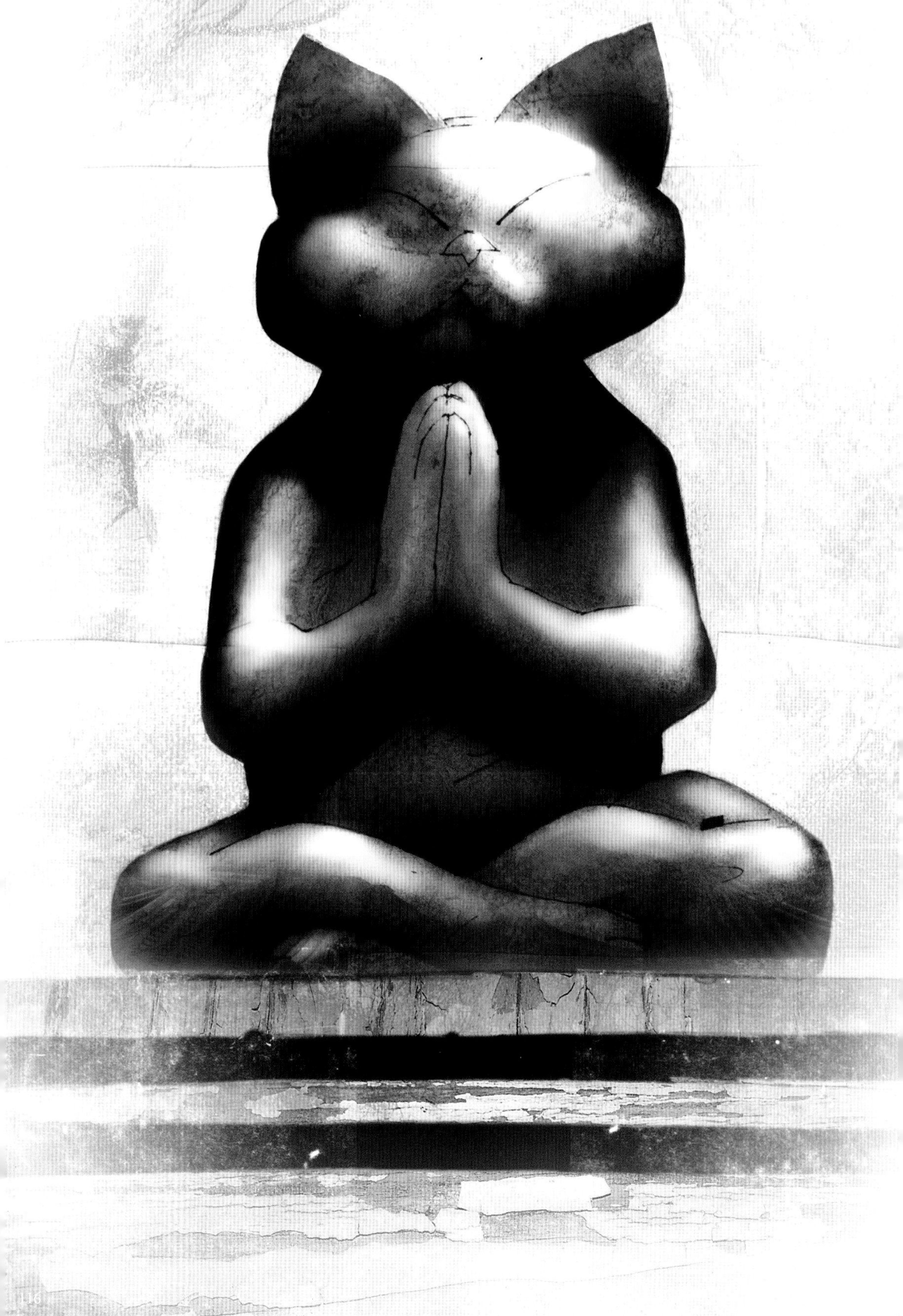

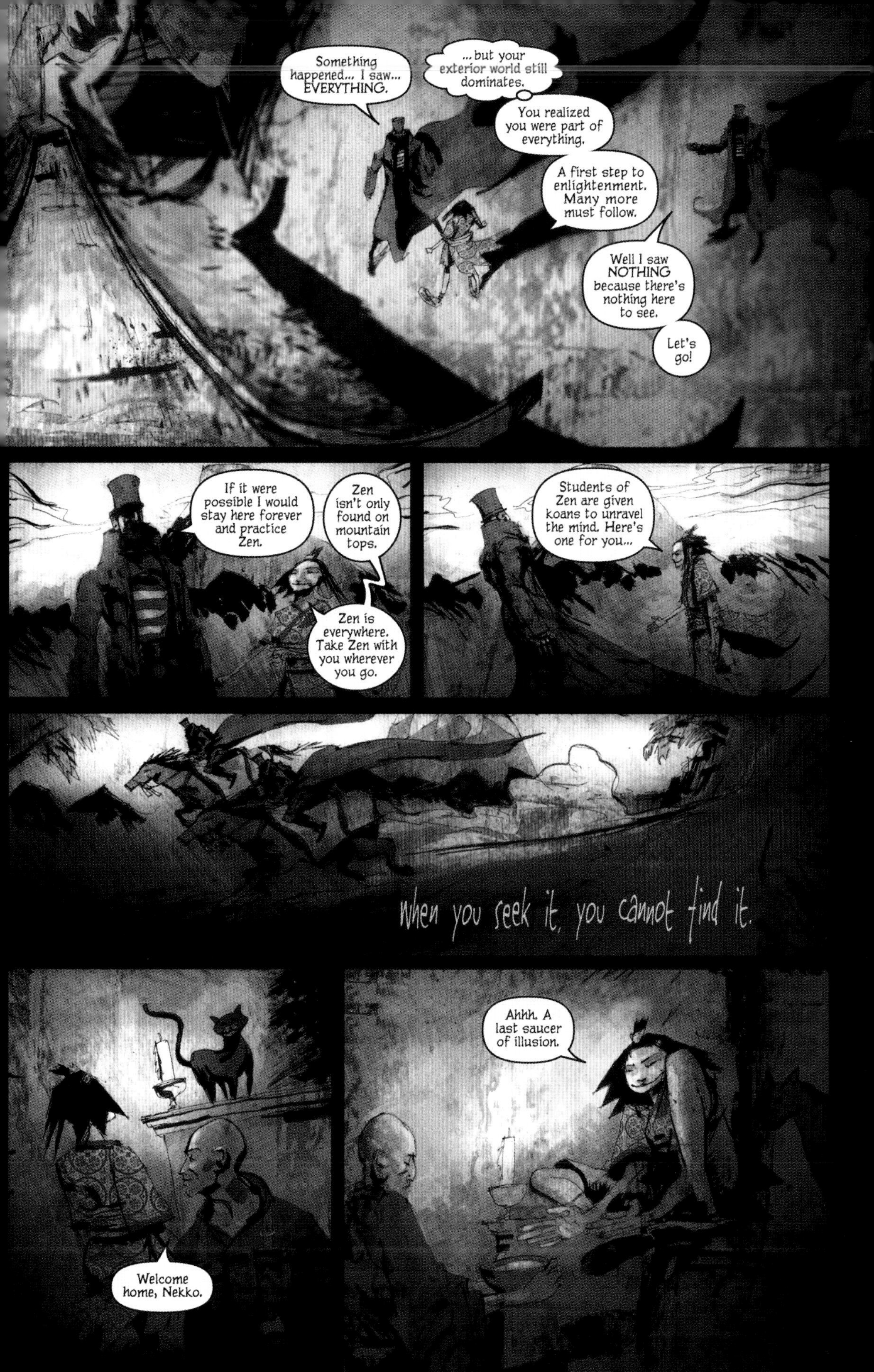
Something happened... I saw... EVERYTHING.
...but your exterior world still dominates.
You realized you were part of everything.
A first step to enlightenment. Many more must follow.
Well I saw NOTHING because there's nothing here to see.
Let's go!
If it were possible I would stay here forever and practice Zen.
Zen isn't only found on mountain tops.
Zen is everywhere. Take Zen with you wherever you go.
Students of Zen are given koans to unravel the mind. Here's one for you...
when you seek it, you cannot find it.
Welcome home, Nekko.
Ahhh. A last saucer of illusion.

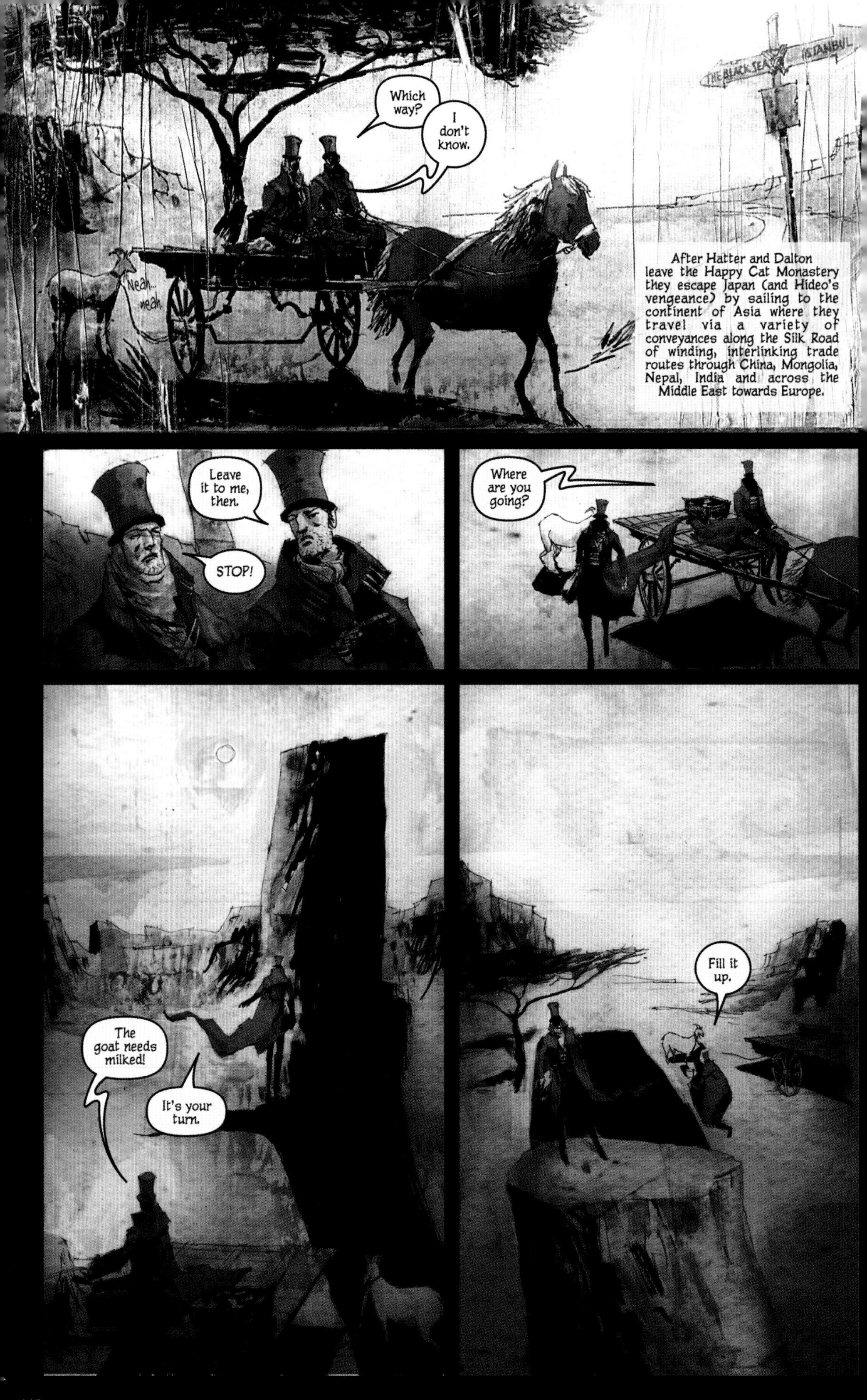
Which way?
I don't know.
THE BLACK SEA
ISTANBUL
Neah... neah.
After Hatter and Dalton leave the Happy Cat Monastery they escape Japan (and Hideo's vengeance) by sailing to the continent of Asia where they travel via a variety of conveyances along the Silk Road of winding, interlinking trade routes through China, Mongolia, Nepal, India and across the Middle East towards Europe.
Leave it to me, then.
STOP!
Where are you going?
The goat needs milked!
It's your turn.
Fill it up.

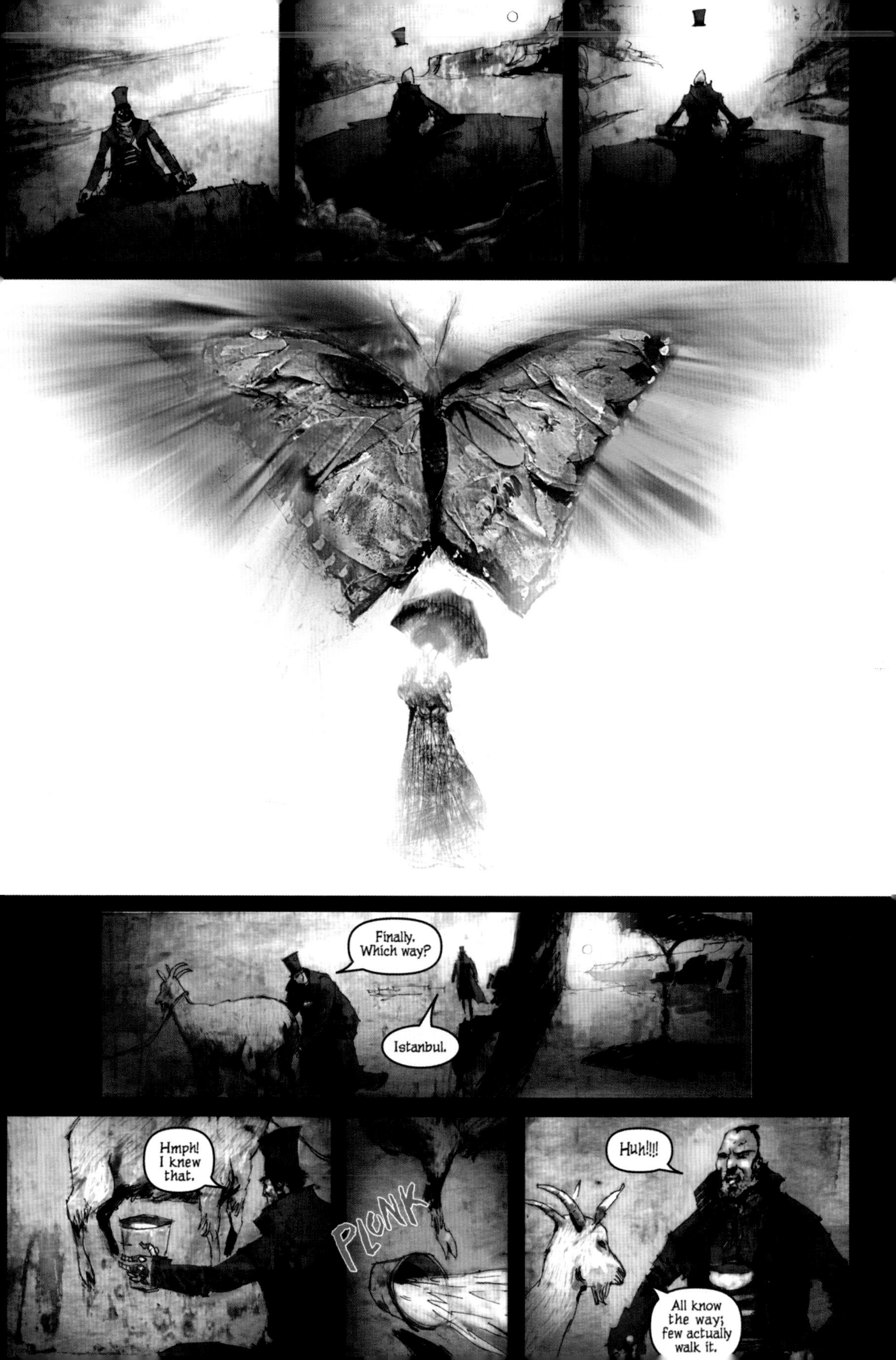

Finally. Which way?
Istanbul.
Hmph! I knew that.
PLONK
Huh!!!!
All know the way; few actually walk it.

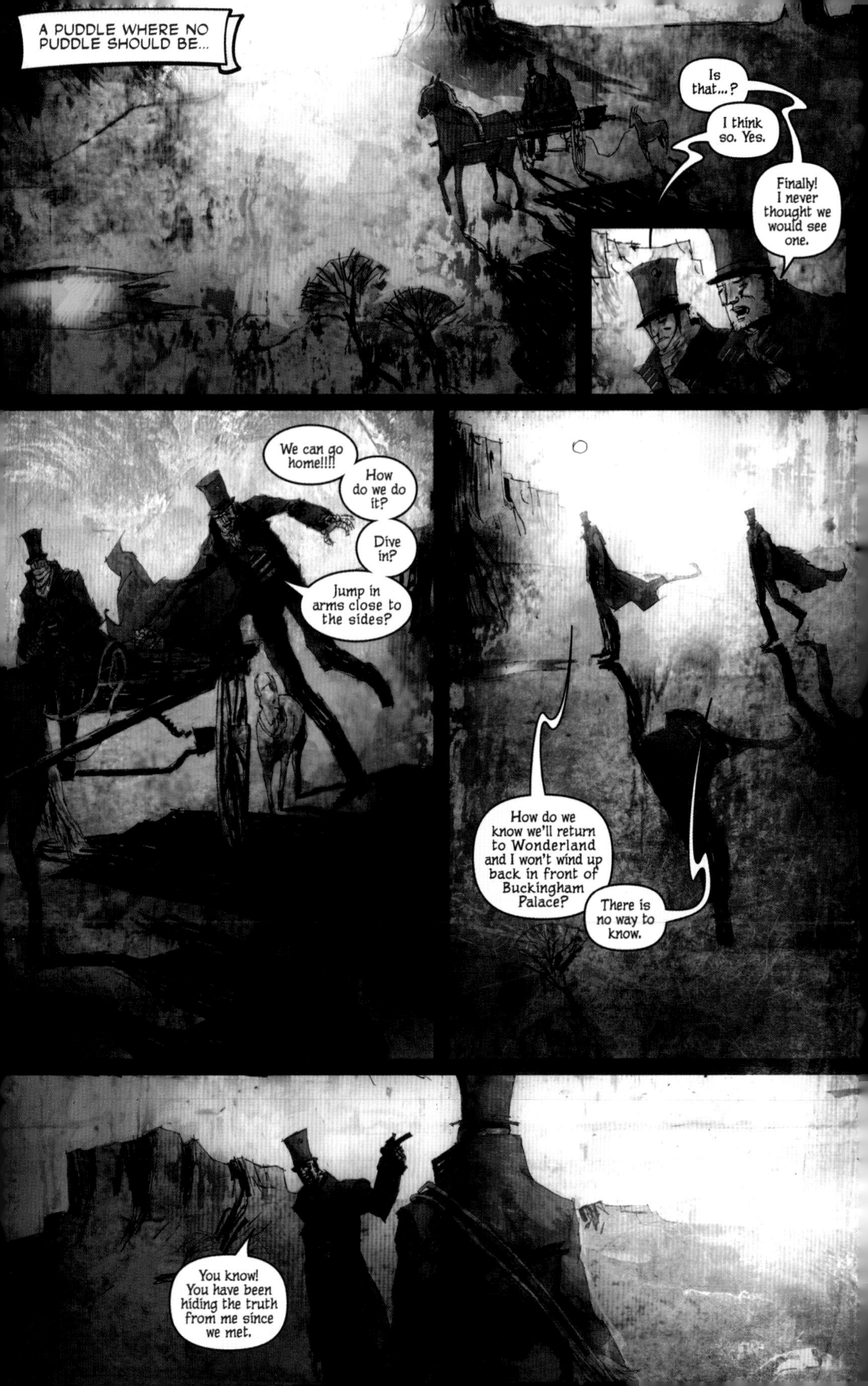
A PUDDLE WHERE NO PUDDLE SHOULD BE...
Is that...?
I think so. Yes.
Finally! I never thought we would see one.
We can go home!!!!
How do we do it?
Dive in?
Jump in arms close to the sides?
How do we know we'll return to Wonderland and I won't wind up back in front of Buckingham Palace?
There is no way to know.
You know! You have been hiding the truth from me since we met.

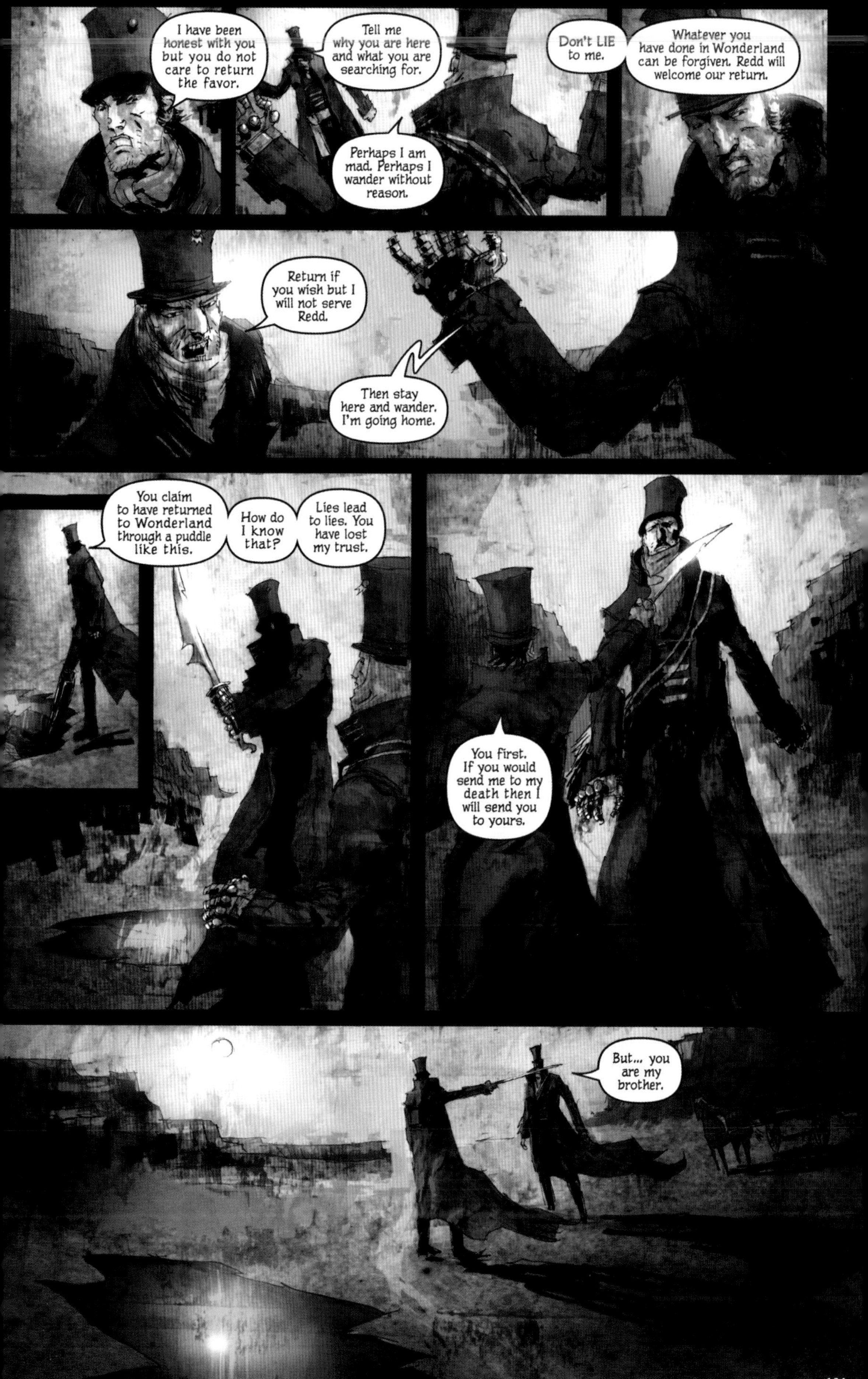
I have been honest with you but you do not care to return the favor.
Tell me why you are here and what you are searching for.
Perhaps I am mad. Perhaps I wander without reason.
Don't LIE to me.
Whatever you have done in Wonderland can be forgiven. Redd will welcome our return.
Return if you wish but I will not serve Redd.
Then stay here and wander. I'm going home.
You claim to have returned to Wonderland through a puddle like this.
How do I know that?
Lies lead to lies. You have lost my trust.
You first. If you would send me to my death then I will send you to yours.
But... you are my brother.

Unless we lose ourselves there is
no hope of finding ourselves.
-Henry Miller

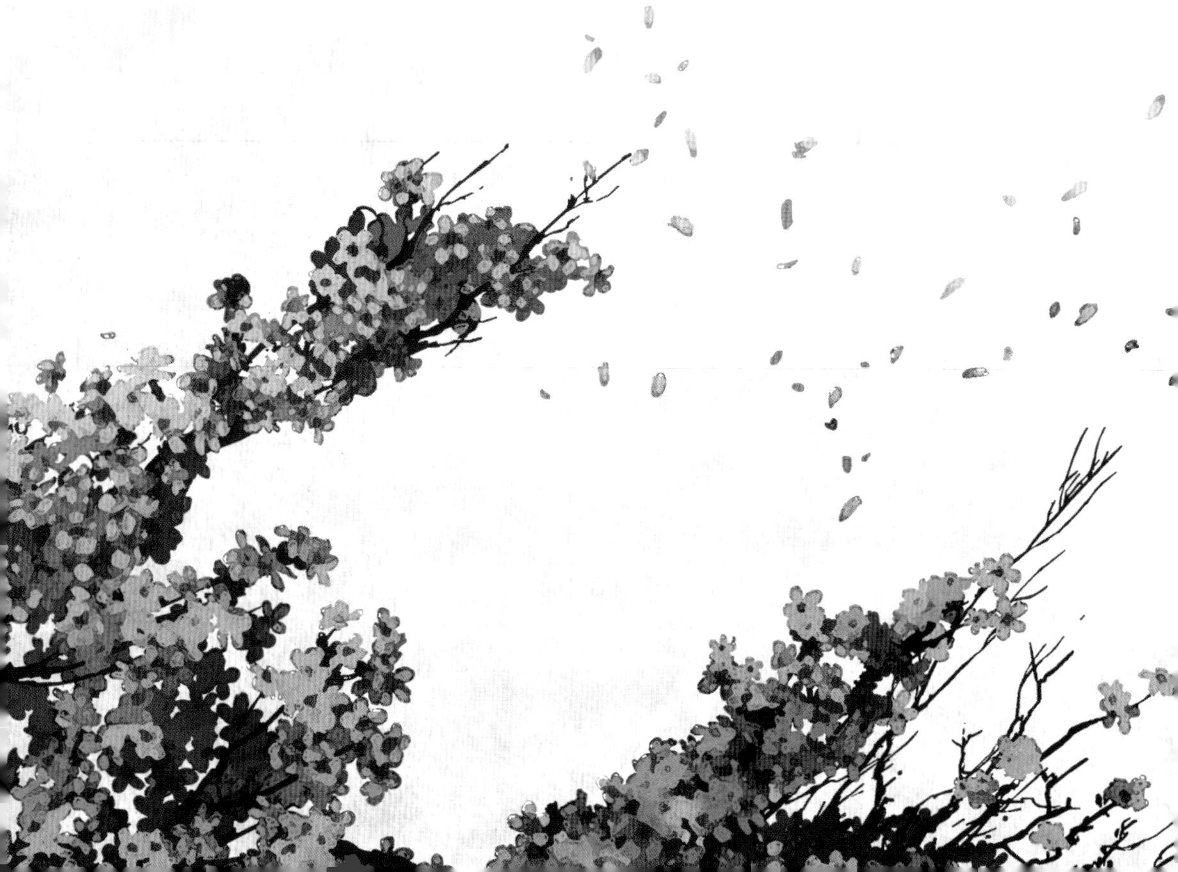

終章 EPILOGUE

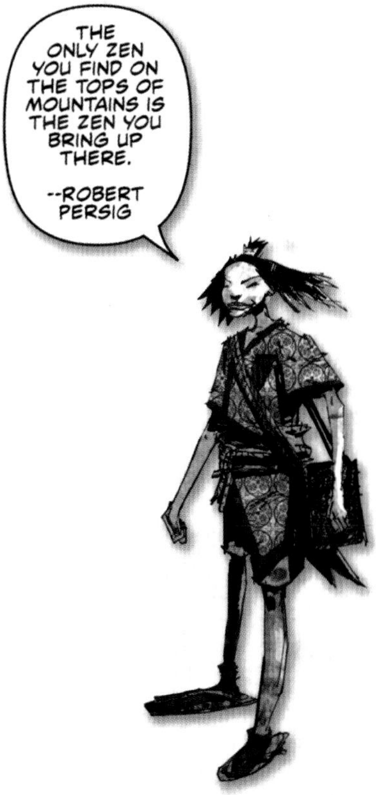
THE ONLY ZEN YOU FIND ON THE TOPS OF MOUNTAINS IS THE ZEN YOU BRING UP THERE.
--ROBERT PERSIG

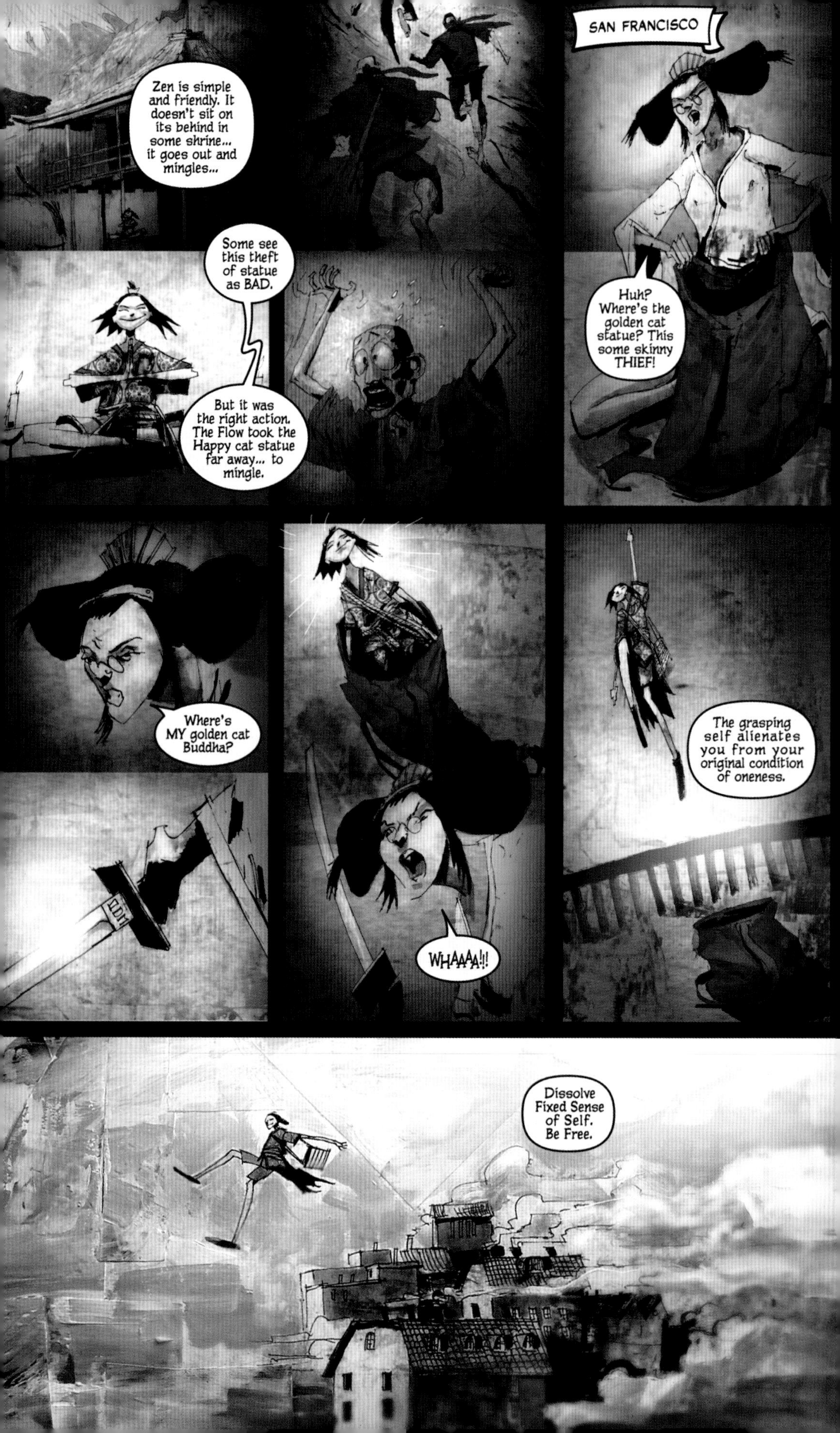

SAN FRANCISCO
Zen is simple and friendly. It doesn't sit on its behind in some shrine... it goes out and mingles...
Some see this theft of statue as BAD.
But it was the right action. The Flow took the Happy cat statue far away... to mingle.
Huh? Where's the golden cat statue? This some skinny THIEF!
Where's MY golden cat Buddha?
WHAAAA!!!
The grasping self alienates you from your original condition of oneness.
Dissolve Fixed Sense of Self. Be Free.

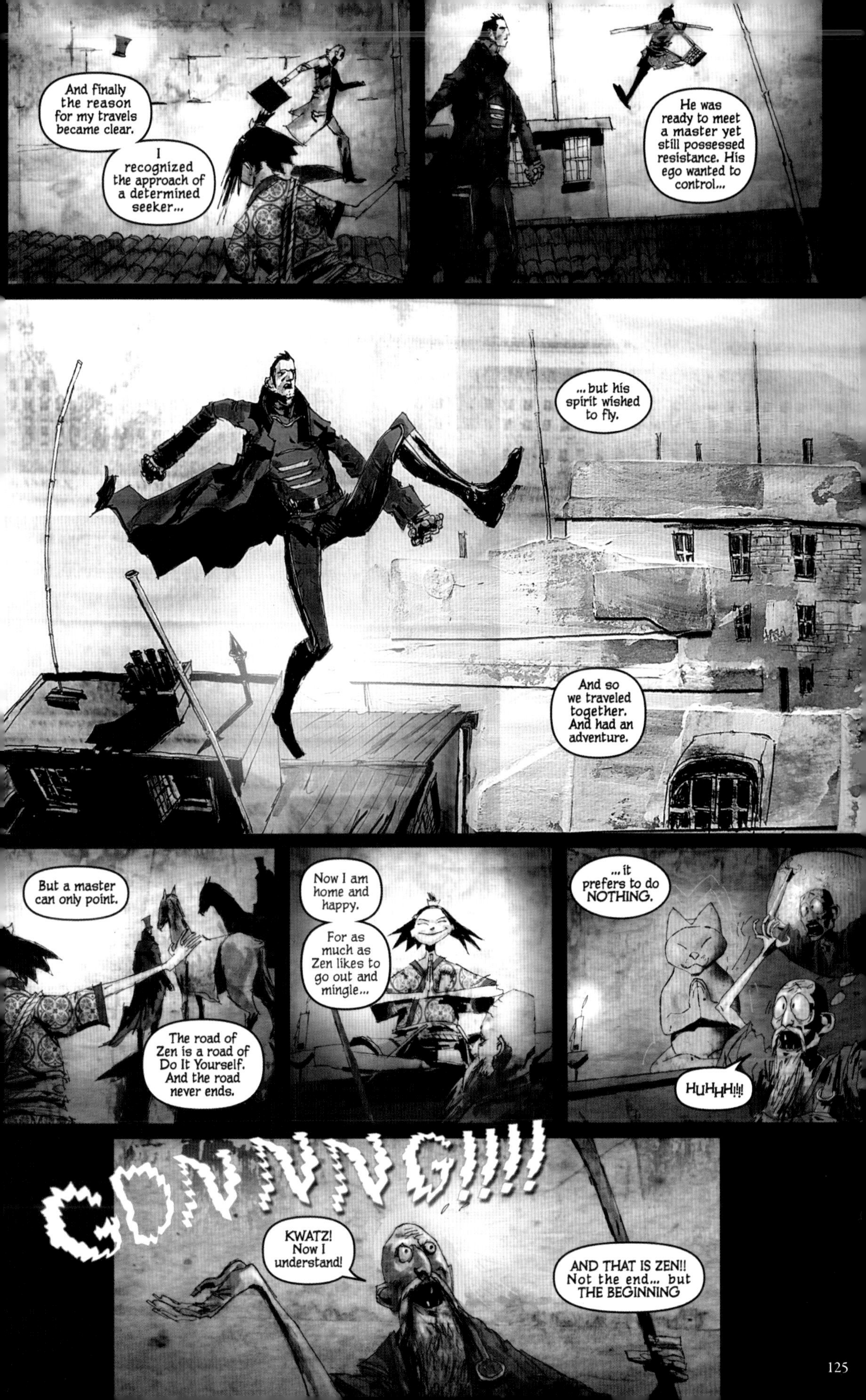
And finally the reason for my travels became clear.
I recognized the approach of a determined seeker...
He was ready to meet a master yet still possessed resistance. His ego wanted to control...
...but his spirit wished to fly.
And so we traveled together. And had an adventure.
But a master can only point.
The road of Zen is a road of Do It Yourself. And the road never ends.
Now I am home and happy.
For as much as Zen likes to go out and mingle...
...it prefers to do NOTHING.
HUHHH!!!
GONNNG!!!!
KWATZ! Now I understand!
AND THAT IS ZEN!! Not the end... but THE BEGINNING

Hatter M
Love
of
Wonder
Volume Five

Love is the only force capable of transforming an enemy into a friend.
-Martin Luther King Jr.

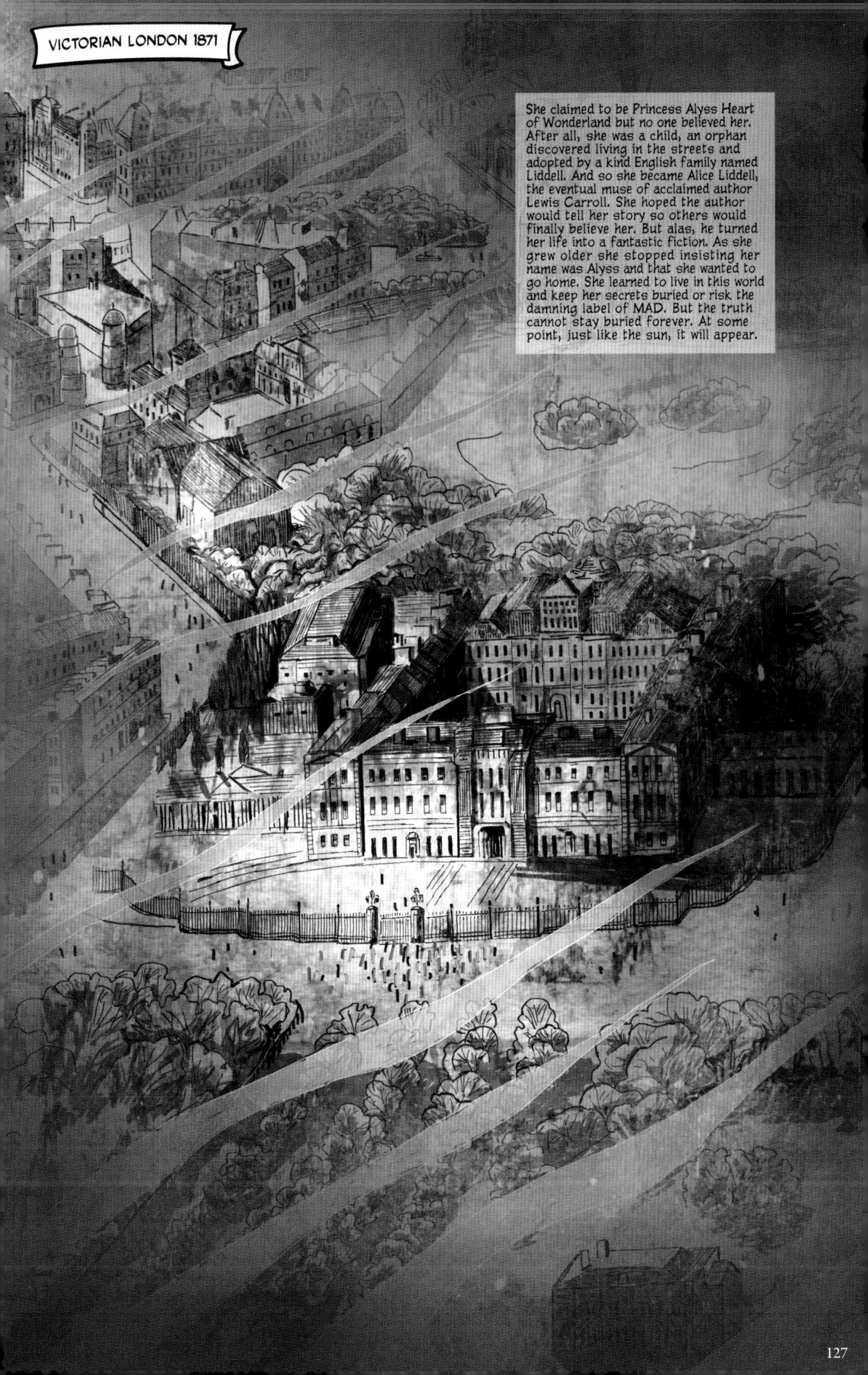
VICTORIAN LONDON 1871
She claimed to be Princess Alyss Heart of Wonderland but no one believed her. After all, she was a child, an orphan discovered living in the streets and adopted by a kind English family named Liddell. And so she became Alice Liddell, the eventual muse of acclaimed author Lewis Carroll. She hoped the author would tell her story so others would finally believe her. But alas, he turned her life into a fantastic fiction. As she grew older she stopped insisting her name was Alyss and that she wanted to go home. She learned to live in this world and keep her secrets buried or risk the damning label of MAD. But the truth cannot stay buried forever. At some point, just like the sun, it will appear.

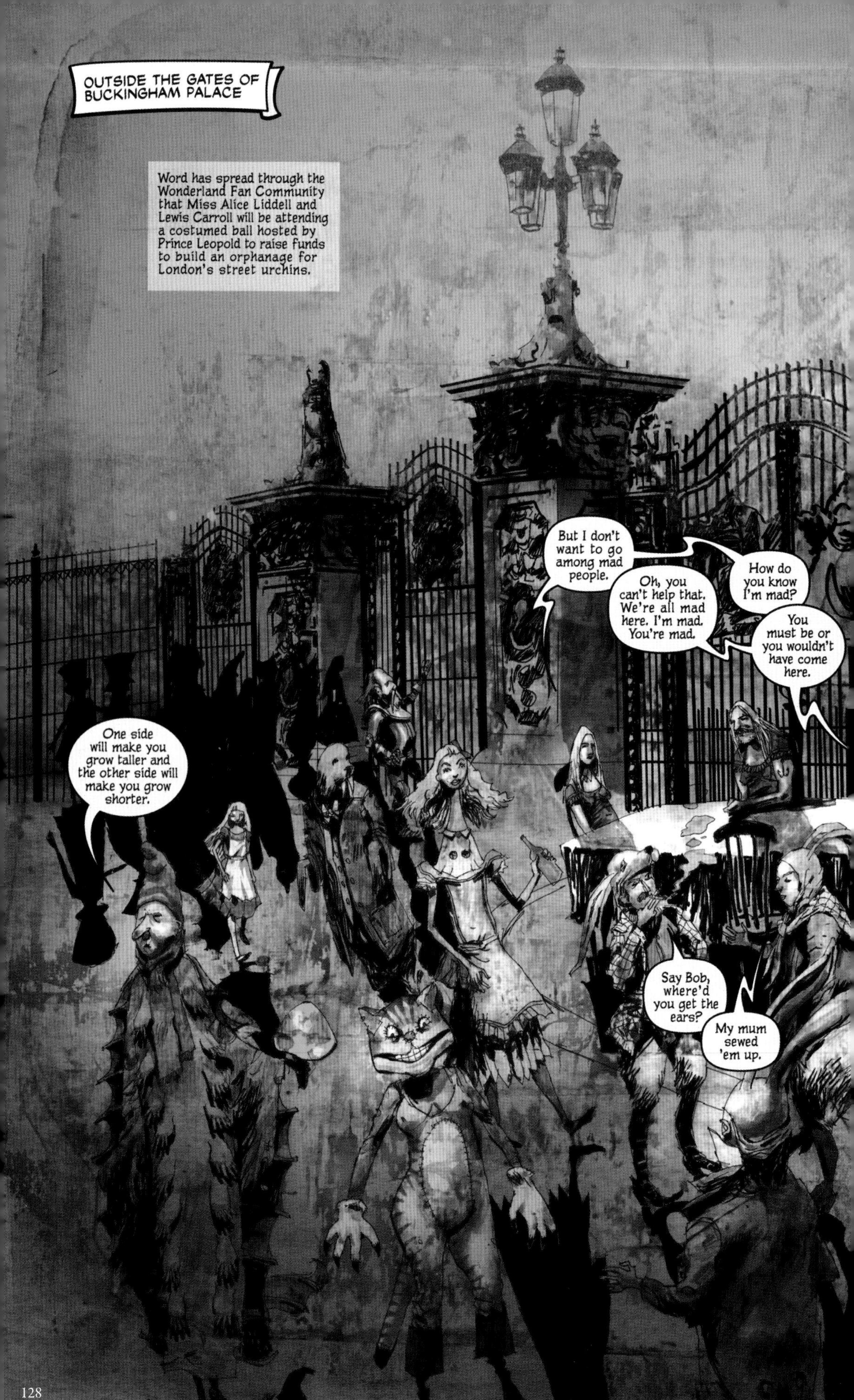
OUTSIDE THE GATES OF BUCKINGHAM PALACE
Word has spread through the Wonderland Fan Community that Miss Alice Liddell and Lewis Carroll will be attending a costumed ball hosted by Prince Leopold to raise funds to build an orphanage for London's street urchins.
But I don't want to go among mad people.
Oh, you can't help that. We're all mad here. I'm mad. You're mad.
How do you know I'm mad?
You must be or you wouldn't have come here.
One side will make you grow taller and the other side will make you grow shorter.
Say Bob, where'd you get the ears?
My mum sewed 'em up.

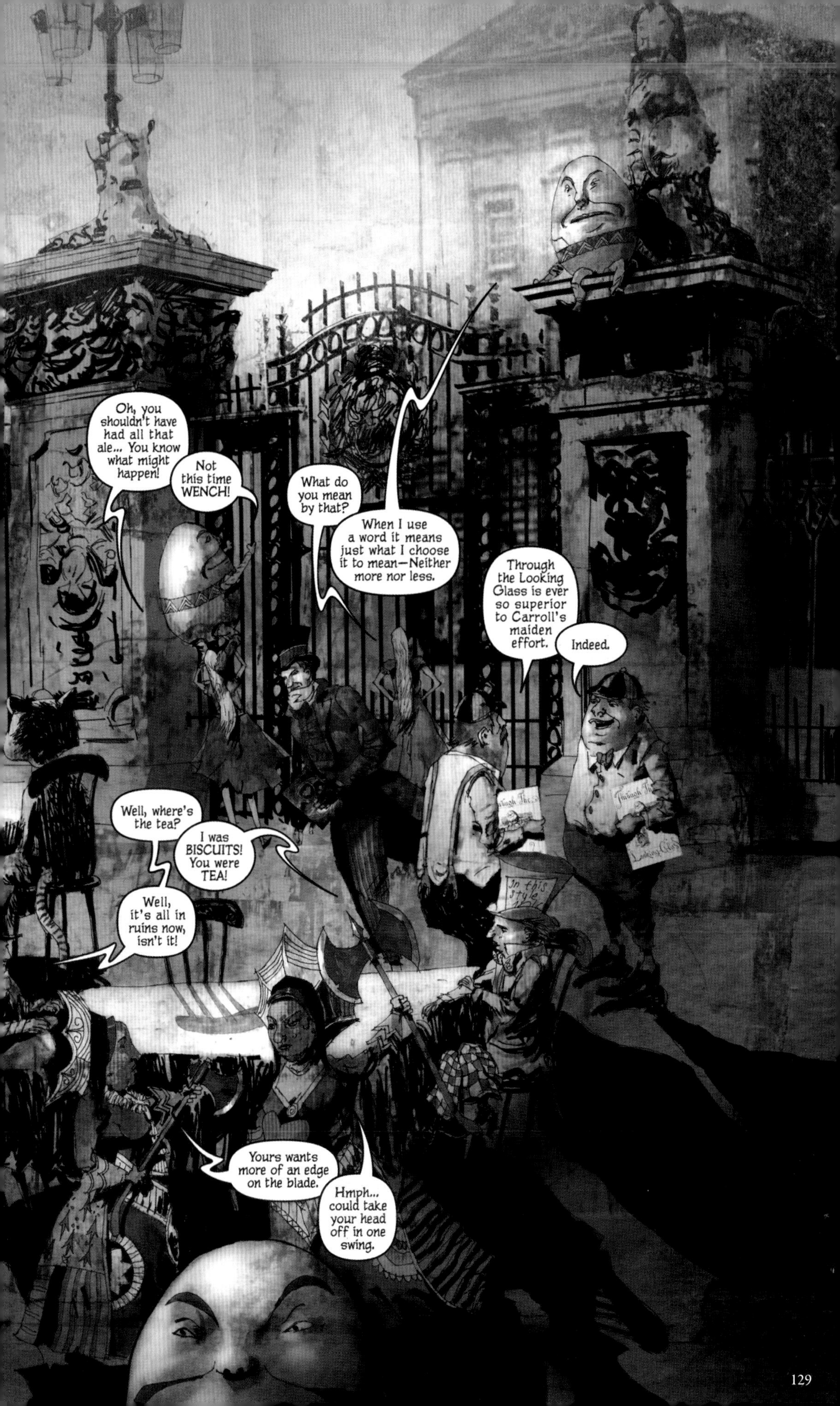

Oh, you shouldn't have had all that ale... You know what might happen!
Not this time WENCH!
What do you mean by that?
When I use a word it means just what I choose it to mean—Neither more nor less.
Through the Looking Glass is ever so superior to Carroll's maiden effort.
Indeed.
Well, where's the tea?
I was BISCUITS! You were TEA!
Well, it's all in ruins now, isn't it!
Yours wants more of an edge on the blade.
Hmph... could take your head off in one swing.

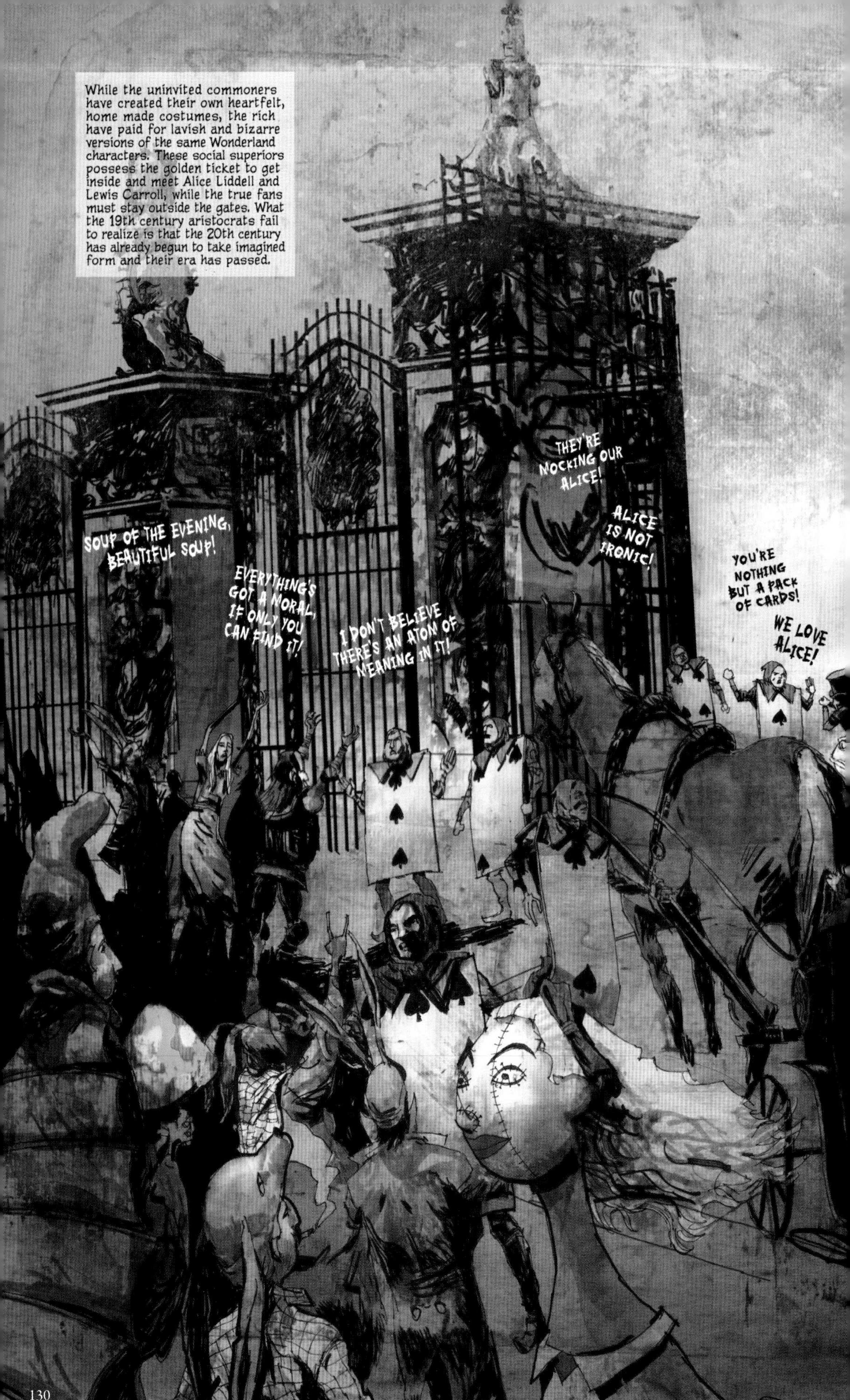

While the uninvited commoners have created their own heartfelt, home made costumes, the rich have paid for lavish and bizarre versions of the same Wonderland characters. These social superiors possess the golden ticket to get inside and meet Alice Liddell and Lewis Carroll, while the true fans must stay outside the gates. What the 19th century aristocrats fail to realize is that the 20th century has already begun to take imagined form and their era has passed.
SOUP OF THE EVENING, BEAUTIFUL SOUP!
EVERYTHING'S GOT A MORAL, IF ONLY YOU CAN FIND IT!
I DON'T BELIEVE THERE'S AN ATOM OF MEANING IN IT!
THEY'RE NOCKING OUR ALICE!
ALICE IS NOT IRONIC!
YOU'RE NOTHING BUT A PACK OF CARDS!
WE LOVE ALICE!

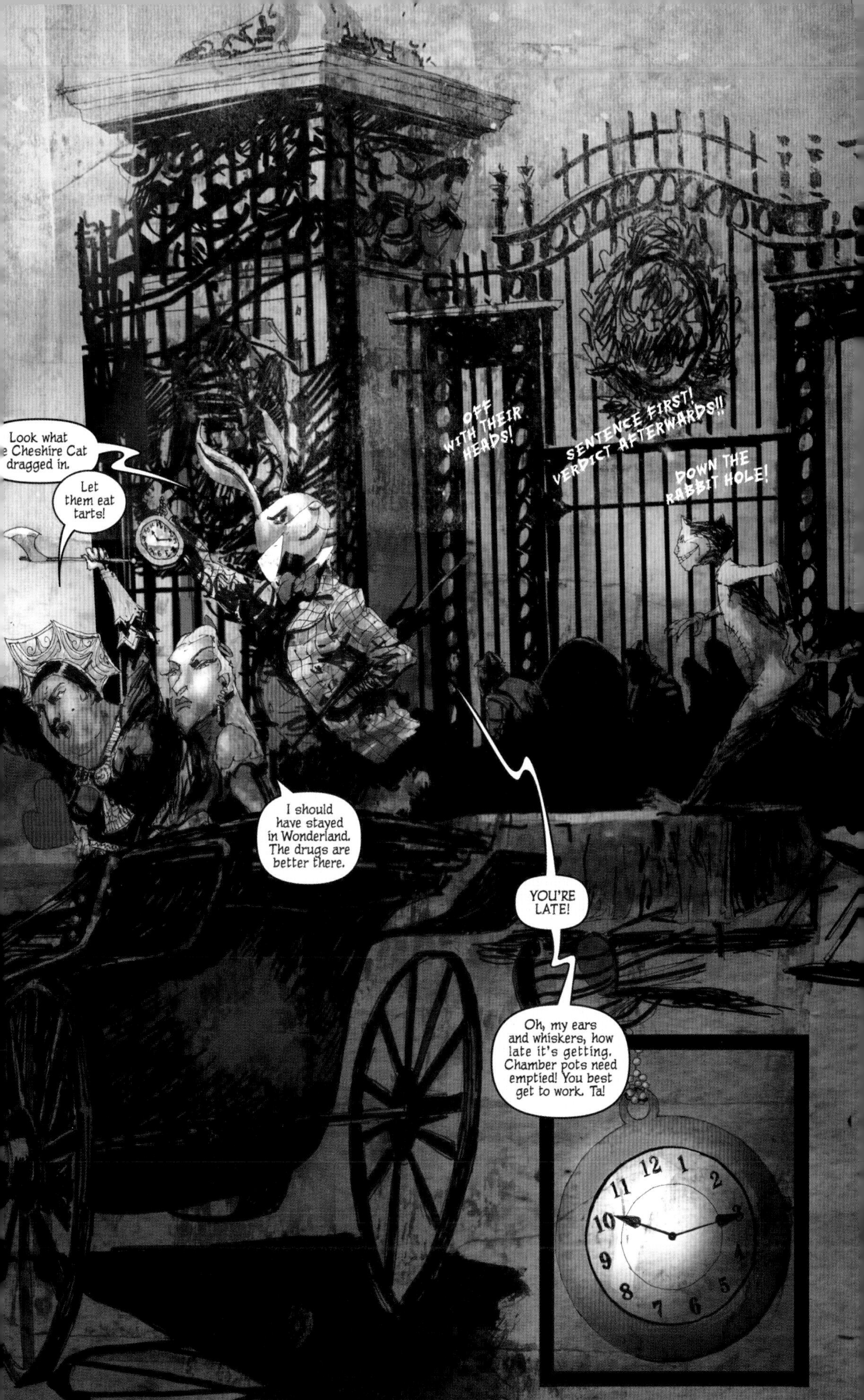
Look what
e Cheshire Cat
dragged in.
Let
them eat
tarts!
OFF
WITH THEIR
HEADS!
SENTENCE FIRST!
VERDICT AFTERWARDS!!
DOWN THE
RABBIT HOLE!
I should
have stayed
in Wonderland.
The drugs are
better there.
YOU'RE
LATE!
Oh, my ears
and whiskers, how
late it's getting.
Chamber pots need
emptied! You best
get to work. Ta!

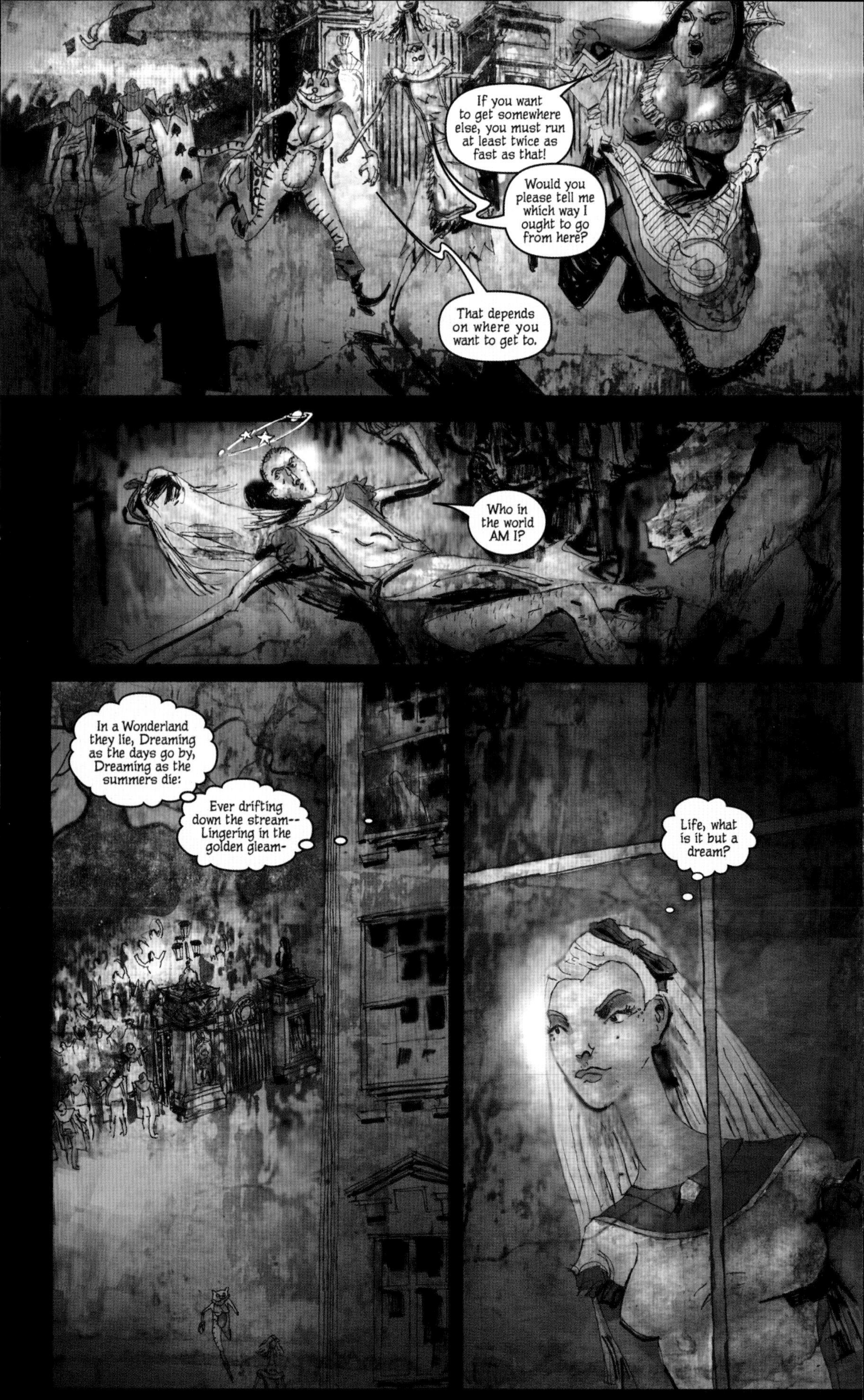
If you want to get somewhere else, you must run at least twice as fast as that!
Would you please tell me which way I ought to go from here?
That depends on where you want to get to.
Who in the world AM I?
In a Wonderland they lie, Dreaming as the days go by, Dreaming as the summers die:
Ever drifting down the stream-- Lingering in the golden gleam-
Life, what is it but a dream?

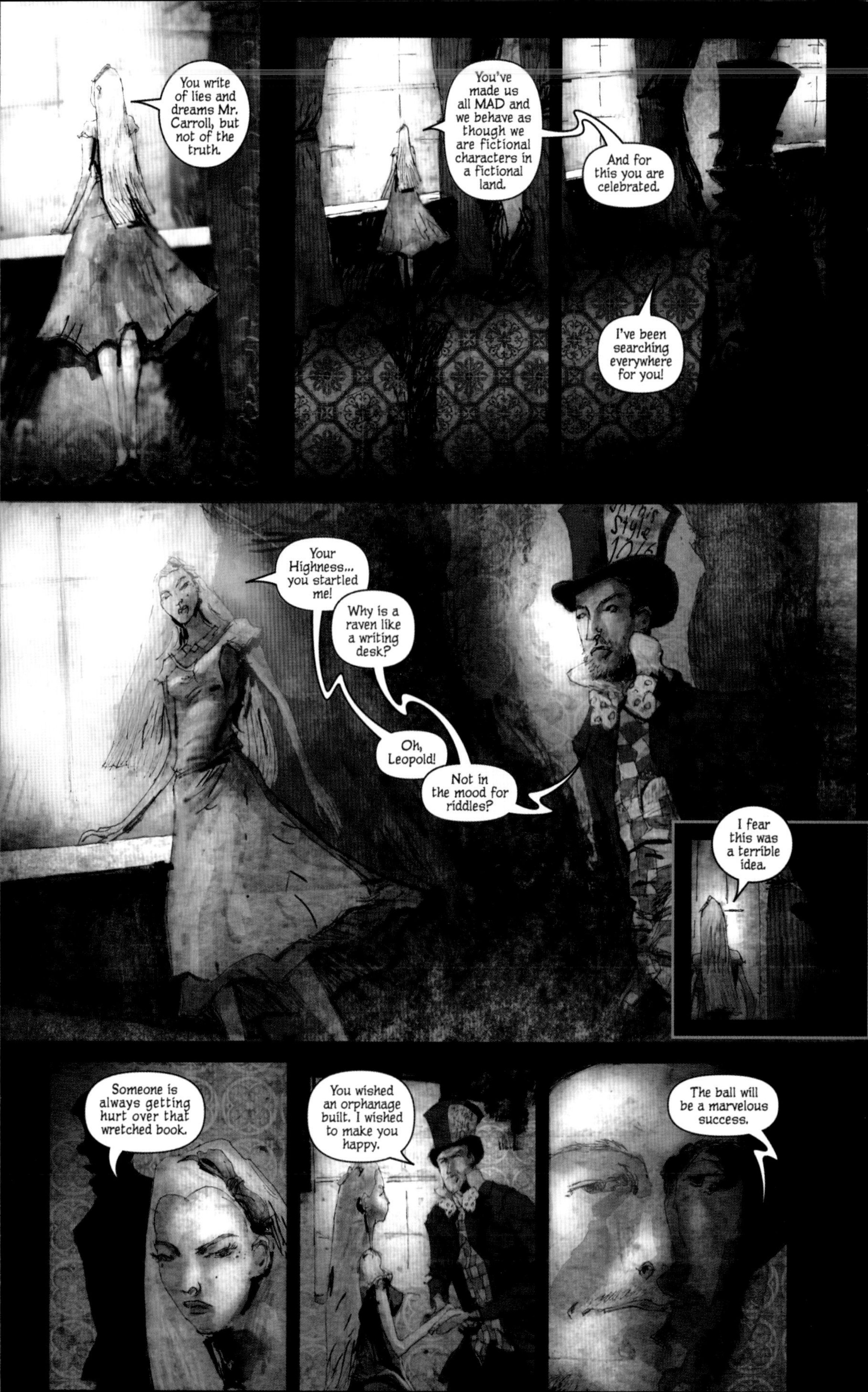
You write of lies and dreams Mr. Carroll, but not of the truth.
You've made us all MAD and we behave as though we are fictional characters in a fictional land.
And for this you are celebrated.
I've been searching everywhere for you!
Your Highness... you startled me!
Why is a raven like a writing desk?
Oh, Leopold!
Not in the mood for riddles?
I fear this was a terrible idea.
Someone is always getting hurt over that wretched book.
You wished an orphanage built. I wished to make you happy.
The ball will be a marvelous success.

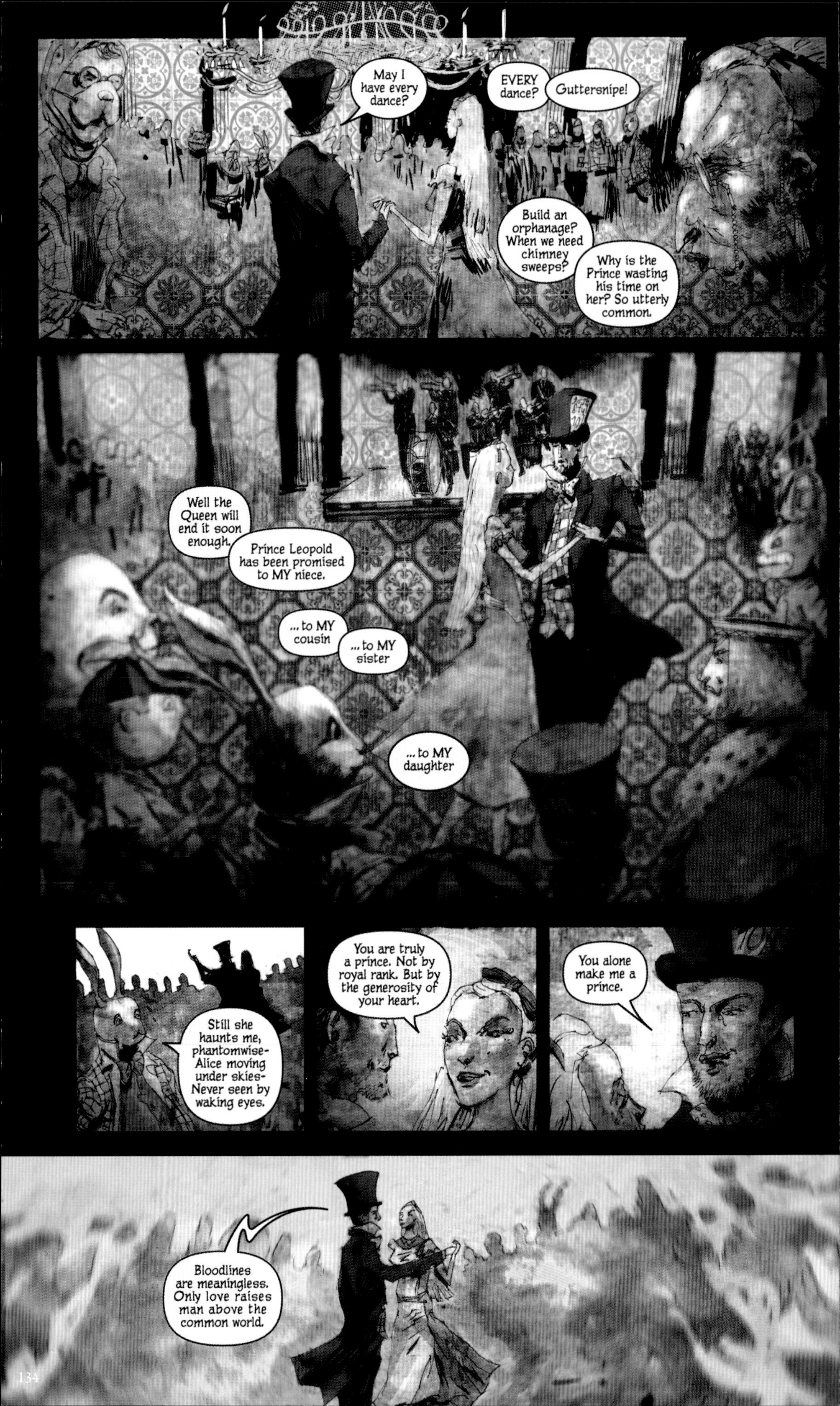
May I have every dance?
EVERY dance?
Guttersnipe!
Build an orphanage? When we need chimney sweeps?
Why is the Prince wasting his time on her? So utterly common.
Well the Queen will end it soon enough.
Prince Leopold has been promised to MY niece.
...to MY cousin
...to MY sister
...to MY daughter
Still she haunts me, phantomwise- Alice moving under skies- Never seen by waking eyes.
You are truly a prince. Not by royal rank. But by the generosity of your heart.
You alone make me a prince.
Bloodlines are meaningless. Only love raises man above the common world.

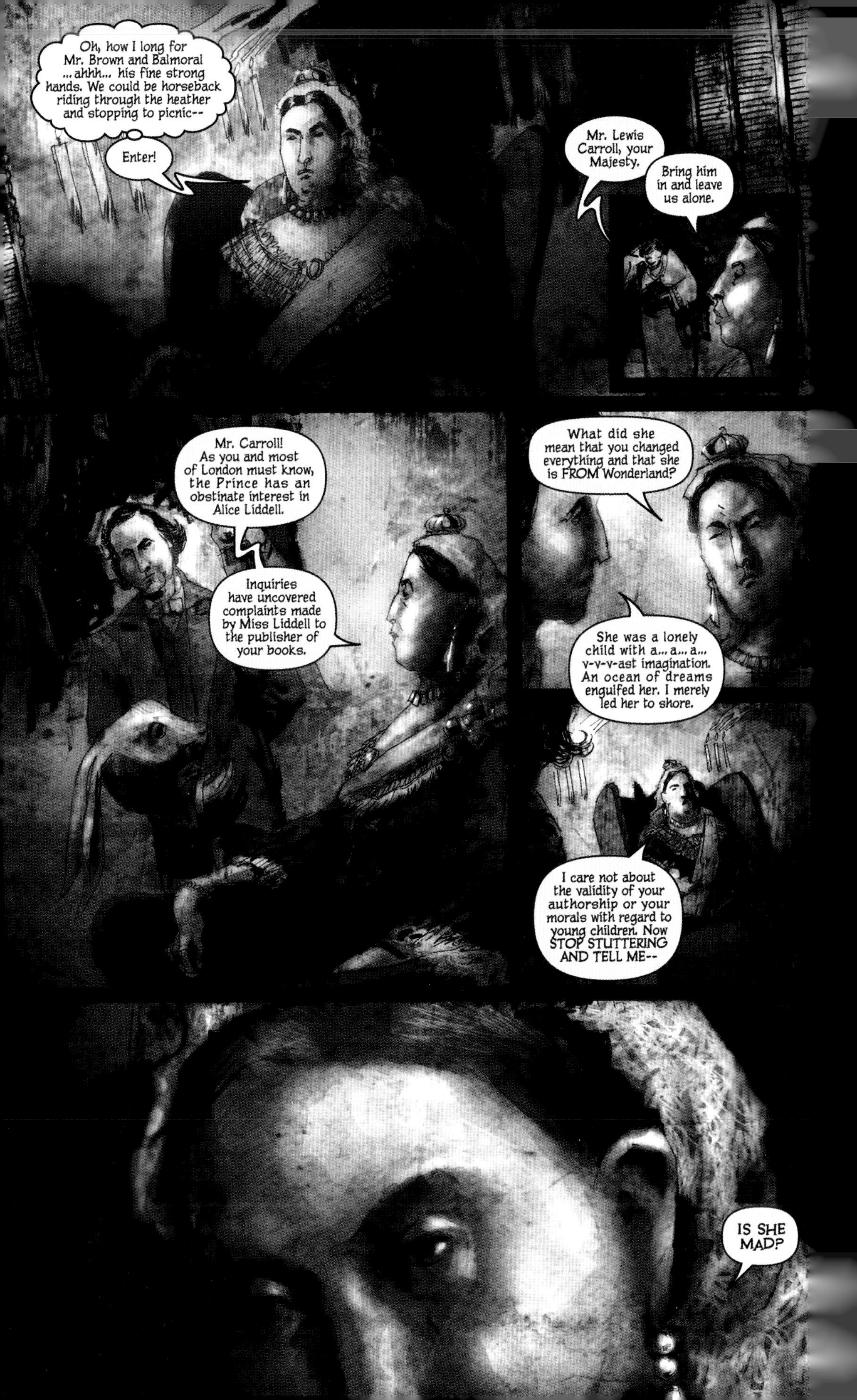

Oh, how I long for Mr. Brown and Balmoral ...ahhh... his fine strong hands. We could be horseback riding through the heather and stopping to picnic--
Enter!
Mr. Lewis Carroll, your Majesty.
Bring him in and leave us alone.
Mr. Carroll! As you and most of London must know, the Prince has an obstinate interest in Alice Liddell.
Inquiries have uncovered complaints made by Miss Liddell to the publisher of your books.
What did she mean that you changed everything and that she is FROM Wonderland?
She was a lonely child with a... a... a... v-v-v-ast imagination. An ocean of dreams engulfed her. I merely led her to shore.
I care not about the validity of your authorship or your morals with regard to young children. Now STOP STUTTERING AND TELL ME--
IS SHE MAD?

One Hand Clapping

Monk: Master, I have just entered the monastery, please teach me.

Joshu (778-897): Have you eaten your rice?

Monk: Yes, I have.

Joshu: Then wash your bowl.

At these words the monk was enlightened.

Did Hatter Madigan achieve satori? We don't know. But it is evident from his travels with Nekko that he cracked open enough to let in some light. And that's all that anyone can expect from Zen. Over the past few years many of us have observed the accepted reality 'cracking open'. This process will only accelerate as the illusionary world spins faster. Practice Zen and your head won't spin as fast as the world. Be still. And know the Truth.

Zazen: seated meditation – the opposite of contemplation – the emptying of the mind of all thoughts in order simply to be.

Hatter was willing to stay at the monastery and continue his studies with Nekko, but Dalton found the Zen surroundings too 'blah'! What Dalton objected to is known as 'wabi' and highly valued in the Zen tradition.

Wabi: spare, impoverished; simple and functional. It connotes a transcendence of fad and fashion. The sprit of wabi imbues all the Zen arts, from calligraphy to karate, from the tea ceremony to Zen archery.

Nekko was a lighthearted master. She saw the humor in life and encouraged Hatter to laugh at his rational thought. Not all masters are as agreeable.

Sanzen: the personal interaction between Zen master and student designed to allow the student to demonstrate his Zen – or lack of it – to the master. The face-to-face confrontation can involve verbal sparring, harsh reprimands, even corporal punishment.

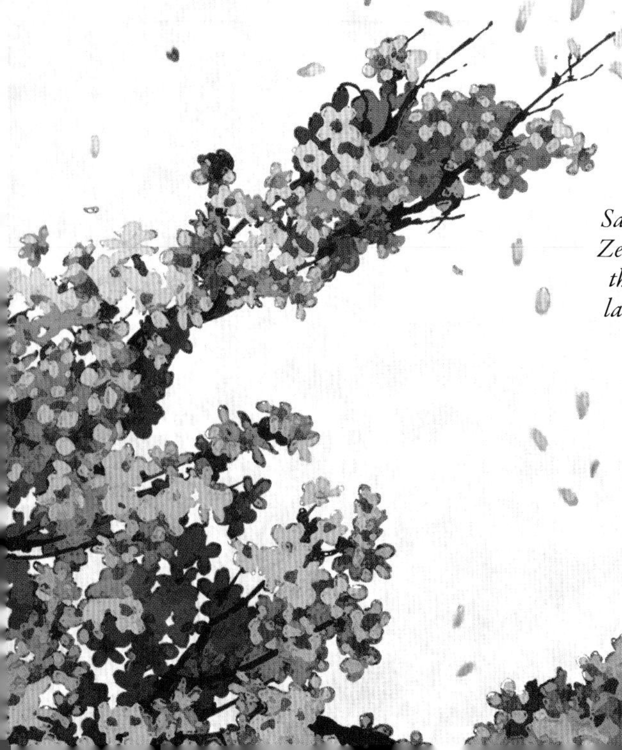

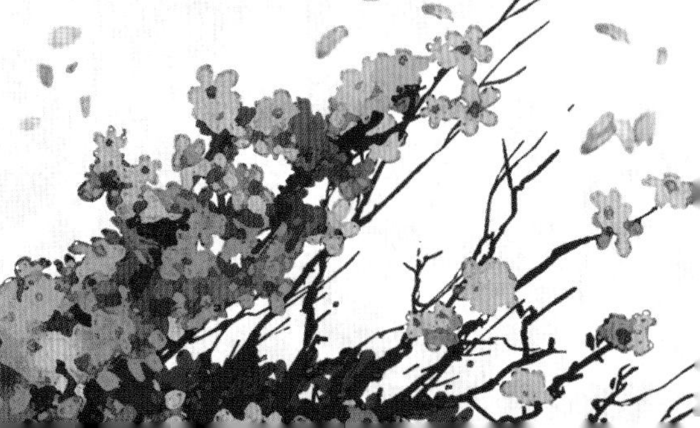

The institute
would like to thank
the latest addition to
our erudite search party,
the renowned scholar,
Demonologist Sonja Midthun.
Her work tracking the Great
Pumpkin Demon and his obsession
with a mysterious Laughing Hat
proved invaluable in reconstructing
the schoolhouse battle only briefly
mentioned in Hatter's journal.

Takedowndo: Martial arts
employing laughter as
ultimate weapon.

Nekko gives Hatter a
koan to ponder as he leaves
the monastery. It is the Zen
proverb 'When you seek it, you cannot
find it'. While most would assume the
answer to the koan to be simple, it is in fact
much more of a challenge. What else does
Hatter seek besides Princess Alyss? What do
you seek? Can you provide an answer that
would impress Nekko and free your mind?
Or will it only make her laugh harder?
HA!

Koan: spiritually instructive conundrums
designed to force the student beyond
logic to sudden illumination.

Hatter's attempts at
writing haiku have been used
in place of his journal entries at the
beginning of each chapter. Haiku
represents the Zen view of ultimate reality
in poetry. Haiku is an art form that expresses
the virtue of knowing when to stop, when
enough has been said. And in keeping with
this philosophy...we will stop here.

KWATZ!

Kwatz!: An exclamation used by Zen
masters to shock a student out of
dualistic thinking.

MANGA CHEAT SHEET

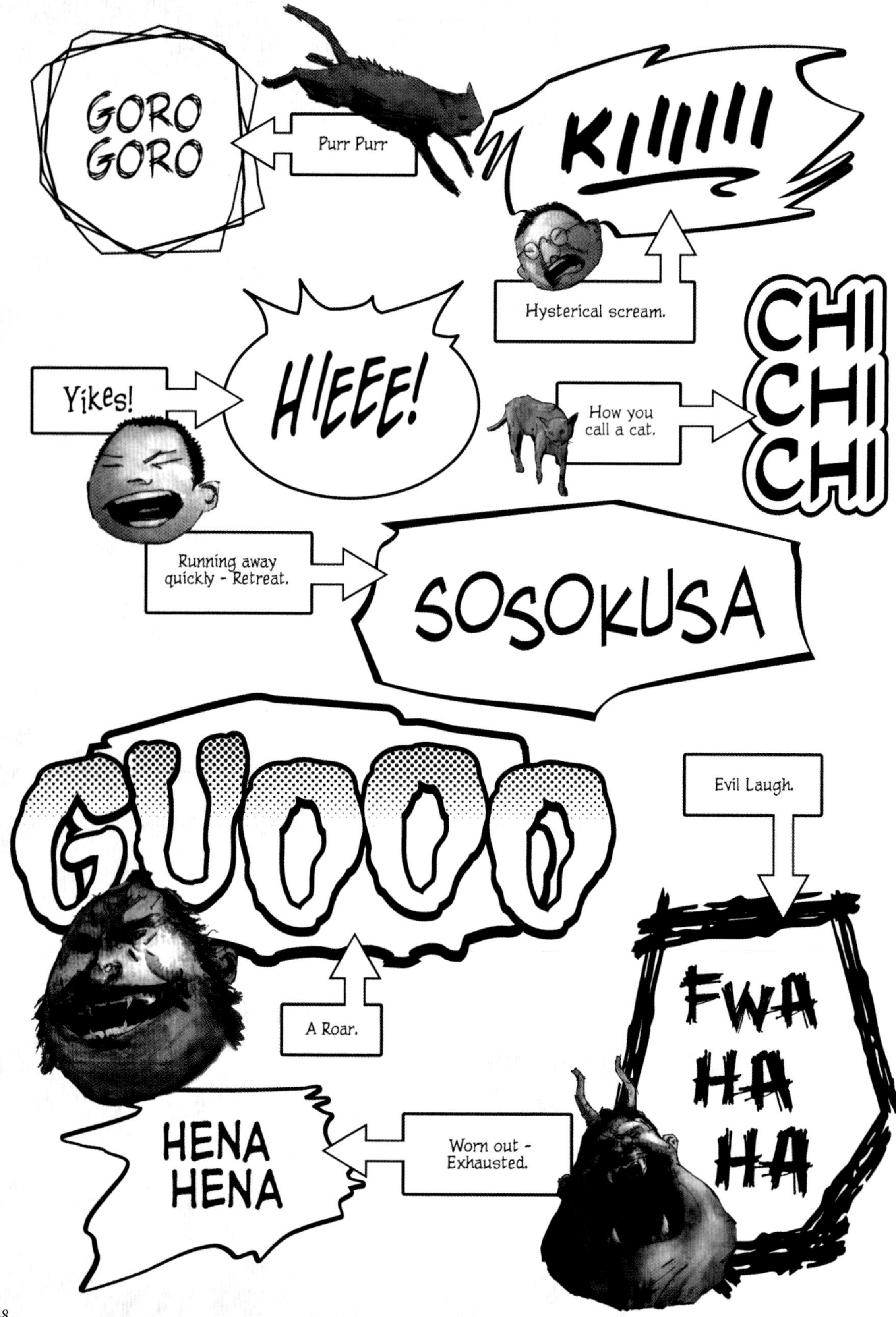
GORO GORO
Purr Purr
KIIIIII
Hysterical scream.
Yikes!
HIEEE!
How you call a cat.
CHI CHI CHI
Running away quickly - Retreat.
SOSOKUSA
GUOOO
Evil Laugh.
A Roar.
FWA HA HA
HENA HENA
Worn out - Exhausted.

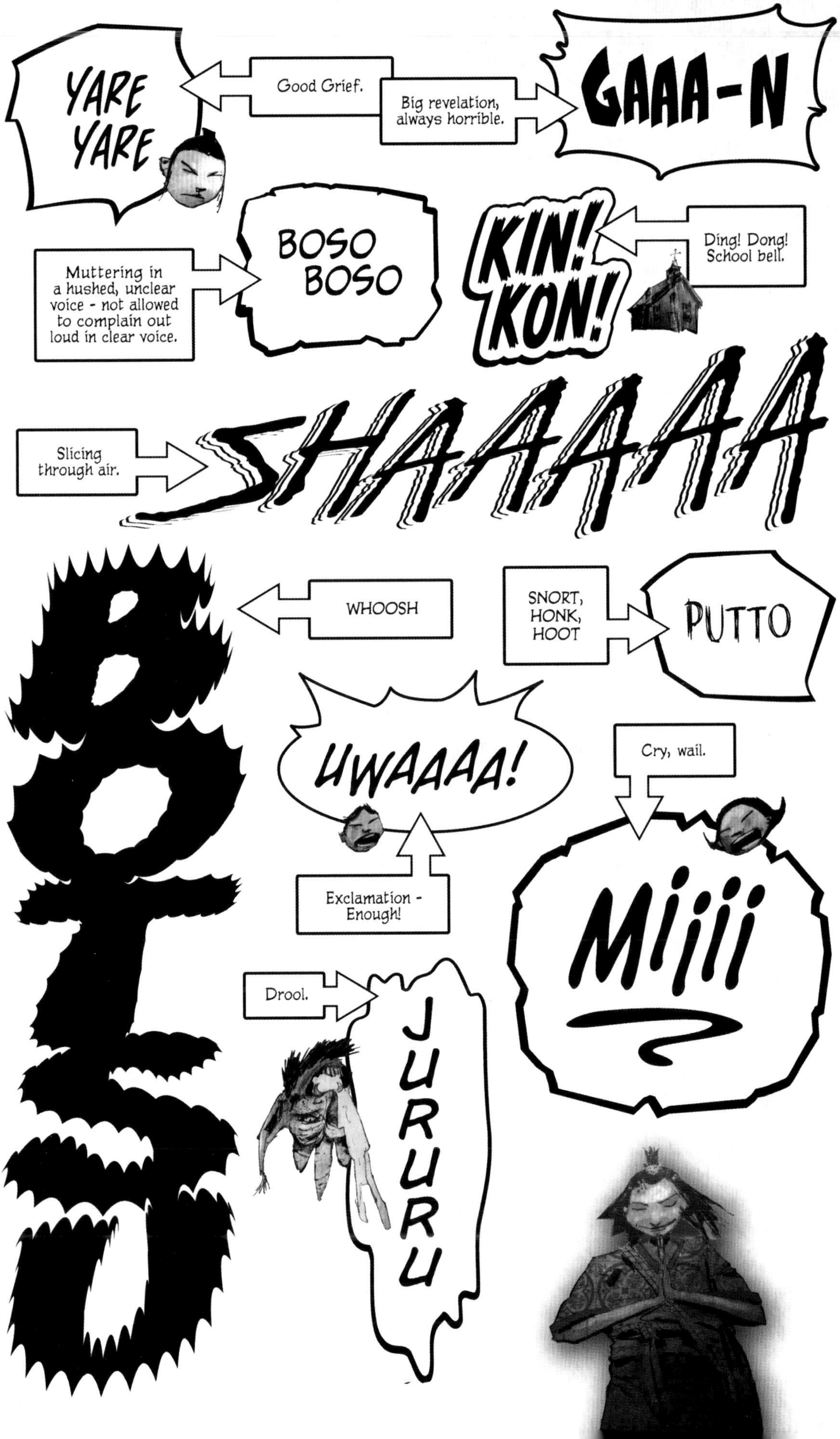
YARE YARE
Good Grief.
Big revelation, always horrible.
GAAA-N
Muttering in a hushed, unclear voice - not allowed to complain out loud in clear voice.
BOSO BOSO
KIN! KON!
Ding! Dong! School bell.
Slicing through air.
SHAAAAAA
WHOOSH
SNORT, HONK, HOOT
PUTTO
UWAAAA!
Cry, wail.
Exclamation - Enough!
Miiii
Drool.
JURURU

ARTIST SAMI MAKKONEN
DREAMS OF DEMONS

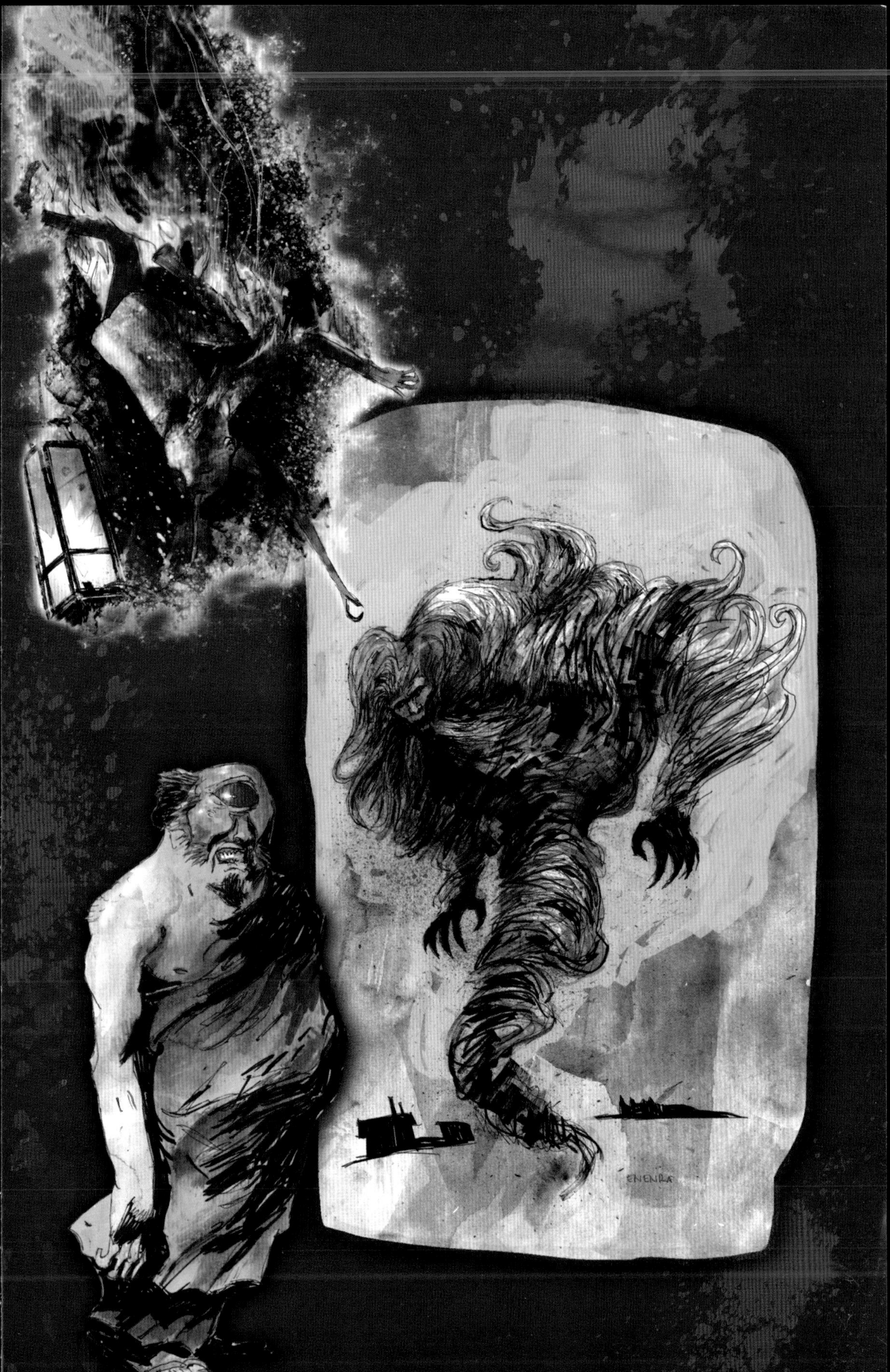
ENENRA

禪

Automatic Pictures Publishing

9200 Sunset Blvd Penthouse 22
Los Angeles CA 90069
automaticstudio@gmail.com

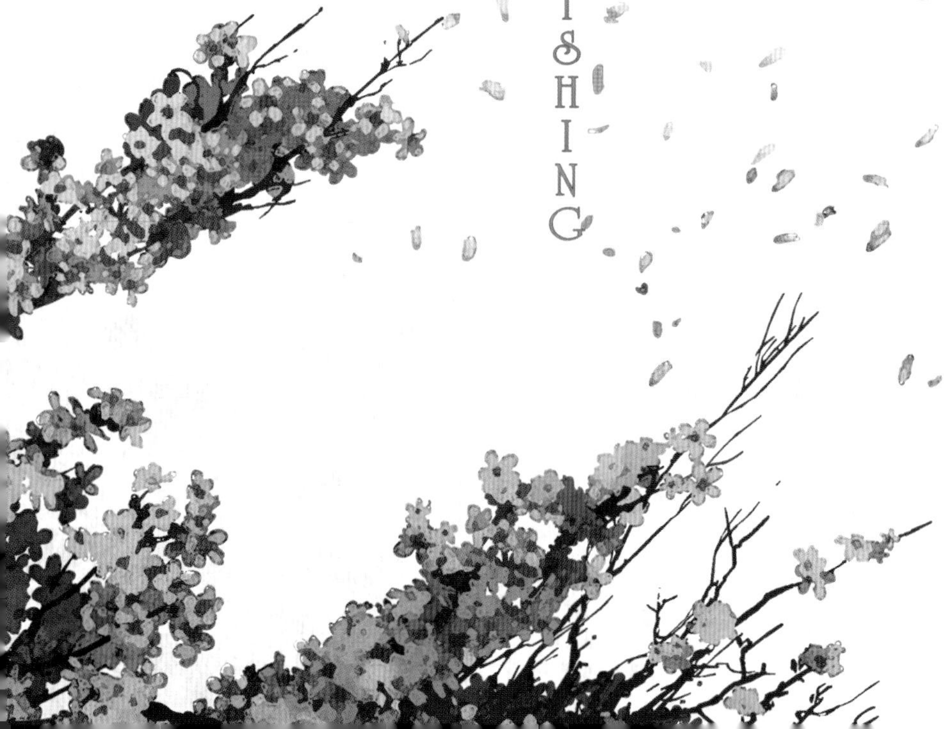